"Ron Sider has offered a faithful, Chr[...]
and fruitful career. This new book giv[...]
pacifist perspective, deeply rooted in Jesus Christ."

—**David P. Gushee**, Distinguished University Professor of Christian Ethics
and director of the Center for Theology and Public Life,
Mercer University

"Sider's sophisticated and coherent case for Christian pacifism magnifies its intellectual as well as existential appeal. War, like sin, may never be abolished. But, as Sider so eloquently argues, nonviolent resistance in the name of Jesus Christ can instigate change by enlivening the gospel with grace and power against the violence of our times."

—**Lisa Sowle Cahill**, Monan Professor of Theology, Boston College

"In trademark fashion, Ron Sider once again invites Christians to consider what they say they believe. *If Jesus Is Lord* is a comprehensive examination of whether Jesus really meant that we should not kill. Focused on the life and teachings of Jesus, but ranging throughout Scripture, church history, and theological tradition, Sider systematically examines the arguments for and against pacifism. He concludes that nonviolent resistance, understood not as a passive alternative to just war theory but as a proactive and creative third way, is the best interpretation of biblical teaching on how to respond to violence in our world. Sider invites readers to imagine the powerful impact of Jesus's teaching in a world where Christians truly practiced this third way, not as a response to an occasional moral dilemma in times of armed conflict but as a way of life. This book is for everyone. You will be a deeper, more creative pacifist or a more thoughtful and compassionate just war theorist after reading *If Jesus Is Lord*."

—**Shirley A. Mullen**, president, Houghton College

"*If Jesus Is Lord* is not a flimsy book of admonitions. Ron Sider takes oft glibly quoted commands, such as 'love your enemies,' and turns them on their head. His writing is challenging and biblically, historically, and theologically grounded. This is Ron Sider at his best. He has been speaking prophetically for a half century and living it out with the grace and love of Jesus."

—**Jo Anne Lyon**, ambassador and general superintendent emerita,
The Wesleyan Church

"Ron Sider meticulously and convincingly explores the meaning of Jesus's message of love for all and the biblical basis for renouncing violence and war.

Essential reading for those who call themselves Christians and for all who seek a world of justice and peace."

—**David Cortright**, director of policy studies, Kroc Institute
for International Peace Studies, University of Notre Dame

"A fine contribution on Jesus's gospel of peace in relation to the Old Testament, views of the atonement, and the early church's stance against killing. Vintage Sider!"

—**Willard Swartley**, professor emeritus of New Testament, Associated
Mennonite Biblical Seminary

"'Jesus intended that his followers should never kill anyone!' After you read *If Jesus Is Lord*, you will be able to reject this claim as unworkable in the real world, but you will not be able to dispute it. This compelling and challenging volume is the lifework of an impressive Christian 'resistance pacifist'!"

—**Miroslav Volf**, Yale Divinity School, director of the Yale Center
for Faith and Culture, and author of *For the Life
of the World: Theology That Makes a Difference*

"Ron Sider is a rare bird among biblical interpreters: he combines well-grounded scholarly attentiveness with a lively practical passion for a world of just peace. He has, moreover, been at it for a long, grace-filled lifetime. It is no surprise then that this book comes at just the right moment for us. It is a moment in which American Christians, across the theological spectrum, are recognizing that our widely shared historical accommodation to cultural religion is a shameful failure and that we must return to Jesus's radical core claims. Sider's exposition of transformative pacifism is based on the cruciality of Jesus, his teaching, and the witness of his life. Many Christians will want to take a deep (spirit-filled!) breath with this book and embrace new resolve about being faithfully present in the world alongside Jesus. Our long-term debt to Sider is deep and beyond calculation. This book is a summons to discipleship in a way that matters."

—**Walter Brueggemann**, Columbia Theological Seminary

"Ron Sider's new book, *If Jesus Is Lord*, is excellent and extremely helpful thinking for our Catholic Nonviolence Initiative. It challenges us to replace simplistic ideas about nonviolent action as naive with more accurate, expanded, and evidence-based information about effective nonviolent tools as an option for resisting evil that could help humanity actually build a more peaceful world. From civil resistance to diplomacy, trauma healing to restorative justice, nonviolent civilian protection to nonviolent communication, the possibilities are legion and largely underdeveloped. Thank you, Ron Sider!"

—**Marie Dennis**, co-president, Pax Christi International

"This book is not merely a case for living as nonviolent Christians; it is a deep and spiritually formative Bible study centered on the life of Jesus. I found it intellectually expansive and emotionally compelling. No one tackles the tough issues like Ron Sider. You just can't go on with your life as before. This book helped me draw closer to Jesus as Lord."

—**Joel C. Hunter**, faith community organizer;
former senior pastor, Northland Church

"Ron Sider has long been an authoritative, faithful, and prophetic voice on issues of Christian faithfulness. *If Jesus Is Lord* creates a timely and compelling challenge to all Christians. His explication of Christian nonviolence, for both individuals and society, is one of the strongest I have seen and draws a clear picture of what it means to truly follow Jesus's beatitude 'blessed are the peacemakers, for they shall be called the children of God.' To live this, one of the most fundamental teachings of Jesus, is central to what it means to believe and follow Christ in our time."

—**Jim Wallis**, *New York Times* bestselling author of *America's Original Sin:
Racism, White Privilege, and the Bridge to a New America,*
president of Sojourners, and editor in chief of *Sojourners* magazine

"Christian pacifism has no better biblical and theological apologist than Ron Sider. In *If Jesus Is Lord*, Sider has presented the most insightful and persuasive treatise for Christian peacemaking. Whatever your posture on war and peace, this insightful tome is a must-read!"

—**Gabriel Salguero**, president, National Latino Evangelical Coalition;
pastor, Calvario City Church, Orlando, Florida

"Ron Sider's book offers an excellent biblically grounded support for Christian peacemaking while also examining differing points of view. It is a great resource for evangelicals today who are seeking to understand the complexities of Jesus's calling to loving one's enemies in an age of violence. In every chapter, Sider presents a compelling invitation to follow Jesus's example of nonviolent and radical love. This book is important reading for all Christians committed to peacemaking."

—**Mayra G. Picos Lee**, board president, Baptist Peace Fellowship of North
America~Bautistas por la Paz; senior lecturer in counseling and director of
the MTS in Latino/a ministries, Palmer Theological Seminary

"Over and over lone voices, the most significant being Ron Sider's, have been calling Christians to think again, probe more deeply, and become more faithful to the paradigm of the cross. But that cross emerged from the teachings and life of Jesus. From Jesus's opening sermon in Nazareth to the cross there is a consistent vision—pacifist to the core—that needs to become our vision all over again. A consistent follower of Jesus is a pacifist, and Ron Sider has demonstrated this one more time. I have been reading Sider for forty years, and this is his best case yet."

—**Scot McKnight**, Julius R. Mantey Professor of New Testament, Northern Seminary

"Ronald J. Sider has spent a lifetime shaking up the religious establishment, blurring the lines of Right and Left with his 'dirty fingernails' theology about peace and social justice. *If Jesus Is Lord* is yet another bold burr in the ethical saddle of the evangelical world. In this provocative and invitational examination of Jesus-centered actions for peace and reconciliation, Sider implores pacifists to be responsive to the range of legitimate critiques against them (you're naive, simplistic, utopian), challenges just war Christians to consider that there are more than two options (kill or do nothing) to defend neighbors, and suggests with bountiful biblical and historical evidence that making peace is less costly than making war. Eminently readable, Sider's book is a biblically based exegesis and a grace-inspired 'third-way' anthem for affirming a justice and Jesus-centered Christianity. Be prepared to be challenged and affirmed at every turn. Sider explores eye-opening 'if' questions about what it means to call ourselves Christians. He begins with, '*If* Jesus is Lord, what does it mean to embrace the full, biblical, nonviolent Christ?' He ends with the question, 'What if most Christians became pacifists?' This book is relevant and impactful for Jesus followers across the spectrum who want to make a difference by reconciling beauty and brokenness in our world today."

—**Susan Schultz Huxman**, president and professor, Eastern Mennonite University

IF JESUS
IS
LORD

Other Books by Ronald J. Sider

Visit the author's website at
https://ronsiderblog.substack.com/.

IF JESUS IS LORD

LOVING OUR ENEMIES IN AN AGE OF VIOLENCE

RONALD J. SIDER

FOREWORD BY STANLEY HAUERWAS

ʙ
Baker Academic
a division of Baker Publishing Group
Grand Rapids, Michigan

Published by Baker Academic
a division of Baker Publishing Group
PO Box 6287, Grand Rapids, MI 49516-6287
www.bakeracademic.com

Printed in the United States of America

Library of Congress Cataloging-in-Publication Data
Names: Sider, Ronald J., author.
Title: If Jesus is Lord : loving our enemies in an age of violence / Ronald J. Sider.
Description: Grand Rapids : Baker Publishing Group, 2019. | Includes bibliographical references and index.
Identifiers: LCCN 2018043307 | ISBN 9780801036286 (pbk. : alk. paper)
Subjects: LCSH: Love—Religious aspects—Christianity. | Violence—Religious aspects—Christianity. | Jesus Christ—Example.
Classification: LCC BV4639 .S527 2019 | DDC 241/.697—dc23
LC record available at https://lccn.loc.gov/2018043307

ISBN 978-1-5409-6214-0 (casebound)

In keeping with biblical principles of creation stewardship, Baker Publishing Group advocates the responsible use of our natural resources. As a member of the Green Press Initiative, our company uses recycled paper when possible. The text paper of this book is composed in part of post-consumer waste.

19 20 21 22 23 24 25   7 6 5 4 3 2 1

CONTENTS

FOREWORD

STANLEY HAUERWAS

Ron Sider has always defied categories. His life and work have belied the generalization that evangelicals, a description that does not do him justice, lack a sense of social and political responsibility. His passion for the poor, the hungry, and the outcast has been a witness that we have sorely needed. He has not let us forget, moreover, that Christians believe that justice is a demanding virtue that tests the soul. Yet his soul has remained gentle and kind. Observing his work on behalf of the have-nots could lead you to think that he believes he has earned the right to take it easy in his later years. But I do not believe Ron Sider knows how to take it easy.

Instead, he has now given us this book developing and defending Christian pacifism. It is a book that has taken a lifetime to write. I do not mean that he has been writing the book for a lifetime, but rather he has through his work on behalf of the poor learned how to live nonviolently. In short this is a book that could have been written only by one who has experienced the demanding life and work of loving one's enemies. By providing close readings of Jesus's work and teachings Ron helps us see that nonviolence is not a side issue in Jesus's ministry but rather is at the very heart of what the kingdom Jesus proclaimed is about. The justice that is Jesus is the justice that is nonviolent.

The pacifism Sider defends in this book, as the title suggests, is "biblical" but that description can mislead. Sider certainly engages in close exegesis of texts, but he does so with a constructive, theological, christological

Stanley Hauerwas is Gilbert T. Rowe Professor Emeritus of Divinity and Law at Duke Divinity School.

perspective. This is but a way to say that Ron helps us see how Scripture must be read christologically. Not every peace is the peace that is Christ, but the peace that is Christ is not restrictive—rather, it is an invitation for all to live lives that are not dominated by fear. Sider's account of nonviolence is not an "ethic" only for Christians but a reality that makes possible common efforts for peace by Christians and non-Christians.

The detailed exegesis matters, and Sider does not skip the hard questions that a biblical account of pacifism raises. His dealing with the texts in the Old Testament in which God commands the killing of Israel's enemies is particularly important. He is well aware that the understanding of nonviolence he develops cannot be justified by any one text of the New Testament. But once the Bible is read as testimony to the risen Christ, it is difficult to avoid the conclusion that Christ has made it possible for a people to exist who can and have survived without killing.

In particular Ron's reading of the Old Testament is important because it can be seen as a way to challenge the oft made criticism "pacifism cannot work." It is alleged that pacifists are unjustified idealists who do not understand the way the world works. Such critiques of pacifists, however, fail to acknowledge that a people has existed for centuries without an army, lived as Jesus seems to have wanted his followers to live, and has often moved to avoid being killed—they are called Jews. Accordingly Sider is quite right as well as insightful to see the significance of Ephesians 2:11–22 for how the Christian commitment to nonviolence draws on God's care of God's chosen people.

Before I die I have given myself the modest task of convincing the Christians in America that as Christians we have a problem with war. I am not expecting the vast majority of Christians to be pacifists or even just warriors. I simply want them to see that there is a profound tension between our worship of a crucified messiah and the support of war. I am well aware that this may be a utopian project, but Ron Sider's book is surely going to be an important aid in that project. So thank God for Ron Sider.

ACKNOWLEDGMENTS

This book owes a huge debt to such a vast number of people (a few of whom I remember; many more I forget; and the overwhelming majority I never knew) that I can only mention a tiny fraction as a way to say thanks to them all.

I acknowledge with deep appreciation the Anabaptist tradition in which I grew up and still live. The courageous and often costly witness to nonviolence of innumerable Anabaptists over five hundred years has shaped my life in more ways than I understand. My devout mother and father, Ida and James Sider, modeled peace in the family. My Brethren in Christ bishop, Bishop E. J. Swalm (one of my early heroes), lived his refusal to kill by going to jail in World War I.

I am grateful for the invitation (to me, then a young person) to give the Bible lectures at the New Call to Peacemaking (1978), sponsored by the Quakers, Mennonites, and Church of the Brethren. Those lectures resulted in *Christ and Violence*, my first small book on the topic of whether Jesus ever wants his followers to kill.

I have been blessed with good friends on the journey. Peace advocate John Stoner has been a good friend for almost fifty years. Richard Taylor, another decades-long friend and peace activist, coauthored a book with me on peace in a nuclear age.

To Merold and Carol Westphal (good friends since graduate school days), who vigorously insisted that this stubbornly proud person needed to agree to his wife's request for marriage counseling to save our marriage, I will be forever grateful. (I actually stopped to talk with them about our troubled marriage on the way home from delivering the peace lectures in 1978!)

To my loving wife and strong partner of fifty-seven years, Arbutus Lichti Sider (who was right in 1978 that we needed marriage counseling!), I can only say thank you from all my heart for walking faithfully with me in the hard period of painful struggle and also in the many decades of joy and peace before and after that time. You have been God's best gift to me after God's incarnate Son.

Two of my students at Palmer Theological Seminary of Eastern University, Ben Pitzen and Merrick Korach, provided invaluable help as they typed and retyped the manuscript.

In my footnotes, I acknowledge some of the vast number of scholars and activists who have shaped my thinking on peacemaking. But I am sure I have also forgotten many.

I owe a special thanks to Bob Hosack, my editor at Baker Publishing for more than two decades. Baker has proved to be an ideal publishing home for me.

Finally, with appreciation, sadness, and dismay, I acknowledge that John Howard Yoder's writings have been important in my thinking. I appreciate the way his incisive writing has been widely influential on the topic of this book. I am deeply saddened that the most brilliant theologian/ethicist in Mennonite history has disgraced himself and negatively impacted the lives of a number of women with terrible sexual and power abuse.[1] And I am dismayed that Yoder stubbornly resisted and refused counsel and correction, contradicting his own theology on communal discernment for many years. I understand why many people believe that Yoder's inexcusable, sinful misconduct over decades means that we should no longer read his works.

It is true that Yoder justified his behavior with fundamentally wrong albeit sophisticated theological/hermeneutical arguments. We must reject his ideas wherever these perverse arguments shape his thinking. And it is especially ironic and pernicious that, as Goossen and others point out, Yoder perpetuated sexual violence even as he preached nonviolence. All this means that we must read Yoder with dismay, caution, and even suspicion.

But I do not think Yoder's sinful behavior means that we should stop reading his writings. Persistent sin and atrocious statements do not mean that everything a person says is wrong. Augustine urged the government to kill heretics and said truly awful things about sex. Martin Luther urged the government to stab and slay peasants and said outrageous things about Jews. Karl Barth had a decades-long adulterous relationship. These terrible failures by Augustine, Luther, and Barth do not mean that we should stop reading and learning from their theological writing. The same conclusion, I believe, applies to Yoder. I therefore continue to learn from Yoder's writing as I grieve his colossal failure.

1. For the details, see the entire January 2015 issue of *The Mennonite Quarterly Review*, especially Rachel Waltner Goossen's lengthy article, "Defanging the Beast."

ABBREVIATIONS

General

AD	*anno Domini*, in the year of our Lord
art.	article
BC	before Christ
ca.	*circa*, about
cf.	*confer*, compare
chap(s).	chapter(s)
ed.	edition, edited by, editor
e.g.	*exempli gratia*, for example
esp.	especially
et al.	and others
i.e.	*id est*, that is
lit.	literally
no(s).	number(s)
p(p).	page(s)
repr.	reprint
rev.	revised
trans.	translated by, translation, translator
v(v).	verse(s)
vol(s).	volume(s)

Old Testament

Gen.	Genesis	Judg.	Judges
Exod.	Exodus	Ruth	Ruth
Lev.	Leviticus	1–2 Sam.	1–2 Samuel
Num.	Numbers	1–2 Kings	1–2 Kings
Deut.	Deuteronomy	1–2 Chron.	1–2 Chronicles
Josh.	Joshua	Ezra	Ezra

Neh.	Nehemiah
Esther	Esther
Job	Job
Ps./Pss.	Psalm/Psalms
Prov.	Proverbs
Eccles.	Ecclesiastes
Song	Song of Songs
Isa.	Isaiah
Jer.	Jeremiah
Lam.	Lamentations
Ezek.	Ezekiel
Dan.	Daniel
Hosea	Hosea
Joel	Joel
Amos	Amos
Obad.	Obadiah
Jon.	Jonah
Mic.	Micah
Nah.	Nahum
Hab.	Habakkuk
Zeph.	Zephaniah
Hag.	Haggai
Zech.	Zechariah
Mal.	Malachi

New Testament

Matt.	Matthew
Mark	Mark
Luke	Luke
John	John
Acts	Acts
Rom.	Romans
1–2 Cor.	1–2 Corinthians
Gal.	Galatians
Eph.	Ephesians
Phil.	Philippians
Col.	Colossians
1–2 Thess.	1–2 Thessalonians
1–2 Tim.	1–2 Timothy
Titus	Titus
Philem.	Philemon
Heb.	Hebrews
James	James
1–2 Pet.	1–2 Peter
1–3 John	1–3 John
Jude	Jude
Rev.	Revelation

Josephus

Ant.	*Jewish Antiquities*
JW	*Jewish War*

Secondary Sources and Collections

ANF	*Ante-Nicene Fathers*
LXX	Septuagint
NPNF¹	*Nicene and Post-Nicene Fathers*, Series 1
TDNT	*Theological Dictionary of the New Testament*. Edited by Gerhard Kittel and Gerhard Friedrich. Translated by Geoffrey W. Bromiley. 10 vols. Grand Rapids: Eerdmans, 1964–77.
TDOT	*Theological Dictionary of the Old Testament*. Edited by G. Johannes Botterweck and Helmer Ringgren. Translated by John T. Willis et al. 8 vols. Grand Rapids: Eerdmans, 1974–2006.

INTRODUCTION

Both in my head and in my heart, I understand and appreciate the just war tradition. Vicious bullies and ruthless dictators—Hitler, Stalin, Pol Pot, ISIS—swagger through history wreaking terrible havoc on hundreds of millions of innocent people. In response, thoughtful, caring Christians (and others) regularly conclude that the only realistic way to stop their vile destruction is to use lethal force. Pacifists who claim that the followers of Jesus should love their enemies and never kill seem, in the face of such massive evil, to be naive, simplistic, utopian.

Even worse, pacifists appear to be fundamentally immoral. They seem to ignore their basic moral responsibility to love—and therefore protect—their neighbors. Standing passively on the sidelines doing nothing to defend neighbors who are being destroyed is irresponsible and wicked.

C. S. Lewis makes the point vividly: "Does anyone suppose that our Lord's hearers understood Him to mean that if a homicidal maniac, attempting to murder a third party, tried to knock me out of the way, I must stand aside and let him get his victim?"[1] Just war Christians regularly charge that pacifists fail to love their neighbors who are threatened. Pacifists, they allege, take no responsibility for history. In fact they prefer tyranny to justice.

I think just war Christians are correct that if there are only two options (to kill or do nothing to defend neighbors), then faithful Christians should kill. Lewis is surely right: Jesus would not want us to step aside and passively watch while an aggressor brutalized others.

The problem with this critique of pacifism is that there are never only two options (to kill or do nothing). There is always a third possibility: to intervene nonviolently to oppose and seek to restrain the aggressor. Nor is nonviolent

---

1. Lewis, *Weight of Glory*, 86. From a 1940 speech ("Why I Am Not a Pacifist") at Oxford to a pacifist society.

resistance to evil a utopian, ineffective approach. In the past one hundred years (and especially the past fifty years) nonviolent resistance to injustice, tyranny, and brutal dictatorship has again and again proved astonishingly successful. Gandhi's nonviolence defeated the British Empire. Martin Luther King Jr.'s nonviolent civil rights movement changed American history. Solidarity's nonviolent campaign defied and conquered the Polish communist dictatorship. A million nonviolent Filipino demonstrators prevailed against the vicious dictator President Ferdinand Marcos.[2] A recent scholarly book examined all the known cases (323) of *both* major armed and unarmed insurrections from 1900 to 2006 and discovered an amazing result: "Nonviolent resistance campaigns were nearly twice as likely to achieve full or partial success as their violent counterparts."[3]

It is simply contrary to the facts of history to say that there are only two options: to kill or to do nothing in the face of tyranny and brutality. I agree that to stand aside and fail to resist evil is cowardly, irresponsible, immoral, and blatantly contradictory to Jesus's command to love our neighbor. But the historical record demonstrates that there is always a third option: vigorous, nonviolent resistance. And it frequently works—in fact, it apparently succeeds more often than violence.

But not always. Sometimes, at least in the short run, nonviolent actions fail. What then should Christians do?

That is the central question of this book. Does Jesus ever want his disciples to kill in order to resist evil and promote peace and justice? When Jesus commanded his disciples to love their enemies, did he mean that they should never kill them?

Later, I will examine the many arguments that allege that Christians today need not, should not, be bound by Jesus's teaching. But if Jesus is true God as well as true man; if the eternal Son became human not only to die for our sins but also to reveal how we should live; if Jesus claimed to be the long-expected Messiah; if central to Jesus's gospel is the announcement that the messianic kingdom where forgiveness and shalom reign is now breaking into history in the new community of Jesus's disciples; and if, in the power of the risen Lord and the Holy Spirit, it is possible for Jesus's disciples to live *now* the norms of Jesus's dawning kingdom; if that is what the New Testament teaches (and this book will seek to show in detail that it is), then it is a huge theological mistake to say that contemporary Christians should ignore or set aside what Jesus taught about killing.

2. See Sider, *Nonviolent Action*, for more examples.
3. Chenoweth and Stephan, *Why Civil Resistance Works*, 7.

For the Christian who embraces historic orthodox teaching about who Jesus is, the most important question for our topic is: Did Jesus mean to teach his disciples never to kill?[4] This book is my answer.

Before starting that detailed argument, however, I need to define how I use the words "coercion" and "violence." I use the word "coercion" to refer to the exercise of influence on others in ways that pressure them to act in a certain way. Legitimate coercion is action that influences others in ways that are in keeping with Jesus's call to love our neighbors (which, as I will argue, excludes killing them). Violence is any action against a neighbor where the intent is to harm the neighbor, including killing the neighbor.[5]

Because we are created as social beings, coercion is inevitable. The most loving acts of parental discipline involve psychological coercion. So do the most loving acts of church discipline or a kind teacher's insistence on deadlines and appropriate behavior. Psychological coercion is an inevitable part of our being social beings living in community. "Coercion is an inherent component of social life."[6] Coercion always involves some exercise of power over another. Duane Friesen outlines several questions to help determine whether the use of such power is moral coercion or immoral violence: the use of power should contribute to shalom, be truthful and not manipulative, not reduce others to impotence (although it may rightly reduce their options for a time), and be nonviolent.[7] It is a mistake to speak of "the ideal of absolute non-coercion in human relations."[8]

Economic boycotts are coercive. So is the physical restraint of a child about to run in front of a car, or of a distraught person about to jump off a high bridge. But these coercive acts are fully compatible with loving the other persons, seeking their best interest and leaving them free to make different choices in the future. Killing a person is fundamentally different from physical restraint prompted by love and exercised to protect persons, or encourage different (moral) choices because killing a person removes any possibility of the person changing.

---

4. I am aware that New Testament scholars in the past two hundred years have argued in great detail whether the Gospels accurately reflect the teaching and actions of Jesus or rather primarily reflect the thinking of the Gospel writers. I do not in this book try to enter into that detailed discussion, although I largely embrace the approach and conclusions of scholars like Craig S. Keener (*Historical Jesus*). Rather, I begin with the church's confession that the biblical canon is God's special revelation that properly functions as the primary source of authority for Christian faith and practice. Therefore my basic question in this book is, What does the biblical canon say to the question of whether Jesus ever wants his followers to kill their enemies?

5. I find especially helpful the distinctions made by Friesen, *Christian Peacemaking*, 143–49.

6. Friesen, "Power," 76.

7. Friesen, "Power," 83–84. See also the helpful essay by Finn, "Morality, Government."

8. Roth, *Choosing against War*, 115.

Violence can be psychological, physical but not lethal, or lethal. Action that damages, and is intended to damage, the dignity or self-esteem of another person is violent. So is action that damages, and is done with the intention to damage, the body or property of another person. Obviously, physically restraining a mentally ill person or boycotting a business because of its unjust activity may cause harm to a person's body or property, but those acts are not violent, because the action does not kill anyone and the intent is to create well-being, not harm.[9] The motive of the person causing harm is a crucial factor in determining whether the action that causes harm is moral coercion or immoral violence. As long as the intent is love and well-being for persons involved and the action leaves all persons free to make different, better choices in the future, the coercive action is not violent.[10] However, even action that causes modest bodily harm or minor economic loss is violent if the intent of the action is to cause harm rather than promote the well-being of the persons involved (which in an economic boycott includes the well-being of large numbers of people being treated unjustly by the person or institution being boycotted).

Coercion (whether psychological, physical, or economic) is morally appropriate as long as the intent and overall effect is the promotion of everyone's well-being and persons are not killed. Violence (whether psychological, physical, or economic) is always wrong, because the action does not flow from love for all persons involved and the desire to promote their well-being. Killing another person always involves violence.

One other comment on definitions: I frequently use the word "pacifism" to describe my position. But by this word, I do not intend to depict a passive (or nonresistant) response to evil and injustice. The biblical pacifism I endorse is not only compatible with a vigorous nonviolent resistance to all evil. As my book *Nonviolent Action* demonstrates, it also demands it.

9. Thus I do not agree with the definition of violence in Stassen and Westmoreland-White, "Defining Violence and Nonviolence," 18. Their definition ("Violence is destruction to a victim by means that overpower the victim's consent") would mean that a morally justified economic boycott that caused some economic loss to an unjust business would be violent. I prefer to call such action morally justified coercion.

10. Hans Boersma finds the key factor distinguishing legitimate and illegitimate nonlethal harm to be the motive of the person causing the harm. Boersma, however, prefers to call even the legitimate nonlethal harm "violence," whereas I find it more clarifying to use the word "violence" only in the case of inappropriate action. See Boersma, *Violence, Hospitality, and the Cross*, 46–47.

1

Jesus's Gospel

Virtually every New Testament scholar, whether liberal or conservative, Catholic or Protestant, agrees that the gospel Jesus announced and proclaimed was "the kingdom of God." This phrase (or Matthew's equivalent, "the kingdom of heaven," which means exactly the same thing) appears 122 times in the first three Gospels—most of the time (92) on the lips of Jesus. Jesus points to the kingdom as the purpose of his coming (Luke 4:43). Both his preaching and his miraculous healings are signs of the kingdom (7:18–28). And Jesus sends out his disciples to announce the coming of the kingdom (Matt. 10:7–8; Luke 10:9).

At the core of Jesus's teaching was the claim that the long-expected messianic time of peace, justice, forgiveness of sins, and restoration of Israel was actually breaking into history in his person and work. But Jesus puzzled and astonished his contemporaries. By his teaching and action, he offered an understanding of the nature and work of the Messiah that was strikingly different from that of popular expectation. He rejected the widespread messianic idea of a conquering military hero. When he publicly made messianic claims in his triumphal entry into Jerusalem, he rode not on a military general's proud warhorse but rather on a lowly donkey. And he taught his followers to love their enemies.

To understand the implications of Jesus's messianic understanding for our topic, we must first explore the messianic expectations of his day, then examine the extent of messianic violence in Jesus's time, and finally develop more fully Jesus's teaching on the dawning kingdom of God. Only then will we be ready to understand Jesus's more specific words and actions with regard to violence.

Messianic Expectations

In 587 BC Babylon conquered the kingdom of Judah, destroyed the capital city Jerusalem and its temple, and took Judah and its leaders into exile in Babylon. Those events fundamentally challenged the basic belief that God had given the land of Israel to Abraham's descendants forever and that the one God of the universe was uniquely present in the temple in Jerusalem. The people's sinful failure to obey God's revealed law, their prophets explained, was the reason for national destruction and exile. But their prophets also held out the hope of a future return from exile and a restoration of their God's presence in a rebuilt temple.

There were modest movements of return from exile under Ezra and Nehemiah in the latter half of the fifth century BC. But no strong independent Jewish kingdom emerged. Many descendants of the ancient Israelites remained scattered throughout the Near East. And those who still lived in the ancient homeland suffered under the rule of oppressive empires. For a century after the Hasmonean revolt, which started in 167 BC, a small Jewish kingdom existed, but the Romans swept through Palestine in 63 BC. Living under the Romans' ruthless rule, the Jews had little sense that the long-expected return from exile had truly happened.

The hope for a Davidic figure who would bring the nation freedom was largely absent for several hundred years after the fall of Jerusalem in 587 BC. But in the Hasmonean period a messianic hope for national restoration grounded in some earlier biblical texts emerged. Yale biblical scholar John J. Collins shows that by the end of the first century BC the idea of the Davidic Messiah as a warrior king who destroys Israel's enemies and brings unending peace "constitutes the common core of Jewish messianism around the turn of the era."[1] "This expectation of a Davidic messiah had a clear basis in the Scriptures and became very widespread in various sectors of Judaism in the last century before the Common Era."[2]

That is not to suggest that there was one uniform messianic understanding in this period. A variety of messianic views existed.[3] The Jewish historian

1. J. Collins, *Scepter and the Star*, 68.
2. J. Collins, *Scepter and the Star*, 95. See also A. Collins and J. Collins, *King and Messiah*, 63–75, and Keener, *Historical Jesus*, 265, for a number of texts of the period that express messianic (often militaristic) hopes.
3. Longman, "Messiah," 28–30; N. T. Wright, *New Testament and the People of God*, 307–20.

Josephus (who is our best source outside of the New Testament for the events in Palestine in the first century AD) talks about various violent rebellious movements (some of which were messianic) in the period leading up to the Jewish War (AD 66–70). These violent movements, Josephus suggests, helped lead to that war. Josephus speaks of an "ambiguous oracle" in the Jewish sacred writings about someone from their country becoming a ruler of the world.[4]

In the Jewish texts from the two hundred years before and after the birth of Jesus that speak of the Messiah, his central task is the liberation of Israel (often using military means) and the cleansing or restoration of the Jerusalem temple. There is no expectation that the Messiah will suffer.[5] But the expectation of a military conqueror is certainly present: "How beautiful is the king, the messiah, who will arise from those who are of the house of Judah! He girds up his loins and goes forth and orders the battle array against his enemies and slays the kings along with their overlords, and no king or overlord can stand before him; he reddens the mountains with the blood of their slain, his clothing is dipped in blood like a winepress."[6] Craig Keener says that "most Jews expected a final war against the Gentiles to culminate this age and inaugurate their redemption."[7]

The texts describing the end of the old age and the arrival of the new messianic age often use powerful apocalyptic language and vivid cosmic imagery. Unfortunately, since the time of Albert Schweitzer at the beginning of the twentieth century, many scholars have thought these texts were talking about the end of the physical world. But more recent scholarship has shown that view to be fundamentally mistaken. In N. T. Wright's words:

> There is virtually no evidence that Jews were expecting the end of the space-time universe. There is abundant evidence that they, like Jeremiah and others before them, knew a good metaphor when they saw one, and used cosmic imagery to bring out the full theological significance of cataclysmic sociopolitical events. There is almost nothing to suggest that they followed the Stoics into the belief that the world itself would come to an end. . . . They believed that the present world order would come to an end—the world order in which pagans hold power and Jews, the covenant people of the creator God, did not. . . . Jews simply did not believe that the space-time order was shortly to disappear.[8]

4. N. T. Wright, New Testament and the People of God, 312.
5. N. T. Wright, New Testament and the People of God, 320.
6. Palestinian Targum on Gen. 48:10; quoted in Hengel, Victory over Violence, 69.
7. Keener, Gospel of Matthew, 168.
8. N. T. Wright, New Testament and the People of God, 333 (italics original). See also N. T. Wright, New Testament and the People of God, 284–85. So too J. Collins, Scepter and the Star,

The apocalyptic language "had nothing to do with a supposed end of the space-time order and everything to do with the great climax to Israel's history, the final liberation of Israel from her pagan enemies."[9]

Very often these texts predicted a violent war that would overthrow the pagans and usher in the age of peace. There are also many passages in the Old Testament that speak of a future leader and time that will bring universal peace. Especially striking are three from Isaiah.

Isaiah 9:5–7 speaks of a coming king who would bring peace and justice:

> Every warrior's boot used in battle
>   and every garment rolled in blood
> will be destined for burning,
>   will be fuel for the fire.
> For to us a child is born,
>   to us a son is given,
>   and the government will be on his shoulders.
> And he will be called
>   Wonderful Counselor, Mighty God,
>   Everlasting Father, Prince of Peace.
> Of the greatness of his government and peace
>   there will be no end.
> He will reign on David's throne
>   and over his kingdom,
> establishing and upholding it
>   with justice and righteousness
>   from that time on and forever.

Isaiah 11:1–9 also talks about a coming descendant of David who will bring peace and justice:

> A shoot will come up from the stump of Jesse [the father of David]; . . .
> With righteousness he will judge the needy,
>   with justice he will give decisions for the poor of the earth. . . .
> The wolf will live with the lamb,
>   the leopard will lie down with the goat. . . .
> They will neither harm nor destroy
>   on all my holy mountain.[10]

---

in his discussion of the frequent phrase, "the end of days" (or the "last days"). The phrase does not mean "the end of history or of the world. . . . In all the prophetic texts, the reference is rather to the end of one era and the beginning of another," 105.

9. N. T. Wright, *Jesus and the Victory of God*, 40; see also 81, 95–97.

10. It is true that Isa. 11:4–6 may suggest a violent war before the age of peace.

And most amazing, Isaiah 2:2–4 says that in the last days,

> the mountain of the LORD's temple will be established
>   as the highest of the mountains;
> it will be exalted above the hills,
>   and all nations will stream to it.

Many peoples will come and say,
>   "Come, let us go up to the mountain of the LORD,
>   to the temple of the God of Jacob.
> He will teach us his ways,
>   so that we may walk in his paths."
> The law will go out from Zion,
>   the word of the LORD from Jerusalem.
> He will judge between the nations
>   and will settle disputes for many peoples.
> They will beat their swords into plowshares
>   and their spears into pruning hooks.
> Nation will not take up sword against nation,
>   nor will they train for war anymore.

We know from the Dead Sea Scrolls and other documents from this period that around the time of Jesus, many Jews understood Isaiah 2:2–4, 9:5–7, and 11:1–9 as predictions of the messianic time. "Isaiah 11 becomes an important proof-text for messianic expectation in the period of the Dead Sea Scrolls."[11] And the New Testament clearly and explicitly applies these passages from Isaiah about peace and justice to Jesus.

Matthew 4:15–16 quotes Isaiah 9:1–2 in connection with the beginning of Jesus's proclamation of the coming of the messianic kingdom. Paul refers to Isaiah 11:1 and 10 in Romans 15:12. Alluding to Isaiah 9:2, the prophet Zechariah points with eager expectation to the Messiah who will "guide our feet into the way of peace" (Luke 1:79). And repeatedly Christian writers of the first three centuries declared that the messianic prophecy of Isaiah 2:4 (Mic. 4:3) was fulfilled in Jesus's prohibition against killing.[12]

Messianic expectations were widespread among the Jews in the period around the time of Jesus's life. But was violence a central part of the expectation?

---

11. J. Collins, *Scepter and the Star*, 25; see also 57–61. It is also true that these documents often describe the coming Davidic Messiah as a warrior. For evidence that Isa. 9:6 was understood to refer to the Messiah, see Mauser, *Gospel of Peace*, 153.

12. Sider, *Early Church on Killing*, 173.

Messianic Violence

There is substantial scholarly disagreement about the extent and nature of movements of messianic violence in the decades around the lifetime of Jesus. Martin Hengel wrote an influential scholarly book called *The Zealots*, in which he argues that the zealots were a major nationalistic messianic party in Judaism at this time. Richard A. Horsley strongly disagrees.[13] Horsley argues that the typical modern portrayals of Jesus as a pacifist depend "basically on 'the zealots' as a foil for Jesus' position and the sayings of Matthew 5:38–48." But that is a mistake because "there was no sustained movement of violent resistance to Roman rule during the first century C.E."[14] Horsley rightly points out that Josephus (ca. AD 37–100) first speaks of the "zealots" as an organized party only in the winter of AD 67–68.[15] The available evidence does not warrant our speaking of a continuous organized zealot party throughout the first century.

What is clear, however, from numerous sources, is that again and again in the three centuries before the Jewish War, oppressive conquerors provoked violent, often religiously motivated, rebellion on the part of the oppressed Jews in Palestine. In this same period, and frequently in close connection, messianic speculation became fairly widespread among the Jews.

In 167 BC, the Hellenistic rulers in Palestine added religious persecution to their heavy taxation. A megalomaniac Syrian monarch actually desecrated the Jewish temple in Jerusalem and replaced Jewish rites with worship of himself. Some Jews refused to comply and were killed. Others, drawing on their holy war tradition and inspired by the religious "zeal" of Phinehas in the Old Testament (who slaughtered those who disobeyed God), organized a guerrilla movement led by Judas Maccabaeus.[16] In a series of bloody battles, they drove the Hellenistic conquerors out of Palestine and secured one hundred years of religious and political freedom. But that was not to last.

In 63 BC, Pompey's Roman soldiers conquered Palestine, inaugurating many centuries of Roman rule. Sometimes they ruled through client kings and sometimes directly through procurators like Pilate. But always the taxation was heavy, and the threat to cherished religious beliefs was frequent. (Pompey walked right into the holy of holies in the temple, where only the high priest

---

13. Horsley and Hanson, *Bandits, Prophets, and Messiahs*. See also Horsley, "Ethics and Exegesis," 3–31; Smith, *Studies in Historical Method*, 211–26.

14. Horsley, *Jesus and the Spiral of Violence*, 318–19.

15. Horsley, *Jesus and the Spiral of Violence*, x.

16. N. T. Wright, *New Testament and the People of God*, 158–59. For Phinehas, see Num. 25:6–13 and 1 Maccabees 2:17–28.

was allowed to enter once a year.) Violent revolts led by Jews, often motivated by religious (sometimes messianic) hope that their God would intervene to save the chosen people, erupted with some frequency. Many of the revolutionaries believed that since God was their only Lord, Jews should not submit to Rome or pay Roman taxes.[17]

The War Scroll of the Essenes (a major Jewish monastic community in the two hundred years before and after the birth of Jesus) illustrates how the holy war tradition (revived under the Maccabees) helped at least some Jews of this period to expect to fight a war against the Romans to usher in the messianic time. The War Scroll talks about how the entire community of the Essenes will fight against the *Kittim* (the Romans). And they believed that God would intervene as they fought to destroy the Romans and inaugurate the messianic kingdom.[18]

Herod the Great ruled Palestine as a client king from about 37 to 4 BC. He built a glorious temple in Jerusalem but also imposed heavy taxes and ruthlessly murdered opponents. He also introduced the cult of the Roman emperor into the Hellenistic areas of his kingdom (building Roman temples honoring Caesar as divine) at a time when the emperor called himself "son of God"—blasphemy, according to devout monotheistic Jews.

Not surprisingly, widespread rebellion broke out when Herod died. It started when Herod was on his deathbed. Contrary to the Jewish prohibition against images, Herod had placed a large golden eagle (a symbol of Roman rule) on a gate of the rebuilt temple. As Herod lay dying, two Jerusalem scribes encouraged their followers to tear down the eagle. But Herod was still alive, and his troops killed the rebels. That only provoked more widespread rebellion against Herod's son and successor, Archelaus, after Herod's death. Teachers of the law led a rebellion, which Archelaus squelched, killing three thousand Jews, many in the temple. Fifty days later, an even larger Jewish crowd attacked the Roman garrison in Jerusalem. They saw, according to Josephus, "a proper opportunity for the recovery of their country's ancient liberty" (*Ant.* 17.269). Religious zeal was clearly a significant part of the rebels' motivation. Furious battles ensued in Jerusalem, killing large numbers of both Roman soldiers and Jewish rebels. Finally, the Roman general in charge of Syria arrived, squelched the rebellion, and crucified two thousand Jewish insurgents (*JW* 2.75; *Ant.* 17.295).[19]

Josephus reports that at this time there were "ten thousand other disorders in Judea" (*Ant.* 17.269). The whole of Judea, Josephus says, was "one

17. Storkey, *Jesus and Politics*, 53.
18. Hengel, *Zealots*, 281–87. See also J. Collins, *Scepter and the Star*, 60. For the meaning of *Kittim*, see 57–58.
19. N. T. Wright, *New Testament and the People of God*, 172–73.

scene of guerilla warfare" (*JW* 2.65). Simon, a former slave of Herod, led a rebel group and proclaimed himself king. A shepherd named Athronges did something similar. These two rebellious outbreaks, N. T. Wright believes, were "would-be messianic movements."[20]

A rebellion also broke out in Galilee in the city of Sepphoris (not too far from Nazareth). The leader was Judas, the son of Hezekiah, a brigand chief with some substantial support in Jerusalem (Hezekiah had been killed several decades earlier by Herod). Judas led a large group of followers, who broke into Herod's arsenal and armed themselves. His motive in part, according to Josephus, was "an ambitious desire of the royal dignity" (*Ant.* 17.272)—quite possibly a messianic claim. But the Romans defeated them, burned the city, and enslaved all the inhabitants (*JW* 2.56, 68).

About ten years later, another rebellion against Rome occurred in opposition to the census and taxation that Quirinius the governor conducted in Judea. "Enrolling in Rome's system meant admitting that the land and the people were not after all sacred to Israel's god."[21] Judas of Galilee and Sadduk, a Pharisee, led the people to revolt against the census. They said that "this taxation was no better than an introduction to slavery and exhorted the nation to assert their liberty" (*Ant.* 18.4). Declaring a message that could easily have been understood to have messianic implications, they told the people that God would assist them if they would join together in daring revolt (*Ant.* 18.5).

From the Essenes' War Scroll, we also know that other Jewish people of this general period believed that when God would intervene at the end of the age, all the devout would join in a holy war of total annihilation of the wicked.[22] Josephus tells us that many people followed Judas and Sadduk and "the nation was infested with this doctrine to an incredible degree" (*Ant.* 18.6; see also Acts 5:37).

Josephus describes Judas of Galilee and Sadduk as the founders of a fourth Jewish "philosophy" alongside that of the Essenes, Sadducees, and Pharisees. Their "philosophy," he says, was almost identical to that of the Pharisees except that Judas and Sadduk "have an inviolable attachment to liberty and say that God is to be their only Ruler and Lord." Nor can even fear of death "make them call any man lord" (*Ant.* 18.23). Josephus says explicitly that it was this fourth philosophy with its religious, perhaps messianic, rejection of Roman rule and taxation that led eventually to the devastating Jewish War (AD 66–70), which destroyed the nation (*Ant.* 18.9–10).

20. N. T. Wright, *New Testament and the People of God*, 173.
21. N. T. Wright, *New Testament and the People of God*, 173.
22. Hengel, *Victory over Violence*, 39–40.

Hostility to and rebellion against Rome continued in the next sixty years after Judas of Galilee's rebellion against Roman taxation. There were at least seven major incidents just during the ten years (AD 26–36) when Pilate was procurator of Judea.[23] In the 40s, Theudas claimed to be a prophet, gathered a substantial number of followers, and promised to divide the Jordan so they could easily cross over—a clear claim to be reenacting the historic exodus from Egypt. But the Romans killed many of his followers and decapitated Theudas (*Ant.* 20.97–99). Sometime between AD 46 and AD 48, two sons of Judas the Galilean were crucified as rebels against Rome. And Josephus says that during a Passover sometime in the years between AD 48 and AD 52, the Romans slaughtered twenty thousand Jews (*Ant.* 20.105–12).

Josephus tells us that in the next decade people he calls bandits (*Sicarii*) attracted many people with their claim to divine inspiration and call for revolutionary change. Someone from Egypt duped thirty thousand Jews, claiming to be a prophet, but he failed (*JW* 2.259–63). According to Josephus, "the imposters and brigands banded together, incited numbers to revolt, exhorting them to assert their independence and threatening to kill any who submitted to Roman domination" (*JW* 2.264).

The evidence is clear. From the time of the death of Herod I in 4 BC, there were repeated violent rebellions against Roman rule in Palestine. Both in Galilee and especially in Jerusalem, "revolution of one sort or another was in the air, and often present on the ground."[24] The sources often indicate a religious motivation. Frequently, N. T. Wright points out, these movements "were led by messianic or quasi-messianic figures."[25] And the Romans frequently squelched them with crucifixion. Violent messianic revolt, grounded in the belief that God would intervene to bring the messianic kingdom if the Jews would dare to rebel, was clearly part of Jewish life in this period.[26]

Even Horsley acknowledges that popular "messianic" revolts occurred in the years before Jesus. With reference to the rebellion in 4 BC at Herod's death, Horsley says, "The three major popular revolts in each of the major outlying

23. N. T. Wright, *New Testament and the People of God*, 174.

24. N. T. Wright, *New Testament and the People of God*, 176. Also: "Violent revolution against Rome was a very live option at this time" (303).

25. N. T. Wright, *New Testament and the People of God*, 173.

26. In *New Testament and the People of God*, N. T. Wright says, "I thus agree broadly with the outline of Hengel's work" (181n76); see also N. T. Wright, *Jesus and the Victory of God*, 290n178. Nigel Biggar agrees that it is "prima facie unlikely" that violent Jewish nationalism had disappeared in Jesus's lifetime (*In Defence of War*, 45–46). Thus both Wright and Biggar largely agree with Hengel's basic interpretation of the period in Palestine in the hundred-plus years between 50 BC and AD 70. See further the critical review of Morton Smith and Richard Horsley in Klassen, "Jesus and the Zealot Option," 131–49.

districts—Galilee, Perea, and Judea—all assumed the same socio-religious form, that of a popular messianic movement."[27]

Hengel sums up this period of imperialistic violence, foreign oppression, and passionate religious nationalism this way: "For the unsophisticated Jewish population, it was almost entirely a history of oppressive exploitation, wars of indescribable brutality and disappointed hopes. The rule of Herod and his sons and the corrupt regime of the procurators—Pilate not least among them—had made the situation in Jewish Palestine so intolerable that apparently only three possibilities remained: armed revolutionary resistance, more or less opportunistic accommodation to the establishment—leaving open the possibility of mental reservations—and patient passive endurance."[28] Remembering this context is essential if we are to properly understand Jesus's gospel of the kingdom of God.

Jesus's Gospel of the Kingdom

As we saw earlier, the first three Gospels make it very clear that the core of Jesus's message is the announcement that the kingdom of God is arriving in his person and work. At the beginning of his Gospel, Mark summarizes Jesus's whole message with the simple words: "The kingdom of God has come near. Repent and believe the good news!" (Mark 1:15). Luke begins Jesus's public ministry with Jesus in the synagogue reading Isaiah 61:1–2—a text often understood in that time as a passage about the coming messianic kingdom.[29] Jesus ends the reading with the words "Today this scripture is fulfilled in your hearing" (Luke 4:21). When John the Baptist sends his disciples to ask Jesus if he is the long-expected Messiah, Jesus points to his miraculous healings of the blind, lame, lepers, and deaf as evidence enough (7:18–23). His actions, Jesus implies, are fulfilling messianic expectations. This becomes especially clear when one compares Jesus's reply to John the Baptist to a fragment from the Dead Sea Scrolls. The latter text reflects an expectation that the Messiah would bring sight to the blind, hearing to the deaf, good news to the poor, and raising of the dead (see 4Q521).[30] And when opponents claim that Jesus is casting out demons by the power of Satan, he replies, "If it is by the Spirit of God that I drive out demons, then the kingdom of God has come upon you" (Matt. 12:28). Past tense! The long-expected kingdom of God has already

27. Horsley, *Jesus and the Spiral of Violence*, 52.
28. Hengel, *Victory over Violence*, 71.
29. E.g., 4Q521 from the Dead Sea Scrolls. Stassen and Gushee, *Kingdom Ethics*, 35.
30. See Perrin, "From Qumran to Nazareth," 224–26.

arrived, and it is happening through the work of Jesus himself—a rather clear, if indirect, claim to be the expected Messiah.

Some scholars have doubted that Jesus ever claimed to be the Messiah. But among the various reasons for thinking that he did is one stark fact. The one thing the Roman judicial and political world knew about Jesus of Nazareth was that he was crucified as a political threat to Rome precisely on the charge of claiming to be king of the Jews, the Jewish Messiah. If Jesus had not claimed to be the Messiah, the disciples would certainly not have applied this politically dangerous title to him after his death. That would have meant creating for themselves the highly dangerous situation of being disciples of someone convicted of treason.[31]

Jesus's declaration that the kingdom of God was arriving would have sparked enormous excitement among Jesus's contemporaries. As N. T. Wright says, "God's kingdom, to the Jew-in-the-village in the first half of the first century, meant the coming vindication of Israel, victory over the pagans, the eventual gift of peace, justice, and prosperity."[32]

But Jesus fundamentally reinterpreted his people's hope for the messianic kingdom. Nowhere is this more clear than in Jesus's rejection of the violent revolutionaries' call to take up arms against the Romans. These revolutionaries who opposed paying Roman taxes would certainly have denounced the Roman law that made it legal for a Roman soldier to demand that a person in a conquered territory carry his bags for one mile. Instead of urging rebellion against that law, Jesus called his followers to carry the bags a second mile! Instead of urging slaughter of the godless conquerors, Jesus urged his people to love their enemies. Luke describes Jesus's triumphal entry into Jerusalem riding on a donkey rather than a warhorse—a powerful indication of Jesus's rejection of violent messianic strategies. And immediately after this account, Luke tells us that Jesus weeps over Jerusalem, foreseeing how the calls for violent revolution will lead to the city's destruction (a tragedy that actually happened in AD 70). Sadly, Jesus says, "If you, even you, had only known on this day what would bring you peace—but now it is hidden from your eyes" (Luke 19:42).[33]

Many Jews in Jesus's day thought the Messiah would come to inaugurate the kingdom if large numbers of people would join the rebels in a huge war

31. Keener, *Historical Jesus*, 266. See also N. T. Wright, *Jesus and the Victory of God*, 514, for the fact that Jesus's frequent self-description "Son of Man" (based on Dan. 7) was understood by some in Jesus's day as a messianic figure.

32. N. T. Wright, *Jesus and the Victory of God*, 204. See too N. T. Wright, *New Testament and the People of God*, 303.

33. See also Mark 13:1–4 and N. T. Wright, *Jesus and the Victory of God*, chap. 8.

against the Romans.[34] Jesus rejects this violent messianic option, calling his
disciples to love their enemies. N. T. Wright puts it this way: Jesus taught that
the kingdom would come "not by military victory, but by a doubly revolutionary method: turning the other cheek, going the second mile, the deeply
subversive wisdom of taking up the cross."[35]

Jesus's teaching on forgiveness also contrasted sharply with other messianic strategies. Some Pharisees taught that if the people kept the law
faithfully, that would hasten the coming of the Messiah. Jesus, however,
teaches that forgiveness was central to the arrival of the kingdom. The
kingdom, Jesus says, is like a merciful king who freely forgives a huge debt
that his servant cannot repay (Matt. 18:23–35). To the horror of the Pharisees, Jesus eagerly forgives even the most notorious offenders—prostitutes,
the woman caught in adultery, and hated tax collectors profiting from col-
laboration with the foreign oppressors. To underline his acceptance, he
shares table fellowship with these social outcasts. When the self-righteous
protest indignantly, he retorts that he came to call not the righteous but
sinners (Mark 2:17).

Jesus forgave sinners in this radical, prodigal way because he knew that
God is like the forgiving father in the parable of the prodigal son. In parable
after parable, Jesus teaches that God takes the initiative to forgive sinners.
"Throughout all the parables, God appears in constantly new variations as
the one who is generous: as the magnanimous, merciful king, as the lender
generously cancelling a debt, as the shepherd seeking the sheep, as the woman
searching for the lost coin, as the father rushing out to meet his son, as the
judge hearing the prayer of the tax collector. Again and again [God] is seen
afresh as the God of infinite mercy."[36] We in turn—as the parable about the
unforgiving servant so vividly shows—are to imitate God's radical forgiveness
in our relationships with others (Matt. 18:23–35).

Jesus not only teaches about a forgiving God. He also claims personal
authority to forgive sins. Jewish sources do not speak of the Messiah forgiving sins on his own authority. But Jesus boldly claims that authority. Jesus
forgives the sins of the paralytic seeking healing. When the religious leaders
object to this blasphemous infringement on God's sole authority to forgive
sins, he retorts, "I want you to know that the Son of Man has authority on
earth to forgive sins" (Mark 2:10).

34. See Josephus, *Ant.* 18.4–6, 9–10, 23; Wright, *New Testament and the People of God*,
174; and Hengel, *Victory over Violence*, 39–40, 58.
35. N. T. Wright, *Jesus and the Victory of God*, 465.
36. Küng, *On Being a Christian*, 276. See Matt. 18:23–27; Luke 7:41–43; 15:3–7, 8–10, 11–32;
18:9–14; cf. Matt. 20:1–15.

Jesus's designation of himself as "Son of Man" in the passage on forgiveness is significant. In Jesus's day, many Jews understood the figure of the "son of man" in Daniel 7 to be a messianic figure. We have Jewish texts of this period that interpret Daniel 7 as a messianic passage that predicts "the Lion of Judah triumphing over the Eagle of Rome."[37] Josephus says that this messianic prophecy "more than anything else incited the Jews to revolt" (JW 6.312–15). As the messianic Son of Man, Jesus did see himself bringing the kingdom. But he brought it through offering forgiveness, not through violence. Jesus understood his offer of forgiveness as a fundamental element of the kingdom breaking into history in his person and work. Forgiveness, not violence and vengeance, was the sign of his messianic kingdom.

Jesus's teaching in general and the Sermon on the Mount in particular spell out how Jesus intends his new messianic community to live. New Testament scholar Richard Hays points out that Matthew understands the Sermon on the Mount not as some impossible ideal but rather as "Jesus' programmatic disclosure of the kingdom of God and of the life to which the community of disciples is called."[38] And Jesus certainly does not think of his disciples as a tiny isolated fringe group in Israel. He says his people should be the salt of the *earth* and the light of the *whole world* (Matt. 5:13–14). By appointing twelve disciples, he shows that his message was for the twelve tribes of Israel—that is, the whole nation. Jesus claimed to be the Messiah of the whole people. His teaching was "a challenge to Israel to *be* Israel."[39]

And that message involved a radical challenge to the status quo at many points. He upsets men who were happy with the easy divorce laws that enabled them to dismiss their wives for many reasons. Instead, he insists that God intended one man and one woman to live together in lifelong union (Matt. 19:3–9; Mark 10:2–12). Jesus also disregarded social patterns that treated women as inferior. According to Jews of the time, a woman's word had no authority in court.[40] It was a disgrace for men to appear publicly with women. A widely used prayer recommended for daily use by Jewish males thanked God that they had not been created a gentile, a slave, or a woman.[41] Jesus, on the contrary, appears publicly with women (John 4:27), teaches them theology (Luke 10:38–42), and honors them with his first resurrection appearance (John 20:11–18).

37. N. T. Wright, *Jesus and the Victory of God*, 514.
38. Hays, *Moral Vision*, 321.
39. N. T. Wright, *Jesus and the Victory of God*, 288 (italics original); see also 251.
40. See Moule, *Significance of the Message*, 9.
41. See Swidler, *Biblical Affirmations of Woman*, 154–57.

Jesus upset political rulers who were smugly satisfied with their domination of their subjects. In the dawning messianic age, servanthood must replace domination.[42] The greatest in the kingdom is the Messiah, who is a servant of all. Therefore, those who aspire to leadership in Jesus's kingdom must likewise be humble servants rather than domineering masters.

Jesus terrified the economic establishment of his day. It would be easier for a camel to squeeze through the eye of a needle, he insists, than for a rich person to enter the kingdom (Matt. 19:24). He summons those with capital to lend to the needy even if they had no hope of recovering their investment (Luke 6:30, 34; cf. Matt. 5:42).[43] He recognized in the rich young ruler the idolatrous materialism that plagues many rich people. Therefore, he summons him—and presumably all others who worship the same idol—to give all his wealth to the poor (Matt. 19:21). And he denounces those who oppress poor widows.

In a daring act that led to his arrest, Jesus attacked the economic oppression and the religious desecration going on in the temple. Many people see only the religious side of Jesus's cleansing of the temple. But the text explicitly says that Jesus objects to both the sacrilege and the robbery: "It is written . . . , 'My house will be a house of prayer'; but you have made it 'a den of robbers'" (Luke 19:46). The chief priests and their collaborators with Rome had a monopoly on the sale of sacrificial animals, which Jewish worshipers who came from any distance had to purchase in order to sacrifice. Apparently, they turned the temple's Court of the Gentiles into a profitable stockyard where they charged very high prices. Jesus denounces their desecration of the gentiles' place of prayer for the sake of economic oppression.[44]

It is hardly surprising that the authorities moved quickly (Luke 19:47) to dispose of Jesus. A person demanding such radical change from the rich and powerful was a dangerous revolutionary. Jesus's uncompromising attack on the status quo wherever it was wrong was *one* fundamental reason he was crucified.

But Jesus's radical challenge to the status quo is only one part of the explanation for Jesus's death. The title Pilate placed on Jesus's cross, "King of the Jews," shows that the Romans crucified him on the political charge of treason (John 19:19; cf. Matt. 27:37; Mark 15:26; Luke 23:38). And the Jewish leaders of the Sanhedrin charged him with blasphemy for acknowledging that he was

---

42. Matt. 20:25–28; Mark 10:42–45; Luke 22:24–28. Notice that already here servanthood is grounded in the cross.

43. See, beyond these brief references, the more than four dozen passages from the Gospels in Sider, *Cry Justice*, and Sider, *Rich Christians*, chap. 3.

44. See Hengel, *Victory over Violence*, 80, who calls this act "an exemplary demonstration against the misuse of the sanctuary to enrich the leading priestly families."

"the Son of the Blessed One" and asserting that they would see him "sitting at the right hand of the Mighty One" (Mark 14:61–64).[45]

Jesus, however, went to the cross, not just because others hated what he said and did. The Gospels also tell us that Jesus thought his death was central to his mission. The Son of Man (his favorite title for himself) came, Jesus says, "to give his life as a ransom for many" (Matt. 20:28). Both Matthew and Mark report that immediately after Jesus affirms Peter's confession that he is the Messiah, Jesus begins to warn the disciples about his coming death (Matt. 16:13–23; Mark 8:27–33). At the last meal with his disciples, Jesus says his blood is "poured out for many for the forgiveness of sins" (Matt. 26:28).

N. T. Wright shows how Jesus saw his death as central to his belief that the kingdom of God that he had announced was actually arriving in his own person. Jesus's contemporaries expected the Messiah to cleanse or rebuild the temple and defeat their enemies. Jesus seems to suggest that his death will accomplish what Jews generally thought the temple accomplished (he had already claimed authority to forgive sins apart from the temple). "In other words," Wright says, "Jesus intended that his death should in some sense function sacrificially."[46] His death would also conquer the real enemy, who was not the Romans but Satan, "who had duped YHWH's people into themselves taking the pagan route, seeking to bring YHWH's kingdom by force of arms and military revolt."[47] Wright continues, "This, then, was how Jesus envisaged the messianic victory over the real enemy. The satan had taken up residence in Jerusalem, not merely in Rome, and was seeking to pervert the chosen nation and the holy place into becoming a parody of themselves, a pseudo-chosen people intent on defeating the world with the world's methods. . . . He would act on behalf of, act in the place of, the Israel that was failing to be what she was called to be."[48]

The cross, then, is central to Jesus's understanding of the kingdom of God. And the resurrection, also, is central to Jesus's and our understanding of the kingdom. If Jesus had remained dead, the only conceivable conclusion for a Jew would have been that Jesus's announcement of the kingdom was false and that Jesus was a failed, false messiah. Too often in the history of Christianity, Christians have focused exclusively (or largely) on only the life and teaching or only the death of Christ. Even the Apostles' Creed and the Nicene Creed move directly from Jesus's birth to his death—as if nothing

45. See N. T. Wright, *Jesus and the Victory of God*, 550.
46. N. T. Wright, *Jesus and the Victory of God*, 604.
47. N. T. Wright, *Jesus and the Victory of God*, 564.
48. N. T. Wright, *Jesus and the Victory of God*, 608–9.

important happened in between.[49] That is to belittle or ignore Jesus's teaching and undermine discipleship and ethical obedience. The widespread (heretical) idea in many evangelical circles that the only important reason Jesus came was to die for our sins is one of the most glaring examples of failure to embrace the full biblical Christ. Tragically, other Christians seem to affirm the (equally heretical) idea that it is only Jesus's teaching (especially his call to love enemies) that is finally important. If we believe with the church through two millennia that the teacher from Nazareth is God incarnate, then we must embrace the full biblical Christ.

This rather brief sketch of Jesus's gospel—his announcement of the kingdom, his teaching about the kingdom, and his actually inaugurating the kingdom in his life, death, and resurrection—provides the context for us to explore in detail what his actions (the next chapter) and teaching (the following two chapters) tell us about our basic question: Does Jesus ever want his disciples to kill?

---

49. J. D. Weaver rightly makes this critique in *Nonviolent Atonement*, 121–26, 209.

2

Jesus's Actions

Do Jesus's actions tell us anything about his thinking about violence? We must examine the story about Jesus's temptations by Satan; his refusal to become king; the triumphal entry; and the refusal, just before his arrest, of defense by legions of angels.

Response to Temptation by Satan

Some writers have suggested that in one or more of the temptations that Jesus faces by Satan in the wilderness (Matt. 4:1–11; Luke 4:1–13), Jesus is responding to and rejecting a misguided, perhaps violent, messianic option.[1] Is the temptation to turn stones into bread a temptation to persuade the masses to follow him as the Messiah because he feeds them? (In fact, according to John, the people did try to force Jesus to become king after the feeding of the five thousand; John 6:1–15.) Is the temptation to leap from the lofty peak of the temple a temptation to win followers as the Messiah by a spectacular, miraculous escape? And is the temptation to receive all the kingdoms of this world from Satan a temptation to be precisely the violent military conqueror so popular in significant messianic speculation in Jesus's day?

Many commentators reject this interpretation.[2] The word for "bread" (Luke 4:3), Joel B. Green notes, is singular. Therefore, he concludes, this

1. E.g., Yoder, *Politics of Jesus*, 24–27; Ringe, *Luke*, 60–61.
2. France, *Gospel of Matthew*, 127, 131.

temptation is not "an attempt to incite Jesus to gain acclaim as a kind of welfare king who provides food for the masses."[3] And the setting of Jesus alone in the wilderness does not suggest a crowd of potential followers to feed and attract.

Alan Storkey makes an interesting case that the temptation to leap from the highest peak of the temple has messianic implications. When Herod the Great rebuilt the temple in Jerusalem, he followed an alternative reading of the Old Testament's specifications of its height, making it four times as high as the original. Fearing that this tall, dazzling structure (which for Jews symbolized the place where God alone rules) might appear to Rome as a dangerous political threat, Herod added a golden eagle on the temple's front door. But this infuriated the Jews. As we saw in the last chapter, when leaders in Jerusalem thought that Herod was dead, they took down this symbol of Roman occupation. But Herod was not quite dead, and he executed several dozen of the rebels. Thus in the popular mind, the temple "was the place where either God rules or Romans rule."[4] If Jesus would safely jump down from this huge height in front of a vast crowd at a festival, it would say to the people that the promised Messiah, who was to deliver them from the Romans, had truly arrived.

This understanding of the temptation to leap from the temple is plausible. But it is by no means certain. Other views are at least as likely.

The offer to give Jesus all the kingdoms of the world if he would only worship Satan has the most plausible political-messianic connotations. In his commentary on Matthew, Craig A. Evans notes that "this is a dream offer for a would-be messianic leader of Israel itching to throw off the Gentile yoke."[5] Jewish messianic hopes in Jesus's day certainly included the idea that a military messiah would defeat the Romans and rule the world from Jerusalem.

In all these cases, Jesus rebukes Satan and rejects his temptation. Whether Jesus (or Matthew and Luke) thinks that in that rejection he is intending to say no to the option of a violent messianic agenda is simply not clear from the texts we have. This interpretation is especially plausible when Jesus is tempted with receiving all the kingdoms of this world, and perhaps when he is tempted with leaping from the pinnacle of the temple. But it is far from certain. We should not base our understanding of Jesus's attitude toward messianic violence on the story of his temptation by Satan.

3. Green, *Gospel of Luke*, 193. However, in Matthew (4:4), the word for bread is plural!
4. Storkey, *Jesus and Politics*, 76–77.
5. Evans, *Matthew*, 87.

Jesus Refuses to be King

All four Gospels describe a feeding of more than five thousand (Matt. 14:13–21; Mark 6:30–44; Luke 9:10–17; John 6:1–15). It is clear in each account that Jesus has become enormously popular. His healing and teaching are attracting huge crowds. People speculate on who Jesus really is: Elijah? A new prophet? Or John the Baptist raised from the dead (Mark 6:14–16)?

Jesus takes a boat with his disciples to the other side of the Sea of Galilee to get some rest away from the crowds. But thousands rush around the north end of the lake and greet him on his arrival. Filled with compassion, he miraculously feeds five thousand men—plus women and children (Mark 6:30–44). All four Gospels tell us this part of the story.

But John adds one comment not in the others: "After the people saw the sign Jesus performed, they began to say, 'Surely this is the Prophet who is to come into the world.'" The next verse makes it fairly clear what they are thinking: "Jesus, knowing that they intended to come and make him king by force, withdrew again to a mountain by himself" (John 6:14–15).

Given what we know about violent messianic movements in Galilee and Judea in the few decades before and after Jesus's public ministry, the implication is clear.[6] (In AD 6, as we saw in chapter 1, Judas of Galilee led a violent revolt against the Romans, promising that God would intervene if the people would join the revolution.) It is likely that behind John's brief words is a major movement of thousands of people who believe Jesus to be the long-expected Messiah to lead the war against Rome and Rome's client rulers. They intend to force Jesus to lead the violent revolution.

Jesus refuses because that is not his understanding of the Messiah. Immediately after noting this scene where Jesus refuses to be king, Richard Hays adds, "At every turn he renounces violence as a strategy for promoting God's kingdom."[7]

It is striking that right after the story of the miraculous feeding, and then Jesus's withdrawal from the crowds, Luke places the story of Jesus asking his disciples who they think he is. Jesus accepts Peter's clear assertion that he is the Messiah (Luke 9:18–20). Equally important, the very next verses in Luke say that Jesus immediately starts to tell his disciples that he must suffer and die. According to Mark, Peter, unable to imagine a dying Messiah, rebukes Jesus. Jesus's response is blistering: "Get behind me, Satan!" (Mark 8:33).

6. See the interpretation of these events in Storkey, *Jesus and Politics*, 86–92 (his details are somewhat speculative, but his basic interpretation is accurate).
7. Hays, *Moral Vision*, 329–30.

Peter clearly is still looking for a conquering military messiah—just like the
masses who want to force Jesus to be king. But Jesus considers that kind of
kingship a satanic temptation. And Hays notes that Jesus imposes "an order
of silence to keep his disciples from proclaiming him as Messiah until he has
redefined the title in terms of the cross."[8]

The Triumphal Entry into Jerusalem

The setting of the triumphal entry is Jesus's final journey to Jerusalem. Jesus's
disciples and a crowd of other pilgrims are traveling to Jerusalem for the approaching Passover festival. As they leave Jericho to walk toward Jerusalem, a
blind beggar calls out to Jesus for healing. His words—"Jesus, Son of David,
have mercy on me!" (Mark 10:47)—could easily be intended to imply messianic
connotations.

This is the setting where Mark places the arrogant request of James and John:
"Let one of us sit at your right and the other at your left in your glory" (Mark
10:37). Like Peter at Caesarea Philippi, they too think of a powerful political Messiah. And Jesus again warns them that suffering for himself and them is coming.

That messianic fervor and speculation would be unusually intense at this
time is not surprising. "It was Passover time, and Passover . . . was the Jewish
festival at which the expectations of God's deliverance always reached fever-
heat among the huge crowds of pilgrims who came to Jerusalem from all over
the world."[9] G. B. Caird has pointed out that Passover "was the time when
the Messiah was expected to appear in Jerusalem."[10] It is at this moment that
Jesus chooses to make a very public messianic claim. Up to this point, Jesus
seems to try to avoid public claims to be the Messiah. But now, C. F. D. Moule,
a long-time Cambridge University New Testament scholar says, Jesus "takes
care that he *shall* be so acclaimed . . . and deliberately rides into Jerusalem,
letting the crowds escort him like royalty."[11]

But Jesus's triumphal entry into Jerusalem does not look at all like the
military procession of a messianic warrior riding on a warhorse. All four

---

8. Hays, *Moral Vision*, 329.
9. Moule, *Gospel according to Mark*, 86.
10. Caird, *Gospel of St. Luke*, 216.
11. Moule, *Gospel according to Mark*, 86 (italics original). Some commentators think Jesus
did not intend to make any messianic claim in his ride into Jerusalem (e.g., Barrett, *Gospel according to St. John*, 349; Cranfield, *Gospel according to St. Mark*, 352–53). But most scholars
disagree. N. T. Wright says, "The so-called 'triumphal entry' was thus clearly messianic" (*Jesus
and the Victory of God*, 491); see also J. Collins, *Scepter and the Star*, 206–7; Green, *Gospel of
Luke*, 683–85; Keener, *Gospel of Matthew*, 493; Senior, *Matthew*, 230.

Gospels tell us that Jesus personally chooses to ride on a humble animal—
Matthew and John say it is a donkey. Furthermore, both Matthew and John
quote from Zechariah 9:9–10 to explain why Jesus chooses a donkey (Matt.
21:5; John 12:15). That passage, which some in Jesus's day understood as a
prediction about the coming Messiah,[12] speaks in vivid terms about a humble,
peaceful figure:

> Rejoice greatly, O daughter Zion!
>   Shout aloud, O daughter Jerusalem!
> Lo, your king comes to you;
>   triumphant and victorious is he,
> humble and riding on a donkey,
>   on a colt, the foal of a donkey.
> He will cut off the chariot from Ephraim
>   and the war-horse from Jerusalem;
> and the battle bow shall be cut off,
>   and he shall command peace to the nations. (Zech. 9:9–10 NRSV)

Both Matthew and John quote part of this text about a peaceful figure. Jesus
is powerfully picturing a very important point. He is the Messiah, but he is
not the violent military conqueror the rebels desire.

Moule has made the point clearly: "Jesus seemed to his friends, as they
recollected the scene, to have ridden into Jerusalem . . . as Messiah, as De-
liverer, but as a peaceful one, not in the guise of a warrior. 'I *am* Messiah,'
he had seemed to say, 'but not the warrior-Messiah whom you are looking
for.'"[13] Craig Keener makes the same point: "Jesus was announcing that he
was indeed a king, but not a warrior-king."[14] Jesus's actions demonstrate that
his rule should not be confused with the revolutionaries' "plans for a national
uprising against Rome."[15]

Vincent Taylor summarizes the incident and the crowd's eventual disap-
pointment:

> Jesus must have observed the growing Messianic tension among His disciples
> and have realized that His teaching about a suffering Messiah had failed. . . .
> By previous arrangement He sends two disciples for the colt, intending to fulfil
> Zechariah's prophecy. Unable to deny that He is the promised Messiah, He seeks

12. See Keener, *Gospel of Matthew*, 493; and France, *Gospel of Matthew*, 777n26.
13. Moule, *Gospel according to Mark*, 87.
14. Keener, *Gospel of Matthew*, 493; see there further references to others (e.g., Robert
Gundry, E. P. Sanders, and Marcus J. Borg).
15. Caird, *Gospel of St. Luke*, 216.

to show to His disciples and to the crowd the kind of Messiah He is, no man
of war, but lowly and riding upon an ass. The crowd is puzzled, but penetrates
His meaning to see that He is not to be the Messiah of their hopes. That is why
they turned against Him.[16]

Refusal to Call on Twelve Legions of Angels

At his arrest in the garden, Jesus rebukes Peter for trying to defend him with
the sword (on that, see chap. 4 below). Jesus then adds, "Do you think I cannot
call on my Father, and he will at once put at my disposal more than twelve
legions of angels?" (Matt. 26:53). One Roman legion contained six thousand
soldiers. So seventy-two thousand angels would represent a formidable force
to resist arrest and even drive out the Romans! We must read this statement
of Jesus in its historical context, where contemporaries of Jesus believed and
taught that God would intervene miraculously to defeat their enemies if the
Jews would rise up in armed rebellion.[17] It is not certain, but very plausible,
to suppose that, here at his arrest, Jesus again faces the temptation of violent
revolution.[18] But Jesus rejects that violent messianic strategy and chooses
the cross.

By themselves, these actions of Jesus would not be enough to say with certainty that Jesus clearly rejected all violence. But the actions we have explored
clearly do not affirm violence. For more clarity on what Jesus intended to
teach on our topic, we turn in the next two chapters to a careful examination
of his relevant teaching.

16. Taylor, *Gospel according to St. Mark*, 452.
17. See chap. 1, "Messianic Violence."
18. See Yoder, *Politics of Jesus*, 46–48.

3

Jesus's Teaching in the Sermon on the Mount

The setting for Jesus's teaching is extremely important. We simply will not accurately understand Jesus's teaching unless we see it as a central part of his announcement that the long-expected messianic kingdom was actually breaking into history in his person and work.

In chapter 1, we saw that many Jews in Jesus's time waited expectantly for the Messiah, who would drive out the Romans, make Jerusalem the center of the world, and bring in an age of peace and justice. We also saw that this messianic hope in no way implied the end of space-time history. The apocalyptic language about a new heavens and earth was rather vivid symbolic imagery to declare that the coming Messiah would bring dramatic sweeping transformation.

Jesus claimed to be the expected Messiah. To be sure, his actions seemed to point to a profoundly different—a nonviolent—messianic strategy. But Jesus certainly claimed, and the early Christians taught, that he was the Messiah. Jesus called on the entire Jewish people to embrace his messianic message and work. Jesus did not see himself as starting a small private circle in the little town of Nazareth. He called on the whole people of Israel to accept him as the Messiah. As N. T. Wright notes, Jesus's teaching was "a challenge to Israel to *be* Israel."[1] Jesus wanted his followers to be the "salt of the *earth*" and the "light of the *world*" (Matt. 5:13–14).

1. N. T. Wright, *Jesus and the Victory of God*, 288 (italics original).

Accepting Jesus as the Messiah meant following his teaching. At the end of the Sermon on the Mount, Jesus pointedly insists that "everyone who hears these words of mine and puts them into practice is like a wise man who built his house on the rock" (Matt. 7:24). And at the very end of his Gospel, Matthew says Jesus sends the disciples into the whole world not only to baptize those who believe but also to teach them "everything I have commanded you" (28:20). The Gospel of John makes the same point with Jesus's words "If you love me, keep my commands" (John 14:15).

Jesus's emphasis on the close connection between repentance and the dawning kingdom he announces underlines this point. Again and again, the Gospels make this connection. In Mark's summary of Jesus's gospel at the beginning of his story about Jesus, Mark writes, "The kingdom of God has come near. *Repent* [*metanoeite*] and believe the good news!" (1:15). According to Luke 5:32, the purpose of Jesus's coming is to call us to repentance (*metanoia*). The noun *metanoia* and its related verb, according to the *Theological Dictionary of the New Testament*, mean "an unconditional turning to God" and an "unconditional turning from all that is against God."[2]

Accepting Jesus's gospel of the kingdom requires a fundamental reorienting of one's thinking and acting.[3] Jesus's teaching shows his followers how they must allow their thought and behavior to be transformed in order to live in the new messianic time that has arrived in Jesus's life and work.

The Sermon on the Mount in Matthew 5–7 is the largest block of Jesus's teaching in the four Gospels. So, we must start there to answer the question: What does Jesus's teaching tell us about whether Jesus wanted his disciples ever to kill?

How Does Jesus Fulfill the Law?

Especially important for the question of Jesus's teaching on killing are the sets of sayings in Matthew 5:21–48, particularly the last two. In each set, Jesus says something like "You have heard that it was said . . . but I tell you." In at least some instances, Jesus refers to a teaching in the Old Testament and then seems to modify or change it. But immediately preceding this block of material, Matthew tells us that Jesus declares he has come not to abolish the Law and the Prophets "but to fulfill them" (5:17). In fact, Jesus insists that "until heaven and earth disappear, not the smallest letter . . . will by any means disappear from the Law until everything is accom-

---

2. "μετανοέω, μετάνοια E II," *TDNT* 4:1000–1006.
3. Roth makes this point well in *Choosing against War*, 80–81.

plished" (5:18). And Jesus condemns setting aside even "the least of these commands" (5:19).

It is not surprising that two quite different interpretations of how Jesus "fulfilled" the Old Testament have emerged. One group argues that Jesus did not set aside any Old Testament law or teaching; he merely corrected misunderstandings of the Old Testament held by some of his contemporaries. The other group insists that Jesus fulfilled some parts of the Old Testament precisely by setting aside some of its provisions and calling his disciples to a different, higher norm. We must briefly explore both arguments.

The first view—which has a long tradition that includes people like John Calvin—insists that "there is no ethical discontinuity between the kingdom of God and the period of the Old Testament."[4] John Stott argues strongly for this view, presenting several arguments for his claim that Jesus is not setting himself against Moses but only rejecting perversions of the law by scribes and Pharisees of his day. Stott argues that the verb in the statement "[you have heard that] it was said" (Matt. 5:21, 27, 33, 38, 43; cf. 5:31) is not the word Jesus normally uses when he quotes Scripture.[5] Furthermore, since Jesus has just declared in Matthew 5:17–20 that not the smallest letter of the law will perish until heaven and earth pass away, he seems to be blatantly contradicting himself if in the subsequent texts he is setting aside the teaching of the Old Testament.[6]

Many New Testament scholars, however, understand Matthew 5:17–20 differently. In his commentary on Matthew, Craig Blomberg says that in the six antitheses of Matthew 5:21–48, Jesus "contravenes the letter of several of the Old Testament laws."[7] In his massive commentary on the Sermon on the Mount, Robert Guelich notes that the "most common answer" that modern biblical scholars give to the question of how Jesus has fulfilled the law was that Jesus "'set forth its ultimate intention' and thus 'completed the Law' generally through his own teaching about the Law."[8] Guelich also notes that the consensus of recent works on Matthew is that the law that remains valid until heaven and earth pass away is "the Law as taught by

4. Charles, *Between Pacifism and Jihad*, 94; see also Charles and Demy, *War, Peace, and Christianity*, 256–58.

5. In Matt. 5, Jesus uses *errethē*, not *gegraptai*. See Stott, *Sermon on the Mount*, 77. But, as R. T. France points out in his commentary, "'It was said' represents a relatively rare passive form of the verb *errethē* which is used in the NT specifically for quotations of Scripture." France concludes that "in the first half of each contrast we should expect to find a quotation of the Mosaic law." France, *Gospel of Matthew*, 195.

6. Stott, *Sermon on the Mount*, 78; see also Keener, *Gospel of Matthew*, 177–80.

7. Blomberg, *Matthew*, 106.

8. Guelich, *Sermon on the Mount*, 139.

Jesus."[9] The word used in Matthew 5:17, where Jesus says he has come to "fulfill" the Law and the Prophets, is *plēroō*. It is a favorite of Matthew's. He uses it sixteen times—in twelve instances to show how Jesus has fulfilled an Old Testament text.[10]

Guelich argues that Jesus sees himself establishing the new relationship with God that Jeremiah (31:31–34), Ezekiel (36:25–27), and Isaiah (2:2–4) have predicted. Jesus thus fulfills the law by bringing that eschatological time of redemption promised in the Old Testament. The context of the greater righteousness demanded by Matthew 5:20 for the new messianic time is spelled out in the following statements of Matthew 5:21–48.[11]

It is quite clear that Jesus claims the authority to challenge widely understood demands of the law. And the early Christians clearly teach that central demands of the Old Testament law are no longer binding: circumcision, food laws, sacrifices in the temple for forgiveness of sins, the Sabbath. Paul teaches that although the law is a divinely given custodian or guardian applicable until the coming of Christ, now "we are no longer under a guardian" (Gal. 3:25). As R. T. France notes, if Matthew 5:17–20 means that the rules of the Old Testament law must be followed "as they were before Jesus came," Matthew would "here be contradicting the whole tenor of the NT by declaring that, for instance, the sacrificial and food laws of the OT are still binding on Jesus's disciples."[12]

The Old Testament includes clear laws that declare certain foods (meat from pigs, camels, rabbits, etc.) unclean. The people of Israel are commanded not to eat them (Lev. 11:1–47; Deut. 14:3–19). But Mark explicitly tells us that Jesus sets these food laws aside: "Don't you see that nothing that enters a person from the outside can defile them? . . . (In saying this, Jesus declared all foods clean)" (Mark 7:18–19). The story of Peter's vision in Acts 10:9–16 and the teaching of Paul underline the way the early church abandoned explicit food laws in the Old Testament.

Jesus's frequent conflict with the Pharisees over the Sabbath is stunning. One of the Ten Commandments (Exod. 20:8) demands Sabbath observance. Strict observance of the Sabbath was one of the most important parts of Jewish life in Jesus's day. The Gospels report sharp conflicts with the Pharisees because they believe Jesus's and his disciples' actions break the Sabbath laws (Mark 2:23–3:6; Luke 13:10–17; John 5:16–18). But Jesus dares to claim authority over the Sabbath: "The sabbath was made for humankind, and not

9. Guelich, *Sermon on the Mount*, 147.
10. E.g., Matt. 1:22; 2:15, 17, 23; 4:14; 8:17; 12:17; 13:35.
11. Guelich, *Sermon on the Mount*, 163.
12. France, *Gospel of Matthew*, 187.

humankind for the sabbath; so the Son of Man is lord even of the sabbath" (Mark 2:27–28). Claiming lordship over a teaching of one of the Ten Commandments certainly suggests that Jesus's "fulfillment" of the Old Testament may involve major modification of its teaching.

Jesus's comments about John the Baptist demonstrate Jesus's belief that his ministry transcends the Law and the Prophets even as it fulfills them. Jesus says that "among those born of women," no one is greater than John. But then Jesus adds that "whoever is least in the kingdom of heaven is greater than he" (Matt. 11:11). Furthermore, Jesus adds that "all the Prophets and the Law prophesied until John" (11:13). In other words, the messianic kingdom breaking into history in Jesus involves a new time that brings a new understanding of the Old Testament and transcends it in some sense.

Jesus is not denying that the Law and the Prophets are God's Word. But he is saying that now that what they foretold has actually arrived: "It will be for Jesus's followers to discern in the light of his teaching and practice what is now the right way to apply those texts in the new situation which his coming has created."[13]

This has an important implication, according to France: "If in the process it may appear that certain elements of the law are for all practical purposes 'abolished,' this will be attributable not to the loss of their status as the word of God but to their changed role in the new era of fulfillment, in which it is Jesus, the fulfiller, rather than the law which pointed forward to him, who is the ultimate authority." This view, France says, "has gained a considerable degree of assent in recent decades."[14] Thus Matthew 5:20 (one cannot enter the kingdom unless one's righteousness exceeds that of the scribes and Pharisees) means that the behavior of Jesus's disciples must be shaped by Jesus's teaching, including the following words in Matthew 5:21–48, not by some careful observance of all the details of the law.[15]

Clearly, contemporary Christian scholars offer two rather different frameworks for approaching the important block of Jesus's teaching in Matthew 5:21–48. In the first, Jesus corrects contemporary misunderstandings of the law but does not set aside any of its ethical demands. In the second, Jesus sometimes fulfills the law by correcting or even declaring some of its demands no longer normative. Careful exegesis of each of the texts will help us decide which framework fits better with the data.

---

13. France, *Gospel of Matthew*, 183.
14. France, *Gospel of Matthew*, 183; his footnote 17 also cites many scholars.
15. See France's paraphrase of Matt. 5:17–20 in France, *Gospel of Matthew*, 190–91.

Six Antitheses

Murder and Adultery

The first two sets of sayings, on murder (Matt. 5:21–26) and adultery (5:27–30), clearly show Jesus strengthening but certainly not setting aside the Old Testament commands. Not only should Jesus's followers not murder; they also should not be angry with a sister or brother but rather seek reconciliation. Not only should they not commit adultery; they also should avoid dwelling on lustful thoughts.

Divorce

The next segment, on divorce, however, appears somewhat different. In Matthew 5:31, Jesus quotes Deuteronomy 24:1, where the Mosaic law forbids a husband who has divorced his wife (who then marries another man) from taking her back later. The Deuteronomic text does not command divorce, but it clearly allows it. Later, in Matthew 19:3–12, the Pharisees ask Jesus why Moses command a man to give his wife a certificate of divorce (19:7). Jesus replies that Moses permitted divorce "because your hearts were hard" but divorce was never God's will (19:8). And Jesus insists that his disciples follow the Creator's original intention, rejecting divorce "except for sexual immorality" (19:9).

This teaching of Jesus does not set aside an explicit Old Testament command. But it does set aside what the Mosaic law allowed. In fact, in his widely used book *Jerusalem in the Time of Jesus*, German scholar Joachim Jeremias says Jesus "unhesitatingly and fearlessly criticized the Torah for permitting divorce."[16]

Oaths

In Matthew 5:33–37, Jesus condemns all use of oaths: "Again, you have heard that it was said to the people long ago, 'Do not break your oath. . . .' But I tell you, do not swear an oath at all. . . . All you need to say is simply 'Yes' or 'No'; anything beyond this comes from the evil one."

We know from many sources that in Jesus's day there was widespread abuse of oaths. Teachers taught and people believed that as long as one did not swear by God, oaths involving the temple or heaven or one's head were not finally binding. Jesus clearly rejects such rationalizing.[17]

---

16. Jeremias, *Jerusalem in the Time of Jesus*, 376.
17. Keener, *Gospel of Matthew*, 194.

But he does more. The Old Testament not only forbids breaking one's oath (e.g., Deut. 23:21–23); it also explicitly *commands* taking oaths. In Numbers 5:19–22, the text directs the priest to have a woman take an oath. Deuteronomy 6:13 declares, "Fear the LORD your God, serve him only and take your oaths in his name." Exodus 22:10–11 explicitly prescribes that a dispute "will be settled by the taking of an oath before the LORD."[18] As France notes, since the Old Testament law sometimes demands oaths, "there is a *prima facie* case to be made that Jesus is here opposing the intention of one aspect of the law."[19] Or, as Blomberg says, "As with his teaching on divorce, he [Jesus] again forbids what the Old Testament permitted."[20]

It is sometimes suggested that Jesus himself took an oath at his trial.[21] But the text does not say that. The high priest certainly tries to have Jesus swear by God. But Jesus simply answers the question without any statement about taking an oath (Matt. 26:63–64).[22] As Craig Keener notes, Jesus "avoided formal oaths."[23] And James 5:12 shows that the early church remembered and sought to live by Jesus's prohibition of oaths: "Above all, my brothers and sisters, do not swear—not by heaven or by earth or by anything else. All you need to say is a simple 'Yes' or 'No.' Otherwise, you will be condemned."

It is interesting that for the first few centuries, the early church, especially in the East, took Jesus's prohibition of oaths literally. That is clear from the statements of many prominent Christian writers, including Justin Martyr, Irenaeus, Tertullian, Origen, and others. But after Constantine this tradition disappeared.[24]

Eye for an Eye

Matthew 5:38–42 is a very important text for our question: "You have heard that it was said, 'Eye for eye, and tooth for tooth.' But I tell you, do not resist an evil person. If anyone slaps you on the right check, turn to them the other cheek also. And if anyone wants to sue you and take your shirt, hand over your coat as well. If anyone forces you to go one mile, go with them two

18. See also Num. 30:3–16.
19. France, *Gospel of Matthew*, 213 (italics original).
20. Blomberg, *Matthew*, 112.
21. Stott, *Sermon on the Mount*, 102.
22. So Keener, *Gospel of Matthew*, 195; Evans, *Matthew*, 128; Bruner, *Matthew*, 1:241.
23. Keener, *Gospel of Matthew*, 195. Robert Guelich says that in Matt. 5:34a and 37a Jesus is "prohibiting the use of all oaths." Guelich, *Sermon on the Mount*, 218.
24. Bruner, *Matthew*, 1:234; apparently exceptions to the literal understanding appeared early in the Latin church.

miles. Give to the one who asks you, and do not turn away from the one who wants to borrow from you."[25]

An "eye for an eye" had been a central principle of Near Eastern law since the famous Code of Hammurabi (eighteenth century BC). And it was certainly "the keynote of criminal justice for the Jewish law, as seen in the Old Testament."[26] Exodus 21:23–25 is clear: "If there is serious injury, you are to take life for life, eye for eye, tooth for tooth." Leviticus states the same standard: "Anyone who injures their neighbor is to be injured in the same manner: fracture for fracture, eye for eye, tooth for tooth" (24:19–20). Deuteronomy 19 prescribes how to punish someone who gives false testimony in court. If the court discerns that a witness has lied, then "do to the false witness as that witness intended to do to the other party. . . . Show no pity: life for life, eye for eye, tooth for tooth, hand for hand, foot for foot" (19:19–21).

Jesus's response to this fundamental Old Testament principle is pointed: "But I tell you, do not resist an evil person" (Matt. 5:39). In a moment, we must examine carefully what the key verb translated in the NIV as "do not resist" actually means. But to try to argue as some do[27] that here Jesus is not setting aside an Old Testament teaching seems to ignore the clear meaning of the text. The most obvious meaning of the text surely supports Blomberg's view that here Jesus "formally abrogates an Old Testament command."[28] John Piper is equally explicit: "Jesus' command not to resist evil (Matt. 5:39–42) demands the opposite of the Old Testament legal principle. . . . They exclude each other; they are contradictory."[29]

Central to an understanding of this passage is the proper translation of the key verb *antistēnai*. The NIV translates it "do not resist" (Matt. 5:39), and a number of people have concluded that Jesus advocates pure passivity, total nonresistance, in the face of evil. Paul Ramsey and Reinhold Niebuhr

25. Luke 6:29–31 also has this statement with some modest variations.
26. Guelich, *Sermon on the Mount*, 219.
27. See, e.g., Charles and Demy, *War, Peace, and Christianity*, 260–61. Their primary arguments are: (1) Such a view would contradict Jesus's statement in Matt. 5:17–20 (but as we saw above, Jesus's actual teaching in 5:21–48 provides the best interpretation of 5:17–20); and (2) that "an eye for an eye" is a legal principle of all law and therefore Jesus could not possibly be setting it aside (but surely what Jesus actually says must overrule our speculation about what he "could not possibly mean"). Also strange is John Stott's argument that "Jesus did not contradict the principle of retribution for it is a true and just principle." It is peculiar to say Jesus could not have meant what he said by simply asserting that the Old Testament norm Jesus sets aside is "true and right." No more convincing is Stott's argument that Jesus's statement "judge not that you be not judged," or the teaching on a final judgment of sin, supports the principle of an eye for an eye. Stott, *Sermon on the Mount*, 105.
28. Blomberg, *Matthew*, 113.
29. Piper, *"Love Your Enemies,"* 89. See further D. Weaver, "Transforming Nonresistance."

have both argued that "Christ-like love is nonresisting love and does not mean nonviolent resistance."[30] And an earlier generation of Mennonite thinkers agreed, using the word "nonresistance" to describe their understanding of Jesus.[31]

But if Jesus in Matthew 5:39 is advocating pure passivity in the face of evil, then Jesus again and again contradicts his own teaching. Jesus unleashes a blistering attack on the Pharisees, denouncing them as blind guides, fools, hypocrites, and snakes (Matt. 23:13–33). He urges his followers to confront members of the church who sin (18:15–17). His cleansing of the temple, when he overturns the tables of money changers and drives out the animals, is anything but passive (Matt. 21:12–17; Mark 11:15–19; Luke 19:45–48; John 2:13–25). And at his trial, when a soldier slaps him on the cheek, he protests rather than turn the other cheek (John 18:22–23).

A careful study of the verb used in this text shows clearly that Jesus is not recommending passivity. *Anthistēmi* is a variant of the word *antistēnai* (used in v. 39) and *anthistēmi* appears in the Greek Old Testament primarily as a military term. In forty-four of seventy-one uses in the Greek Old Testament, the word refers to armed resistance in military encounters (e.g., Lev. 26:37; Deut. 7:24; 25:18; Josh. 7:13; 23:9; Judg. 2:14).[32] Josephus, the first-century Jewish historian, uses the word fifteen of seventeen times to refer to violent struggle. The Greek lexicon by Liddell and Scott defines the word to mean "set against especially in battle."[33] Ephesians 6:13 uses the word *antistēnai* to refer to the spiritual battle against Satan when Christians are armed with the full armor of God. "In short, *antistēnai* means more in Matt. 5:39a than simply to 'stand against' or 'resist.' It means to resist *violently*, to revolt or rebel, to engage in an insurrection."[34]

N. T. Wright summarizes the meaning of the word this way: "The word 'resist' is *antistēnai*, almost a technical term for revolutionary resistance of a specifically military variety. Taken in this sense, the command draws out the implication of a good deal of the sermon so far. The way forward for Israel is not the way of violent resistance . . . but the different, oblique way of creative non-violent resistance. . . . Jesus' people were not to become part of the

---

30. Ramsey and Hauerwas, *Speak Up*, 73; Niebuhr, "Why the Christian Church Is Not Pacifist."
    31. See especially Hershberger, *War, Peace, and Nonresistance*, 43–64, 170–233.
    32. Wink, "Neither Passivity nor Violence," 114.
    33. Liddell and Scott, *Greek-English Lexicon*; quoted in Wink, *Jesus and Nonviolence*, 107.
    34. Wink, "Neither Passivity nor Violence," 115. The related word *stasis* is used in Mark 15:7 to refer to Barabbas's violent insurrection and in Acts 19:40 to rioting. See also the use of variations of the basic word to refer to violent revolt (Acts 5:37) and attacks on Christians by Jews (Acts 16:22; 17:5).

resistance movement."[35] In his new translation, N. T. Wright translates verse 39 this way: "Don't use violence to resist evil."[36]

After prohibiting a violent response to evil, the text describes a proper response in four concrete situations. In each case, the commanded response is neither violent nor passive. Jesus calls his disciples not to turn aside passively or hit back but rather to confront the evil nonviolently.[37] "By doing more than what the oppressor requires, the disciples bear witness to another reality (the kingdom of God)."[38]

Walter Wink has proposed an interpretation of verses 39b–41 that, if correct, greatly strengthens the claim that in these statements Jesus is suggesting a vigorously activist (although certainly nonviolent) response to evil and injustice.[39] Some scholars agree with Wink.[40] Others do not. But his argument merits careful evaluation.

Turn the other cheek. The text says, "If anyone slaps you on the right cheek, turn to them the other cheek also" (5:39b). Hays notes that there is widespread acceptance by commentators that someone could strike a person on the right cheek only with the back of the hand and that such an action would be the kind of insult that a superior would deliver to an inferior.[41] (To test this theory, face someone and notice how much easier it is to slap that person's right cheek with the back of your right hand than it is to hit the right cheek with your right fist.) We know from documents of the time that a backhanded blow to the right cheek was a huge insult, "the severest public affront to a person's dignity."[42] Ancient documents also show that the fine for

35. N. T. Wright, *Jesus and the Victory of God*, 291. Wright (291nn179–80) cites and agrees with Walter Wink's basic analysis of *antistēnai*. Guelich has argued for a more narrow understanding of verse 39a, saying the text only condemns opposing an evil person in court (*Sermon on the Mount*, 220). But Richard Hays points out that although *antistēnai* can refer to a legal setting, this word is "not a technical term for legal opposition" and it does not normally have this sense in the rest of the New Testament. Furthermore, the narrow meaning does not make much sense of either 5:39b or 5:41, 42 (Hays, *Moral Vision*, 325–26). Bruner (*Matthew*, 1:248–49) also rejects Guelich's view.

36. N. T. Wright, *Kingdom New Testament*, 9. So too Glen Stassen and David Gushee, who translate the verse: "Do not retaliate or resist violently or revengefully, by evil means" (*Kingdom Ethics*, 138). There is another ambiguity in verse 39a. The NIV translates, "Do not resist an evil person." But the Greek word translated "person" is in the dative, and therefore it could equally be a masculine or a neuter. In the latter case, the word refers to evil generally, not an evil person.

37. Bruner, *Matthew*, 1:251.

38. Hays, *Moral Vision*, 326.

39. Wink, *Engaging the Powers*, 175–84; Wink, *Powers That Be*, 98–111.

40. E.g., Stassen and Gushee, *Kingdom Ethics*, 139; Fahey, *War and the Christian Conscience*, 35–38; Kraybill, *Upside-Down Kingdom*, 182; Neufeld, *Killing Enmity*, 23–25.

41. Hays, *Moral Vision*, 326. Hays himself is not fully convinced.

42. Keener, *Gospel of Matthew*, 197.

striking an equal with the (insulting) back of the hand was double that for a blow by one's fist.[43] But no penalty followed for striking slaves that way. A backhanded slap was for inferiors, like slaves and wives.[44]

If that is the proper context for understanding the saying, then Jesus's advice to turn the other (left) cheek conveys a surprising suggestion. Normally, an inferior would simply accept the insult (or on occasion fight back). But by turning the left cheek to the person insulting one, one almost forces the attacker to use his fist if he wants to strike again. (It is much harder to hit the left cheek with a backslap than with a fist.) The effect, Wink believes, is that the inferior person astonishes the superior by a dramatic act that asserts the inferior's dignity, not by striking back but by forcing the attacker either to stop or use his fist and thus treat the inferior as an equal. Thus Jesus is urging a nonviolent but nonetheless activist response to evil. One cannot assert with certainty that this is Jesus's intended meaning.[45] But that conclusion is certainly plausible.

Sued for one's coat. "If anyone wants to sue you and take your shirt [inner garment], hand over your coat [outer garment] as well" (Matt. 5:40).[46] The setting refers to a typical first-century context where debt was widespread among the poor. Jesus tells many parables about people in debt. Rome's client king in Galilee, Herod Antipas, taxed the people heavily to pay tribute to Rome. Many poor people fell into debt.[47]

In Jesus's example, the person taken to court for an unpaid debt is obviously very poor, owning nothing of worth to repay the debt except clothes. Such an impoverished person has no hope of winning against the richer person and so loses the inner garment as payment on the debt. Probably the reason the text says the person is being sued to give up the inner garment is because the Old Testament specifically forbade taking the outer garment as collateral for more than the daytime, because the poor person needed an outer garment to use as a blanket while sleeping.[48]

---

43. Gundry, *Matthew*, 95.

44. Wink, *Engaging the Powers*, 176.

45. Bruner disagrees with Wink's argument about the slap on the right cheek but agrees that Jesus is calling the person to confront the evil, not run away or hit back. See Bruner, *Matthew*, 1:251.

46. The words for "shirt" and "coat" are *chitōn* and *himation*, respectively, which Liddell and Scott say mean the inner garment worn next to the skin (*chitōn*) and the outer garment (*himation*). Liddell and Scott, *Greek-English Lexicon*, 829, 1993.

47. Wink, *Engaging the Powers*, 178.

48. See Exod. 22:25–27; Deut. 24:10–13, 17. The word for "garment" in the LXX is *himation*. Luke 6:29b has the debtor being sued for the outer garment. Matthew's version corresponds better with Old Testament law. Gundry, *Matthew*, 95.

But why would Jesus tell this kind of poor person who has just lost an inner garment to give the person who is owed money the outer garment as well? Since many poor people had only one outer garment, that would mean stripping naked in court. And nakedness was a terrible disgrace in Palestinian Jewish society.[49]

Wink's explanation is certainly plausible. The disgrace for nakedness fell not only on the naked person but also on those viewing the naked person.[50] By stripping naked, the debtor exposes the cruelty not only of the creditor but also of the oppressive system the creditor represents. "The entire system by which debtors are oppressed has been publicly unmasked."[51] Rather than recommending a passive response to injustice, Jesus urges a dramatic nonviolent protest.

The second mile. "If anyone forces you to go one mile, go with them two miles" (Matt. 5:41). The context for this saying is clearly Roman imperialism. The word translated "mile" is a Roman word, not a Jewish word.[52] And the word translated "forces you" is the verbal form of the technical term (*anga-reia*) widely known in Roman law to refer to the legal right of Roman soldiers to compel subject people to carry their packs for one mile.[53] Matthew 27:32 uses precisely this word to describe the way Simon of Cyrene is compelled to carry Jesus's cross. There is also a large literature that demonstrates both that Roman soldiers often abused this right and that colonized people hated this burdensome obligation.

Earlier, in chapter 1, we saw how angry, violent rebellion against Roman rule and its collaborators kept erupting among the Jews in the century around the time of Jesus. These violent revolutionaries certainly urged fellow Jews to refuse to carry the baggage of oppressive Roman soldiers.[54] What Jesus recommends "is the precise opposite of what the zealots advocated doing in their revolutionary sedition against the Romans."[55] The words used and the context demonstrate that Jesus is clearly rejecting a widespread, popular attitude toward the oppressive Roman imperialists.

49. Keener, *Gospel of Matthew,* 198.
50. Gen. 9:20–27.
51. Wink, *Engaging the Powers,* 179. Stassen and Gushee agree with Wink; see *Kingdom Ethics,* 154.
52. France, *Gospel of Matthew,* 222.
53. See the massive literature cited in Wink, *Engaging the Powers,* 371–72nn17–19. There is no extant Roman law limiting the right to one mile, but scholars have generally believed that was the law (371n17).
54. Rome's client king, Herod Antipas, ruled Galilee in Jesus's day, so it is possible Matt. 5:41 refers to Herod's soldiers. See Wink, *Engaging the Powers,* 373n28.
55. Schweizer, *Matthew,* 130. So too Bruner, *Matthew,* 1:255.

But is he recommending passivity? Is he urging fellow Jews to affirm Roman oppression? Again, Wink's interpretation is intriguing and plausible. The soldier knows the colonized person has a legal obligation to carry his pack one mile. He also knows the law forbids the Roman soldier forcing the person to carry it more than one mile. And he knows his commander may punish him severely for breaking this law. So when they reach the end of the first mile, the soldier asks for his pack back. "Imagine then the soldier's surprise when, at the next mile marker, he reluctantly reaches to assume his pack and the civilian says, 'Oh no, let me carry it another mile.'" Now the soldier is in trouble. He may be disciplined by his superior. So he begs to be given back his pack. "Imagine the situation of a Roman infantryman pleading with a Jew to give back his pack! The humor of this scene may have escaped us, but it would scarcely have been lost on Jesus' hearers, who must have been regaled at the prospect of thus discomfiting their oppressors."[56]

With this action, the oppressed Jew seizes the initiative and asserts personal dignity—all in a nonviolent way fully compatible with loving the oppressor without endorsing the oppression.

Economic sharing. "Give to the one who asks you, and do not turn away from the one who wants to borrow from you" (Matt. 5:42). It is important to note that Jesus does not say give whatever a person asks. Rather, he teaches his followers to respond in love to those in economic need. On occasion, a loving concern for the best interests of the other may prompt rejection of some of the specifics of the request. Jesus is not urging some idealistic, impractical, utopian behavior that ignores practical reality.[57] But here and elsewhere he does call his disciples to doable, albeit costly, economic sharing that reflects the fact that the messianic kingdom has already begun. In that new kingdom, Jesus's followers abandon every rigid eye for an eye, even in the economic realm.

"Love Your Enemies"

You have heard that it was said, "Love your neighbor and hate your enemy." But I tell you, love your enemies and pray for those who persecute you, that you may be children of your Father in heaven. He causes his sun to rise on the evil and the good, and sends rain on the righteous and the unrighteous. If you love those who love you, what reward will you get? Are not even the tax collectors doing that? And if you greet only your own people, what are you doing more

56. Wink, *Engaging the Powers*, 182.
57. Stassen and Gushee, *Kingdom Ethics*, 132–37, make the point that Jesus's ethical demands in the Sermon on the Mount are realistic and doable.

than others? Do not even pagans do that? Be perfect, therefore, as your heavenly Father is perfect. (Matt. 5:43–48)

There is no dispute about the source of the traditional summons to "love your neighbor," which Jesus mentions in verse 43. It is a verbatim quote from the Greek translation of Leviticus 19:18. In his scholarly analysis of pre-Christian Jewish thinking on love for neighbor, John Piper has shown that the neighbor whom one was obligated to love was normally understood to be a fellow Israelite.[58] A different attitude toward gentiles was expected.

But who are those who call people to "hate your enemy"? Who does Jesus have in mind? We know that the Manual of Discipline of Jesus's contemporaries the Essenes (known to us from the Dead Sea Scrolls) explicitly says, "Love all the sons of light . . ., and . . . hate all the sons of darkness."[59] And for some of the Jewish revolutionaries of Jesus's day, "the slaying of the godless enemy out of zeal for God's cause was a fundamental commandment, true to the rabbinic maxim: 'Whoever spills the blood of the godless is like one who offers sacrifice.'"[60]

But might Jesus also be thinking of Old Testament passages? There is certainly no Old Testament text that explicitly commands hatred of enemies. In fact, there are Old Testament passages that urge kindness toward enemies. If you find your enemy's lost donkey, return it (Exod. 23:4–5). If your enemy is hungry, feed him (Prov. 25:21).[61]

But a number of scholars argue that there is material in the Old Testament that does teach hatred of God's enemies and hatred of the enemies of the people of God.[62] Speaking of those who hate God, the psalmist says, "I have nothing but hatred for them; I count them my enemies" (Ps. 139:21–22). And Psalm 137 says of Babylon, an enemy nation that conquered Judah, "Happy is the one who repays you according to what you have done to us. Happy is the one who seizes your infants and dashes them against the rocks" (137:8b–9). Thus Guelich concludes, "Matthew 5:43 in one sense stands in continuity with the teaching of the Old Testament. . . . The premise of 5:43 sets forth the common understanding of the Law in the Old Testament."[63] It is impossible for modern readers to be certain whether Jesus is thinking of

58. Piper, *"Love Your Enemies,"* 30–32. See also, Schweizer, *Matthew*, 132.
59. Quoted in Schweizer, *Matthew*, 132. See also Josephus, *JW* 2.139.
60. Quoted in Hengel, *Victory over Violence*, 75.
61. See also 1 Sam. 24:5–7, 18; Job 31:29; Prov. 24:17.
62. So Bruner, *Matthew*, 1:268; Gundry, *Matthew*, 96–97; Guelich, *Sermon on the Mount*, 227; Keener, *Gospel of Matthew*, 203. Old Testament texts certainly command punishment of enemies (e.g., Deut. 25:17–19).
63. Guelich, *Sermon on the Mount*, 226–27.

his contemporaries or Old Testament texts. Perhaps he is thinking of both. But in any case, his command represents a radical challenge to virtually every person and culture. It urges the very opposite of the reciprocity principle embedded in the norm of an eye for an eye.

But who are the enemies Jesus summons his disciples to love? It is interesting that in Matthew 5:43 ("love your neighbor and hate your enemy") the words for "neighbor" and "enemy" are singular. But verse 44 uses the plural: "Love your enemies." Every class of enemy seems to be included.[64]

Richard Horsley has argued that the word for "enemies" (*echthroi*) used by Jesus refers not to foreign or military enemies but to personal enemies, because of local squabbles in small Palestinian villages. Therefore, this summons to love one's enemies has nothing to do with the question of whether Jesus opposes killing violent enemies.[65]

Duke New Testament scholar Richard Hays, however, argues convincingly that Horsley is wrong. There is nothing in Matthew's text that suggests the kind of precise social situation in small villages that Horsley imagines. Furthermore, the lexicographical evidence does not support Horsley. "The term *echthroi* is generic. It is often used in biblical Greek of national or military enemies."[66] For example, in Deuteronomy 20:1 (LXX), the text says, "When you go to war against your enemies [*echthroi*] and see horses and chariots and an army greater than yours, do not be afraid of them." (It is also interesting that this verse follows immediately after Deuteronomy 19:21, which commands an eye for an eye—the principle that Jesus specifically rejects.) After a major review of recent scholarly literature on the topic, Heinz-Wolfgang Kuhn concludes that the enemies Jesus calls his disciples to love include everyone. "The directive is without boundaries. The religious, the political, and the personal are all meant. Every enemy is meant."[67]

Martin Hengel, one of the leading scholars on the nationalist, revolutionary Jewish movements of Jesus's time, thinks that Jesus's command to love one's enemies "was formulated with direct reference to the theocratic and nationalistic liberation movement in which hatred toward an enemy was regarded as a good work."[68] There is no way to prove that decisively. But the fact that, in the immediately preceding section, Jesus has urged his followers

64. So France, *Gospel of Matthew*, 225.
65. Horsley, "Ethics and Exegesis." See also Horsley, *Jesus and the Spiral of Violence*, esp. 261–73.
66. Hays, *Moral Vision*, 328.
67. Quoted in Klassen, "'Love Your Enemies,'" 11. So too Schrage, *Ethics of the New Testament*, 76.
68. Hengel, *Christ and Power*, 19.

to carry the packs of Roman soldiers not just the legally mandated one mile but also a second mile demonstrates that Jesus is thinking about the situation the violent Jewish revolutionaries hated. If in verse 41 Jesus is talking about how to respond to Roman imperialists, it is very likely that his command to love enemies includes the people the revolutionaries seek to kill.

Jesus's stated reason for loving one's enemies is important. His disciples should act that way so "that you may be children of your Father in heaven" (Matt. 5:45). Since God sends the sun and rain on both good and evil people, Jesus's disciples must act in love toward everyone, both friends and enemies. As one of the beatitudes says, the peacemakers are "called children of God" (5:9).

The final verse of this section ("Be perfect, therefore, as your heavenly Father is perfect"; Matt. 5:48) could be understood to demand an impossible ideal that drives us to repentance rather than calls us to discipleship. But the word translated "perfect" (*teleios*) is used by Paul and often translated "mature" (e.g., 1 Cor. 2:6; Phil. 3:15). In 1 Corinthians 14:20, Paul uses this word to urge Christians to stop being children and instead think like "adults" (*teleioi*).[69] "Jesus is not frustrating his hearers with an unachievable ideal but challenging them to grow in obedience to God's will."[70]

But we dare not minimize Jesus's costly summons. His words echo the Old Testament call to "be holy because I, the LORD your God, am holy" (Lev. 19:2). "The community of Jesus' disciples is to reflect the holiness of God in scrupulous obedience to the will of God as disclosed through the teaching of Jesus, who has taken the place of Moses as the definitive interpreter of the Law."[71] The messianic kingdom has begun, and it is now possible and imperative for Jesus's disciples to demonstrate (imperfectly but powerfully) the character of God. And that, according to Jesus, includes loving one's enemies.

The same teaching about loving enemies appears in the Gospel of Luke. There too, as in Matthew, it is a major part of Jesus's first ethical teaching.[72]

It is hard to exaggerate either the originality or the importance of Jesus's direct command to love our enemies. It contradicts the practice of every society known to historians. No precise parallel to Jesus's words has been found. New Testament scholars point out that the saying appears in both the earliest sayings tradition of Jesus's words (scholars call it Q) and then Luke (6:27, 35) as well as Matthew. This leads Hengel to say that "this Magna Charta

69. See France, *Gospel of Matthew*, 228–29; Bruner, *Matthew*, 1:276.
70. Blomberg, *Matthew*, 115; so too Yoder, *War of the Lamb*, 146–47.
71. Hays, *Moral Vision*, 329.
72. Luke 6:27–36. There are some differences from Matthew in the Lukan version, but the call to love enemies and thus be children of God is central to both.

of *agape*" is what is "actually revolutionary in the message of Jesus."[73] John Howard Yoder notes that there is no other ethical issue about which the New Testament says Jesus's disciples are like the heavenly Father when they act a certain way.[74]

Also striking is the fact that Matthew 5:38–48 is probably the most frequently cited biblical text when one collects all the statements about killing from the early Christian writers before the time of Constantine. Ten writers in at least twenty-eight different places cite or refer to this passage and note that Christians love their enemies and turn the other cheek. In nine instances, they link this passage from Jesus with a statement that Christians are peaceable, ignorant of war, or opposed to attacking others. Sometimes they explicitly link Jesus's saying to a rejection of killing and war.[75] In every single instance where pre-Constantinian Christian writers mention the topic of killing, they say that Christians do not do that, whether in abortion, capital punishment, or war.[76] And Jesus's statement about loving enemies is one of the reasons cited.

Sidestepping Jesus's Teaching

It is not surprising that Christians over the centuries have developed numerous ways to weaken or set aside Jesus's call to love our enemies. His teaching directly contradicts our natural instincts. It challenges the practice of all civilizations. We must examine the most common arguments for setting aside this radical teaching.[77]

Jesus came to die. Many Christians think that the only important reason Jesus came was to die as the substitute for our sins. The gospel is the good news that we are forgiven through the cross and can go to heaven when we die. Jesus's ethical teaching is at best relatively unimportant and perhaps irrelevant.

The problem with this understanding is that it simply ignores Jesus's full teaching about his gospel. As we saw in chapter 1, Jesus's gospel was the good news that the long-expected messianic kingdom was now breaking into history. Certainly one fundamental part of that good news is that God forgives sinners and that Jesus's death on the cross has accomplished our reconciliation with God. But equally central to Jesus's understanding of the gospel is the

---

73. Hengel, *Was Jesus a Revolutionist?*, 26–27.
74. Yoder, *War of the Lamb*, 79.
75. Sider, *Early Church on Killing*, 171–72.
76. Sider, *Early Church on Killing*, 163–95, esp. 190–95.
77. Among the more extensive listings of these arguments are Yoder, *Politics of Jesus*, 4–8; Hays, *Moral Vision*, 320.

fact that the new messianic time of peace and justice has already begun and Jesus's disciples are now summoned to live according to Jesus's teaching.

Jesus's message is spiritual, not social. Somewhat similar to the previous view, this position believes that Jesus's message relates to the inner spiritual life of individuals, not to life in society.

Again, as we saw in the previous point, Jesus's gospel of the kingdom relates both to the disciples' inner spiritual life and to the new socioeconomic reality that was arriving in Jesus's dawning messianic kingdom.

Jesus taught an interim ethic. Since Albert Schweitzer at the beginning of the twentieth century, many scholars have thought that Jesus expected an almost immediate end to our space-time world. Since the world was about to end, Jesus could proclaim a radical ethic for this brief interim—an ethic that would be totally unrealistic if the world were to continue.[78]

The problem with this argument, as N. T. Wright clearly demonstrates, is that there is virtually no evidence that any Jew in Jesus's day thought that the arrival of the messianic kingdom meant the end of our space-time world.[79] The apocalyptic language used to describe the arrival of the messianic kingdom was figurative language to underline the sweeping societal change that the Messiah would bring.[80] Since Jesus was not thinking of a very near end to our space-time world, the idea of his teaching an interim ethic for the short time before the world ended makes no historical sense. It is a fiction of modern scholarship.

Jesus's radical ethics is for a special class of Christians. In the Middle Ages, Catholic thinkers developed the idea that Jesus's hard sayings (his "counsels of perfection" like his call to love enemies) apply only to especially religious people, such as monks and nuns. Ordinary Christians may live by less-demanding standards.

The problem with such a view is that there is not a hint from Jesus or in the rest of the New Testament of such a double standard. Jesus understands himself as the Messiah for all Israel. His ethical teaching is for everyone who accepts his gospel that the kingdom is now arriving and that it is possible and important for his disciples to live all that he has taught. In fact, he explicitly commands his followers to teach the new disciples in "all nations" to "obey everything I have commanded you" (Matt. 28:19–20).

---

78. George Weigel says: "This hope for a decisive, world-ending act of God in history colored much of the preaching of Jesus" (*Tranquillitas Ordinis*, 26). Therefore, it is a mistake to look to Jesus for an ethic of war and peace. See also Niebuhr, *Interpretation of Christian Ethics*.

79. N. T. Wright, *Jesus and the Victory of God*, 40, 81, 95–96; and N. T. Wright, *New Testament and the People of God*, 333–34.

80. See above, chap. 1, "Messianic Expectations."

Jesus's radical ethics calls us to repentance, not discipleship. Believing that Jesus's radical ethics are impossible to live, some Christians (Martin Luther, among others) argue that the purpose is to reveal our sinful failure and thus drive us to confess our sins and seek forgiveness rather than reveal how Jesus wants his disciples to live.

Jesus's high demands rightly lead us to repentance. But there is not a hint from Jesus that that is all he intends. In fact, repeatedly it is clear, as we saw in the previous point, that Jesus summons his disciples to obey all that he commands.[81]

Jesus's ethics is for some future eschatological kingdom, not the present. Dispensational theology used to teach that since the Jews rejected Jesus as the Messiah, the messianic kingdom was postponed until the millennium. Therefore, Jesus's ethical teaching in the Sermon on the Mount and elsewhere does not apply today in the church age.

This view fails to grasp Jesus's basic understanding of the gospel: the kingdom is now breaking in, and his disciples can and should live now according to his teaching. Furthermore, it is strange to say that a teaching like "love your enemies" is not for the present (when Christians *do* have real enemies) but only for the millennium (when evil has been conquered and enemies no longer exist).

Jesus's command not to kill enemies applies to private not public roles. Various versions of this argument are probably the most common way that Christians have asserted that Jesus's command to love enemies does not mean that Christians should never kill others. (As soldiers or public officials carrying out a judicial decision on capital punishment, Christians rightly kill.) Jesus's teaching about how to respond to a slap of the hand or a demand for one's clothing shows that he is talking about how to respond to personal injury, not about public life.[82] Paul Ramsey argues that Jesus is talking about how one person responds to a single individual who oppresses one, not how one responds in a complex social setting when there are multiple neighbors under attack from evil persons.[83]

Proponents of this view often argue that Romans 12:9–21 (do not repay evil for evil; leave vengeance to God) applies to the personal life of Christians in the church. Romans 13:1–7 (government is God's servant to punish the evildoer) prescribes the public responsibilities (including serving in the army) that Christians have as citizens. Since one of the Ten Commandments

81. See also introduction to chap. 3.
82. Charles, *Between Pacifism and Jihad*, 96. See also Charles and Demy, *War, Peace, and Christianity*, 252.
83. Ramsey, *Basic Christian Ethics*, 42.

prohibits killing but the Old Testament clearly commands the death penalty
and war, the proper conclusion is that as a private individual, one dare not kill,
but as a person serving in a public role, one rightly kills. That, it is argued,
is the assumption behind Romans 12–13.[84]

Martin Luther's two-kingdom theology is one common version of this
private-public distinction.[85] Every Christian, Luther says, lives in two kingdoms. In the "kingdom of Christ" (seen most clearly in the church), the individual Christian loves enemies and does not resist evil. But in the "kingdom
of the world," the same person occupies a public office (perhaps as judge or
soldier) and rightly restrains evil, even with the sword. Thus Luther writes
that when Christians went to war and "struck right and left and killed," there
"was no difference between Christians and the heathen." These Christian
soldiers "did nothing contrary to this text [Matt. 5:38–39]. For they did it
not as Christians but as obedient members and subjects, under obligation to
a secular person and authority."[86]

Careful consideration of this widely used argument is essential. I believe
this argument: (1) ignores the historical context of Jesus's teaching; (2) contradicts what seems to be the most obvious meaning of the text; (3) relies on
pragmatism to set Jesus aside; (4) historically, has sometimes led to very bad
consequences; and (5) ignores the first three centuries of Christian teaching
about killing.

First, in his historical context, Jesus claimed to be the Messiah of the
entire Jewish people. He intended his teaching, as N. T. Wright points out,
to show Israel how it should live. Jews of all kinds—common people and
religious leaders, ordinary folk and members of the Sanhedrin—heard his
teaching. And it is clear that Jesus disagreed with the devout, violent Jewish
revolutionaries of his time who, according to Josephus, urged the Jews to
rebel against the Roman imperialists and their Jewish collaborators. Rejecting
the widespread expectation of a military messiah, Jesus clearly chose to be
a peaceful Messiah who called his followers to love even their enemies—and
those enemies, as the saying about carrying Roman soldiers' packs a second
mile demonstrates, included the hated Romans.

Jesus advocated love, even for political enemies, as his response to several
centuries of violent Jewish attitudes to foreign oppressors. And there is certainly no hint that Jesus's reason for objecting to the violence of the revolutionaries was that they were unauthorized individuals whose violent sword

84. Charles, *Between Pacifism and Jihad*, 96–97; Stott, *Sermon on the Mount*, 105–13. For
a detailed response to this interpretation of Rom. 12–13, see below, chap. 6, "Romans 13."

85. See the discussion of Luther in Cahill, *Love Your Enemies*, 101–8.

86. Luther, *Sermon on the Mount*, 196; quoted in Sprinkle, *Fight*, 140–41.

would have been legitimate if the religiopolitical leaders of the Sanhedrin had just given the order. Rather, his point was that the revolutionaries' whole approach to enemies was wrong. They offered one messianic strategy. Jesus offered another. But both appealed to the entire Jewish nation to follow their vision and teaching.

The premonitions of national disaster in Jesus's teaching show that Jesus realized that the only way to avoid destruction was through a rejection of the revolutionaries' call to armed revolt. Right after the story of Jesus's triumphal entry (riding on a donkey, not a warhorse), Luke tells us that Jesus weeps over Jerusalem as he predicts its destruction and laments its failure to understand "what would bring you peace" (Luke 19:41–44). Jesus also says the temple itself will be torn down (Mark 13:1–2).[87] Revolutionary violence, Jesus realized, would lead to national destruction, as it did in the Jewish revolt (AD 66–70) just a few decades later. Jesus's messianic vision offered an entirely different approach. He called the Jewish people to embrace his vision of a peaceful messianic kingdom where people loved their enemies rather than killed them. That kingdom, he said, was now breaking into history, and he invited the entire Jewish people to embrace it. Understood in its historical setting, Jesus's call to love enemies clearly cannot be limited to the personal sphere of private life.

Second, the personal-public distinction seems to contradict the most natural, literal meaning of the text. There is no hint in the text of such a distinction. It is true that one or two of Jesus's concrete examples refer to personal life. That is true of the slap on the cheek. To some extent, that is also the case with the statement about how the debtor should respond. But in that case, the setting is a court of public law. The call to carry the Roman soldier's pack a second mile clearly speaks of the public political setting where Roman imperialists had the legal right to make oppressive demands. And Jesus's call to reject the principle of an eye for an eye refers to the foundational principle of all Near Eastern jurisprudence—that is, the very center of public life, not some personal private sphere. Swiss New Testament scholar Edward Schweizer is surely correct: "There is not the slightest hint of any realm where the disciple is not bound by the words of Jesus."[88]

The members of the Sanhedrin and other officials surely heard Jesus's teaching. The most natural conclusion is that Jesus intended his words to be normative not just in private but also in public life. The burden of proof would

87. See also Luke 23:26–30. Perhaps, Luke 12:54–56 and 13:1–5 are also allusions to Jerusalem's destruction. See also N. T. Wright, *Jesus and the Victory of God*, 182–86, 335–36, 416–17, 424.
88. Schweizer, *Matthew*, 194.

seem to rest on those who want to argue that Jesus's statement about loving enemies referred only to the way the individual should act in private life.

Third, an essential ethical pragmatism often underlies the argument that Jesus could not have meant that his followers should never use lethal violence. In a sinful world that often tramples on nonviolent persons, it is argued, violence is necessary to defend oneself and others. Jesus's love ethic, Niebuhr said, is an "impossible ideal" that simply will not work in the real world. This factual claim may or may not be accurate.[89] But what is surely most important for Christians, however, is the essential pragmatism of the argument. The *pragmatic* question of whether Jesus's ethic works in the short run—that is, whether it enables us and others to avoid suffering—dare not be decisive in our analysis of what Jesus actually means. If one confesses, as the church has for two millennia, that Jesus is truly God incarnate, then one simply dare not tell Jesus that his teaching is impractical in the real world and therefore may, even should, be set aside.

Fourth, the consequences of this dualistic distinction between private and public have often been disastrous. Christians have justified their participation in terrible evil on the pretext that it is not right for them to challenge official orders. The failure of most German Protestants to oppose Hitler's atrocities is sometimes attributed in part to Luther's two-kingdom ethics.[90] In 1933, German Christians argued that "the church is obliged to obey the state in every earthly matter." And they concluded that "unconditional allegiance" to the Nazi state was fully compatible with allegiance to Christ.[91]

Finally, the writings of Christians in the first three centuries clearly do not support the personal-public distinction. In every instance where they discuss killing, they say that Christians do not and should not kill. That holds in both the private realm of abortion and infanticide and also the public realm of capital punishment and war.[92] Writing in the first decade of the fourth century, the Christian orator Lactantius insists, "When God forbids us to kill, . . . [God] warns us against the commission of those things which are esteemed lawful among people. Thus it will be neither lawful for a just man [a Christian] to engage in military service . . . nor to accuse anyone of a capital charge, because it makes no difference whether you put a person to death by

89. See Sider, *Nonviolent Action*, for numerous examples of successful nonviolent action against injustice and dictatorship.

90. For a historical analysis of the doctrine of the two kingdoms, see Duchrow, *Lutheran Churches*. See also Hertz, *Two Kingdoms*.

91. Hertz, *Two Kingdoms*, 184–85.

92. Sider, *Early Church on Killing*, 165–95. For abortion, see 165–66; for infanticide, 110–11; for capital punishment, 166–68; for war and military service, 168–90.

word or rather by sword, since it is the act of putting to death itself which is prohibited."[93] Repeatedly, the early Christian writers reject the view that Christians may kill in the public role of soldier or executioner.

It is often argued that the Old Testament material requires some distinction between the personal and public roles with regard to murder, capital punishment, and war. If that is correct, then something unusual must have happened to produce this reversal of thinking represented in the early Christian writers' insistence that killing of every sort, not just private murder by unauthorized individuals, is wrong. Their explanation is Jesus, who, they said, prohibits every kind of killing. Origen, probably the most widely read Christian author in the middle of the third century, explicitly discusses the distinction between the "former economy" of Israel, where killing in war was allowed, and the teaching of Christ: "For Christians could not slay their enemies or condemn to be burned or stoned, as Moses commands" (Origen, *Against Celsus* 4.9; 7.26).[94] The most likely explanation for this significant change is that Jesus himself called his disciples to reject killing in every area of life, both private and public. That is certainly what early Christian writers thought.

The most natural interpretation of the Sermon on the Mount seems to confirm that Christians in the first three centuries were right in thinking that Jesus intended to teach his followers never to kill. In the next chapter, we will examine other aspects of Jesus's teaching.

93. Lactantius, *Divine Institutes* 6.20; Sider, *Early Church on Killing*, 110.
94. Sider, *Early Church on Killing*, 73, 76.

4

Other Teachings of Jesus

In addition to the major text explored in the last chapter, there are a number of additional places where Jesus's statements seem to point toward a rejection of violence.

Jesus's Inaugural Sermon

Luke 4:16–30 depicts Jesus in the synagogue in his hometown reading from Isaiah 61:1–2. As we saw earlier, some Jews in Jesus's day understood this text to be speaking of the messianic time.[1] What is striking for our purposes here is that Jesus seems to end his reading in the middle of verse 2. He omits the words "the day of vengeance of our God." Nothing in the text specifically tells us why Jesus does not include those words on God's vengeance on Israel's enemies that popular messianic expectation eagerly awaited. But some scholars have thought that the central point of the narrative is the rejection of Jewish expectations of vengeance on their enemies and instead the expansion of God's covenant to include all people.[2]

The following verses lend weight to that interpretation. The people of the town ask, "Isn't this Joseph's son?" (Luke 4:22)—suggesting that they question Jesus's implied claims for himself. In response, Jesus elaborates on the fact that a prophet is not accepted in his hometown. And then Jesus refers

1. See chap. 1, "Jesus's Gospel of the Kingdom."
2. E.g., Jeremias, *Jesus' Promise to the Nations*, 41–46. So too Cowles, "Case for Radical Discontinuity," 24–25.

to two prominent Old Testament prophets who ministered to and healed people who were Israel's national enemies. In spite of the fact that there were many widows in Israel in Elijah's day, Jesus says, Elijah was sent to a Baal-worshiping widow in the pagan city of Sidon (4:26; cf. 1 Kings 17:8–24). Furthermore, Jesus says, there were many Israelites with leprosy in Elisha's day, but he healed Naaman the Syrian (Luke 4:27). Naaman was not just a pagan; he was also the commander of the Syrian army, which had recently defeated Israel (2 Kings 5:1–19). Naaman was a national enemy! Jesus's two references point out that prominent Old Testament prophets acted in love toward their national enemies. The implication seems to be that Jesus's messianic kingdom welcomes and loves even national enemies. Not surprisingly, the devout Jews of Nazareth are furious at this implication. They try to throw Jesus off the high cliff at the edge of the town (Luke 4:28–29).

Jesus and the Samaritans

Jesus's attitude toward and interaction with the Samaritans provide a striking example of loving one's enemies.

In Jesus's time, Jews and Samaritans hated each other. The Samaritans were probably a mixed racial group, descendants of Jews who intermarried with gentiles who were introduced into the area by a foreign conqueror.[3] By at least the fourth century BC, the Samaritans had built their own temple on Mount Gerizim as a rival to the temple in Jerusalem. The Samaritans' version of the Pentateuch declared that Mount Gerizim, not Jerusalem, was where God was to be worshiped.[4] Sometime around 129 BC the Hasmonean (Jewish) ruler actually destroyed the Samaritans' temple on Mount Gerizim. Then about AD 6–9, one night during the sacred Jewish feast of Passover, some Samaritans dumped human bones in the porches of the Jerusalem temple and scattered them all over the sanctuary (*Ant.* 13.255–56; 18.29–30). Conflict, even bloody encounters, often occurred when Jewish pilgrims from Galilee traveled through Samaria on their way to Jerusalem for festivals (e.g., *JW* 2.231, 234). We see this bitter hostility exemplified in the Gospels when Jesus is refused lodging because he is on his way to Jerusalem (Luke 9:52–53) and even refused a drink by the Samaritan woman (John 4:9). When Jews accuse Jesus of being a "Samaritan and demon-possessed" (8:48), they reflect this intense hatred. The Jews forbade intermarriage with Samaritans and considered them to be gentiles.

3. For a somewhat extensive discussion of the Samaritans and the mutual hatred between Jews and Samaritans, see Jeremias, *Jerusalem in the Time of Jesus*, 352–58.
4. Keener, *IVP Bible Background Commentary*, 205.

Seen in this context, Jesus's dealings with Samaritans provide an astonishing example of loving national enemies. He praises the faith of a Samaritan, rejects his disciples' desire to call down fire from heaven on Samaritans who insult him, accepts a Samaritan woman as one of his earliest "evangelists," and makes a Samaritan the hero of one of his most famous parables.

After Jesus heals ten lepers, only one—a Samaritan—returns to thank him. Jesus pointedly notes that only this "foreigner" has come back to say thanks. And then Jesus praises him for his faith (Luke 17:18–19).

Once as Jesus is traveling through Samaria to Jerusalem, he tries to find shelter in a Samaritan village. But the Samaritans refuse, as they often did, because he is on pilgrimage to Jerusalem (Luke 9:51–56). In response, Jesus's disciples want to call fire down from heaven to destroy these enemies—just like Elijah, who had done that to kill his enemies (2 Kings 1:9–16). Jesus rejects that violent response and simply goes to another village. Citing this incident, Richard Hays comments, "At every turn, he renounces violence as a strategy for promoting God's kingdom."[5] In his commentary on this story, G. B. Caird notes that just a bit earlier in his Gospel, Luke describes the transfiguration, where Elijah and Moses appear with Jesus and then disappear. Caird comments, "This is why Elijah had to disappear from the mountain to give place to Jesus, with his new way of loving his enemies."[6]

Jesus's engagement with the Samaritan woman at the well is also striking. She refuses his request to give him a drink because "Jews do not associate with Samaritans" (John 4:9). But Jesus persists in talking to her and eventually reveals that he is the Messiah she is expecting. In response, she invites her whole village to come to see Jesus. And Jesus gladly accepts the villagers' invitation to stay for two days (4:21–42). Rather than the frequent, often bloody, conflicts between Samaritans and Jews on pilgrimage to Jerusalem, trust for former enemies emerges.

When Jesus makes a hated Samaritan the hero of one of his powerful parables, he must have incensed many of his Jewish listeners. In the parable, two Jewish leaders (a priest and a Levite) ignore and fail to help a half-dead victim of robbers lying naked by the roadside. But then a Samaritan traveler stops, gently cares for the wounded man, puts him on his donkey, transports him to the nearest inn, and pays the innkeeper to care for him. At the end of the story, Jesus forces the learned expert on the Jewish law to admit that it is really the hated Samaritan who has acted as a neighbor. Rubbing it in, Jesus tells him to imitate the Samaritan (Luke 10:25–37)!

5. Hays, *Moral Vision*, 329–30.
6. Caird, *Gospel of St. Luke*, 140.

Every Jewish listener to Jesus's words would know without any question that Jesus was making a hero out of their nation's enemy. Love for one's enemy is a central implication of this parable.[7] Indeed, all Jesus's encounters with Samaritans seem to teach the same point.

Healing a Centurion's Servant

Matthew 8:5–13 tells the story of a centurion who begs Jesus to heal his sick servant.[8] As a military commander in charge of one hundred Roman soldiers, he represents the hated Roman imperialists who control the land of the Jews. He is a visible symbol of the foreign conquerors whom the violent Jewish revolutionaries want to overthrow—a "member of the despised colonial-imperial occupying power."[9]

But Jesus offers to come to his house to heal his servant (Matt. 8:7). And when the centurion humbly responds that he is not worthy for Jesus to visit his home and that all he wants is for Jesus to speak a word of healing, Jesus is amazed at his faith: "Truly I tell you, I have not found anyone in Israel with such great faith" (8:10). But even more amazing is Jesus's next sentence: "I say to you that many will come from the east and the west, and will take their places at the feast with Abraham, Isaac and Jacob in the kingdom of heaven" (8:11). Jesus tells the centurion that his dawning messianic kingdom is not just for Jews. It is for people from everywhere.

This story not only depicts Jesus associating with and healing the servant of the most visible symbol of the Jews' national enemy. It also clearly implies that Jesus's dawning kingdom welcomes those enemies as members.[10]

Paying Roman Taxes?

The question of whether devout Jews should pay Roman taxes was hotly debated in Jesus's day. In AD 6, Judas of Galilee led a major violent revolt, sharply condemning the payment of Roman taxes.[11] At Jesus's trial before

7. See Klassen, *Love of Enemies*, 82–83, 107n13 for a number of scholars who have seen this parable as an illustration of love for enemy.
8. In Luke's account of this incident (7:1–10), we learn that the centurion is a friend of the Jews. But in spite of his personal friendship, his very office makes him a symbol of the Roman imperialists.
9. Bruner, *Matthew*, 1:378.
10. This text says nothing negatively or positively about whether being a soldier is compatible with being Jesus's disciple. For that discussion, see below, chap. 6, "Soldiers in the New Testament."
11. See above, chap. 1, "Messianic Violence."

Pilate, the Jewish leaders accuse Jesus of opposing the payment of taxes to Caesar (Luke 23:2)—a charge, if true, that would certainly result in death.

All three Synoptic Gospels tell us of a group of Herodians and Pharisees who try to trick Jesus with the question, "Is it right for us to pay taxes to Caesar or not?"[12] Should devout Jews living according to the Torah pay taxes to a pagan conqueror? They know that if Jesus says no, the Romans will promptly execute him for treason. They also know that if he says yes, he will lose credibility with large numbers of Jews who hate Roman imperialism and look for the Messiah to lead a successful battle against Rome. Supporting the payment to Rome would mean to many, if not most, Jews that he was not the Messiah.[13]

Jesus asks his questioners to show him a specific coin, the Roman denarius. Jesus knows that stamped on this coin of Caesar (especially minted for the payment of the Roman tax) are the words "Tiberius, Caesar, worshipful son of the divine Augustus."[14] On the back of the coin is an image of the emperor's mother sitting on the throne of the gods.[15] Not only does Jewish theology reject any claim to divinity by a man. It also forbids making an image of a person. Jesus's clever action forces his opponents to admit that they carry this blasphemous coin—even in the temple, where the debate occurs (Luke 20:1). Jesus has exposed their hypocrisy.

Jesus's response—"then give back to Caesar what is Caesar's, and to God what is God's" (Luke 20:25)—cleverly avoids the trap they have set. He does not say the Jews should refuse to pay the Roman tax—thus clearly distancing himself from the violent Jewish revolutionaries.[16]

But does he urge the Jews to pay the Roman tax? "Give back to Caesar what is Caesar's" could mean that since they have already compromised their Jewish values by carrying Caesar's blasphemous coin in their purses, then they have no excuse for refusing to pay the tax. A number of commentators think Jesus's words mean that he did support paying the tax as long as people were clear that only God and not Caesar was owed total submission.[17] But it is also possible that his listeners would have heard a studied ambiguity—especially since the final words of the story indicate that his questioners were astonished at how cleverly he avoided the impossible dilemma with which they thought they had trapped him. Whether or not Jesus's listeners understood his answer

---

12. Luke 20:20–26; Mark 12:13–17; Matt. 22:15–22.

13. Lasserre, *War and the Gospel*, 87; see also Bruner, *Matthew*, 2:397; Blomberg, *Matthew*, 330.

14. Bruner, *Matthew*, 2:398.

15. Douglass, *Non-Violent Cross*, 190.

16. Blomberg, *Matthew*, 332.

17. E.g., Bruner, *Matthew*, 2:400–403; France, *Gospel of Matthew*, 833–34.

to be ambiguous about paying the Roman tax, certainly nothing in the account suggests that Jesus supports the call for violent revolt against Rome.

Dealing with Conflict in the Church

In Matthew 18, Jesus provides a process for dealing with sin in the church (vv. 15–20). First, go alone to the person sinning and seek restoration. Second, if the first step fails, have two or three others join the conversation. If that fails, take it to the whole church.

There is nothing in this text that speaks about killing. But the text does present a nonviolent way to resolve conflict. To be a human community is to have conflict and sinful behavior. The typical response is to use violence to solve the problem. Jesus's teaching here offers a nonviolent procedural alternative.[18] In his commentary on Matthew, Frederick D. Bruner calls this text the "Magna Carta of confrontation" because it combines genuine confrontation of evil with "the *nonviolence* of the large Sermon on the Mount."[19] Thus this passage fits well with Jesus's general rejection of violence.

"Father, Forgive Them"

Luke tells us that after the soldiers nailed Jesus to the cross, Jesus uttered the amazing words "Father, forgive them, for they do not know what they are doing" (23:34).[20] By any ordinary understanding, people who nail you to a cross are enemies. But Jesus offers even these wicked people his love and forgiveness. Jesus's action and words on the cross are a powerful illustration of his teaching to love our enemies.

From the biblical story of Lamech to Homer's depiction of Achilles's thirst for revenge, we see humanity's natural inclination to seek revenge rather than offer forgiveness. After killing a man for striking him, Lamech says, "If Cain is avenged seven times, then Lamech seventy-seven times" (Gen. 4:24). Jesus alludes to this story when Peter asks how many times he should forgive a brother or sister (Matt. 18:21). Peter suggests that seven times would be enough! But Jesus replies, "I tell you, not seven times, but seventy-seven times"

18. See the discussion in Yoder, *Body Politics*, 1–13; and A. Kreider, E. Kreider, and Widjaja, *Culture of Peace*, 62–68.

19. Bruner, *Matthew*, 2:224 (italics original).

20. Some important manuscripts do not include these words. But G. B. Caird notes that "it is well attested in other manuscripts, and most modern textual critics accept it as a genuine part of the text." Caird, *Gospel of St. Luke*, 251.

(18:22).[21] Forgiveness, even for enemies, is Jesus's example and his summons to his followers. And forgiveness for enemies, Miroslav Volf points out, is the only way to break the spiral of vengeance.[22]

Jesus and the Suffering Servant of Isaiah 40–55

Modern scholars have disagreed sharply over whether Jesus saw himself and his work as related to Isaiah's suffering servant.[23] N. T. Wright has argued convincingly that Isaiah 40–55 and especially the servant song in Isaiah 52:13–53:12 was central to Jesus's understanding of his mission.

For Jews in Jesus's day, Isaiah 40–55 was important for their expectation that God would soon end their exile, punish the pagans who held them captive, and return to Zion as king. And there is clear evidence that some Jews at this time understood the servant in Isaiah in a messianic way.[24] But these Jewish thinkers definitely did not speak of a *suffering* Messiah.[25] The idea that the Messiah would suffer and die had "no precedent in Judaism."[26]

The servant song in Isaiah 52:13–53:12 was central to the widespread Jewish views in Jesus's day that their exile would end, their present suffering would cease, and divine wrath would fall "on the pagan nations that had oppressed Israel."[27] Jesus shared much of that basic vision but challenged it "precisely at the point where his contemporaries were expecting a military victory over Israel's enemies."[28]

Jesus announced the dawning of the messianic kingdom. "But, unlike the other kingdom-announcers of his time from Judas the Galilean to Simeon ben Kosiba [would-be messiah during the Jewish War], Jesus declared that the way to the kingdom was the way of peace, the way of love, the way of the cross."[29] Unlike the Maccabean martyrs and more-recent religious rebels, Jesus "saw as

---

21. Some translations say "seventy times seven" but "seventy-seven," with the clear allusion to Gen. 4:24, is almost certainly correct. See Bruner, *Matthew*, 2:236; France, *Gospel of Matthew*, 701.

22. Volf, *Exclusion and Embrace*, 121–25.

23. Oscar Cullmann argues strongly for this identification (*Christology of the New Testament*, 51–82). See N. T. Wright, *Jesus and the Victory of God*, 601n218, for a list of some of the major works on the topic.

24. N. T. Wright, *Jesus and the Victory of God*, 588–89. Michael B. Shepherd shows that the Targum on Isaiah clearly identifies the servant of Isaiah as the Messiah. Shepherd, "Targums," 55.

25. N. T. Wright, *Jesus and the Victory of God*, 590.

26. J. Collins, *Scepter and the Star*, 235.

27. N. T. Wright, *Jesus and the Victory of God*, 591.

28. N. T. Wright, *Jesus and the Victory of God*, 591.

29. N. T. Wright, *Jesus and the Victory of God*, 595.

pagan corruption *the very desire to fight paganism itself.* Israel had become a hotbed of nationalistic revolution; suffering would come of it, specifically in the form of Roman swords, falling masonry and above all crosses planted outside the capital city."[30] What Jesus predicted actually occurred just a few decades later when the Romans destroyed Jerusalem in the Jewish War of AD 66–70. Drawing on Isaiah's picture of the suffering servant, Jesus offered a different, peaceful messianic strategy that included loving enemies, even when that involved being crucified.

"All Who Draw the Sword Will Die by the Sword"

All four Gospels tell us that at Jesus's arrest someone (Peter, according to John 18:10–11) draws a sword and strikes a person coming to arrest Jesus. And in each Gospel, Jesus rebukes his would-be defender and commands him to stop using the sword. In John, the explanation is that Jesus must drink the cup his Father has given (18:11). Mark and Luke give no reason for Jesus's command. But in Matthew's account, Jesus says, "Put your sword back in its place, for all who draw the sword will die by the sword" (26:52).

Some commentators argue that since Jesus does not say "throw away your sword" but rather says, put it "in its place," Jesus means that there is a proper place for the sword—that is, when authorized by government.[31] But the text certainly does not say that in any clear way. Furthermore, the text in Matthew offers a general reason—"all who draw the sword will die by the sword"—for Jesus's rebuke of Peter. It is easy to see how this general reason could imply an application to all uses of the sword. Thus R. T. France comments that Jesus's words about "'those who take up the sword' are quite general and provide *prima facie* support for the belief that physical violence, and particularly retaliatory violence, is incompatible with following Jesus (see 5:39 for the principle of nonresistance)."[32] Hays quotes Ulrich Mauser, who says, "If anything in Matthew's Gospel, this scene at the arrest is the authentic interpretation of the sentence in the Sermon on the Mount, 'Do not resist an evildoer' (Matt. 5:39)."[33]

This text does not explicitly say that Jesus's disciples should reject all violence. But that implication of Jesus's general statement certainly fits well with his other actions and teachings.

---

30. N. T. Wright, *Jesus and the Victory of God*, 596 (italics original).
31. Bruner, *Matthew*, 2:672. So too Martin Luther.
32. France, *Gospel of Matthew*, 1013. So too similarly Schweizer, *Matthew*, 495.
33. Mauser, *Gospel of Peace*, 80; quoted in Hays, *Moral Vision*, 322.

Jesus's Disciples Must "Take Up Their Cross"

We have seen how Jesus's messianic understanding differed sharply from widespread views in his time. Many Jews expected a militaristic Messiah who would lead the war against the Romans. Some taught that God would intervene to send the Messiah and bring victory if the Jewish people would dare to take up the sword.[34]

Both his actions and his teaching show that Jesus rejected that violent path. Instead, he chose the cross. And, repeatedly, Jesus taught that his disciples must take up their own cross.

All three Synoptic Gospels describe the same sequence of events. Peter confesses that Jesus is the Messiah.[35] Jesus immediately predicts his rejection by the Jewish leaders and his death.[36] Peter (still failing to understand Jesus's peaceful messianic understanding) takes Jesus aside and rebukes him for talking about rejection and death. In response, Jesus denounces Peter as Satan for his violent understanding.[37] In all three Gospels, Jesus's demand that his disciples also take up their cross follows immediately. Very clearly, each evangelist intends to teach that Jesus's disciples must follow Jesus in choosing the cross rather than violence.

Again and again, Jesus repeats the demand that his disciples take up their cross.[38] "Whoever does not take up their cross and follow me is not worthy of me" (Matt. 10:38). "Whoever wants to be my disciple must deny themselves and take up their cross and follow me" (16:24). He warns his disciples that they will have to drink the cup and be baptized with the baptism that Jesus himself will experience (Mark 10:39). Jesus's actions and teaching reject the use of violence. And he seems to expect his disciples to do the same.

All through the Gospels it is clear that Jesus intends his disciples to live what he has taught. At the end of the Sermon on the Mount, Jesus describes two men, one foolish, one wise. "Everyone who hears these words of mine and puts them into practice is like a wise man who built his house on the rock" (Matt. 7:24). Only those who do the will of Jesus's Father will enter the kingdom (7:21). In the final scene in Matthew's Gospel, as Jesus is about to leave his disciples, he commands them not only to make disciples of all nations but also to teach "them to obey everything I have commanded you"

34. See chap. 1, "Messianic Violence."
35. Matt. 16:13–16; Mark 8:29; Luke 9:18–20.
36. Matt. 16:21; Mark 8:31; Luke 9:21–22.
37. Matt. 16:22–23; Mark 8:32–33. Luke omits this embarrassing failure of Peter.
38. See Lasserre, *War and the Gospel*, 67.

(28:20). And in the Gospel of John, Jesus says, "If you love me, keep my commands" (14:15). Hays is surely correct: "Matthew does not regard the discipleship of the Sermon on the Mount as an impossible ideal. It is, rather, the way of life directly commanded by Jesus, who possesses 'all authority in heaven and on earth.'"[39]

39. Hays, *Moral Vision*, 323. So too Hauerwas, *Peaceable Kingdom*, 85.

5

Peace in the Rest of the New Testament

What evidence is there that early Christianity, as represented in the New Testament outside Jesus's words and actions, understood and carried on what we have seen in Jesus?

Early Christianity retained the essential framework of Jewish belief and expectation but with dramatic modifications. They embraced the Jewish belief that God had called Abraham and his descendants to be God's special people in order to bless all nations (Gen. 12:1–3). They accepted the basic Jewish apocalyptic expectation of a messianic time when the kingdom of God would arrive in power to defeat evil and bring dramatic restoration. But their belief that Jesus was the long-expected Messiah and that he had, in his life, death, and resurrection, already inaugurated (but not yet completed) the kingdom of God profoundly transformed their understanding. They no longer defined the kingdom in terms of the Torah's food laws, sacrifice at the temple, or an exclusive relationship with Abraham's descendants. All people are equally welcome in Jesus's new messianic kingdom. "The *story* of the new movement is told without reference to the national, racial or geographical liberation of Israel. The *praxis* of the kingdom (holiness) is defined without reference to the Torah. . . . This early Christian kingdom-language has little or nothing to do with the vindication of ethnic Israel, the overthrow of Roman rule in Palestine, the building of a new temple on Mount Zion, the establishment of Torah-observance, or the nations flocking to Mount Zion."[1] That is the framework for what the New Testament tells us about the early Christian understanding of peace.

Frequent Use of the Word "Peace"

That the concept of peace was important for the early church is clear simply from the widespread use of the word "peace" (*eirēnē*). It appears at least ninety-nine times in the New Testament. It appears (as a noun or verb) at least once in every book except 1 John. Half of those appearances are in Paul's writings.[2]

The angels' song of peace on earth (Luke 2:14) reverberates throughout the New Testament. It is hardly surprising that peace became a central motif for the earliest Christians. They believed that the eschatological age of peace had broken into the present. Jesus the Messiah was the fulfillment of the prophetic vision of messianic shalom. In Christ, they experienced peace with God, peace with Christian brothers and sisters in the new messianic community, and inner peace of mind. The word "peace" is everywhere. So prominent is the concept of peace that early Christians sometimes describe their entire gospel message as the "gospel of peace." Again and again, Paul describes God as the "God of peace." Continually and in every way, the Lord gives peace. "Now may the Lord of peace himself give you peace *at all times and in every way*" (2 Thess. 3:16). The New Testament speaks of the "God of peace," the "gospel of peace," peace in the addresses of the New Testament letters, peace in the church, and peace with everyone.

God of peace. At least six times the New Testament writers identify God as the "God of peace."[3] At the end of the second letter to Corinth, Paul urges the Christians there to live in peace, promising that the "God of love and peace will be with you" (2 Cor. 13:11). And Hebrews describes the one who raised Jesus from the dead as the "God of peace" (Heb. 13:20). Most of the instances of the phrase the "God of peace" are in Paul's writings. This phrase, which is extremely rare in Jewish literature prior to and around the time of Jesus, is a favorite of the apostle.[4]

The gospel of peace. Ephesians 6:15 speaks of the "gospel of peace." In the story of Cornelius, Peter sums up his whole message as the "good news of peace through Jesus Christ" (Acts 10:36). The Greek text in Acts 10:36 is

1. N. T. Wright, *Jesus and the Victory of God*, 218–19 (italics original).
2. Klassen, *Love of Enemies*, 110; see 129n1 for a long list of scholarly work on Pauline thinking on peace.
3. Rom. 15:33; 16:20; 2 Cor. 13:11; Phil. 4:9; 1 Thess. 5:23; Heb. 13:20. Also the "peace of God" in Phil. 4:7 and the "Lord of peace" in 2 Thess. 3:16.
4. Mauser, *Gospel of Peace*, 106.

euangelizomenos eirēnēn. The first word is the verb form of the Greek word for "gospel." Literally, they are "evangelizing" or "gospeling," and the object (or content) of their evangelizing is the word "peace." The meaning is that those messengers proclaim the gospel of peace.[5]

In describing how Christ overcomes the fierce hostility between Jew and gentile, Ephesians 2 uses the word "peace" four times. Both Jew and gentile are accepted with God on exactly the same basis—namely, Christ's death on the cross. As a result, Christ "is our peace" (v. 14) and makes peace (v. 15). "He came and preached peace to you who were far away and peace to those who were near" (v. 17). In this passage the word "peace" essentially becomes a word to describe the full work of salvation that Christ brings. Luke's summary of the angelic message at Christ's birth carries a similar implication: Luke implies that the whole message about Christ can be suggested with the words "Glory to God in the highest heaven, and on earth peace" (Luke 2:14). Also in 2 Thessalonians 3:16—"May the Lord of peace himself give you peace at all times and in every way"—the word "peace" seems to summarize the full salvation in Christ.

Peace in the addresses of New Testament letters. Since "grace" was part of the standard beginning of Greek letters and "peace" played the same role in Jewish letters, it is not surprising that "grace and peace" begin almost all of Paul's letters as well as a number of other New Testament letters.[6] But Ulrich Mauser has argued that these words convey the apostle's belief that the letter in some way conveys a message of grace and peace from God. In addition, Paul often ends his letters with a reference to peace. "Peace, then, is regularly a part of the opening, and frequently a part of the ending, of Paul's letters. The word has the dignity and value to summarize the essential content of each of the apostle's writings."[7]

Peace in the church. Frequently, the New Testament uses the word "peace" to refer to harmony in the church. After urging Christians not to harm those with weak consciences about food or special days, Paul reminds Christians that "the kingdom of God is not a matter of eating and drinking, but of righteousness, peace and joy in the Holy Spirit. . . . Let us therefore make every effort to do what leads to peace" (Rom. 14:17–19). Similarly, after urging the Corinthians to prevent the issue of speaking in tongues from producing chaos and disruption, he ends with the reminder that "God is not a God of disorder but of peace" (1 Cor. 14:33).[8]

5. The same Greek text appears in Rom. 10:15 in a number of manuscripts.
6. See all the instances cited in Mauser, *Gospel of Peace*, 107.
7. Mauser, *Gospel of Peace*, 108.
8. Other texts also speak of peace in the church: 2 Cor. 13:11; Eph. 4:1–3; 1 Thess. 5:13; Heb. 12:14.

"Live at peace with everyone." Some places where the New Testament speaks of peace, the word seems to have a more general meaning. Romans 12:18 certainly refers to more than other Christians.[9] After telling the Corinthian Christians how to deal with a nonbelieving spouse, Paul concludes, "God has called us to live in peace" (1 Cor. 7:15). The book of James points out that fights, quarrels, and killing arise from covetousness. "But the wisdom that comes from heaven is first of all pure; then peace-loving. . . . Peacemakers who sow in peace reap a harvest of righteousness" (James 3:17–18).

Summary. The good news is a "gospel of peace." God is a "God of peace." Jesus is the "Lord of peace." And God's will is "peace in the Holy Spirit." Christians are urged to live at peace both in the church and in the larger world.

Obviously, none of the texts just cited say anything explicit about whether Christians may ever kill.[10] But all these texts certainly demonstrate that peace—with God, with other Christians, and with everyone—is a central concern of the entire New Testament.

Peter and Cornelius

Acts 10 tells the amazing story of how a devout Jew breaks important Jewish norms to preach the gospel to a Roman centurion, the visible representative of the hated national enemy. Cornelius, the centurion, lives in Caesarea, a city with Roman soldiers, who typify the essence of Roman military power. He commands occupation troops that enforce Roman rule on reluctant Jews. Furthermore, as a gentile, Cornelius represents the kind of person whom devout Jews like Peter would not eat with or enter the house of.[11]

Cornelius, however, is "God-fearing" (i.e., he is very sympathetic to Jewish belief), and God sends him a message telling him to invite Peter to his home. To prepare Peter for this highly unorthodox activity, God gives Peter a vision, which includes clean and unclean animals. The Old Testament law commands Jews to avoid eating unclean animals. So Peter's response is no. He says, "I have never eaten anything impure or unclean" (Acts 10:14).[12] But in the vision, Peter is told to change his thinking about strict Jewish food laws—and, by implication, gentiles too. So in spite of strict Jewish custom, Peter invites the gentile messengers from Cornelius to stay overnight in a Jewish house and then

9. So too probably Heb. 12:14.
10. Although James 3:17–18 perhaps moves in this direction with its call for peace rather than "fights, quarrels and killing."
11. Keener, *IVP Bible Background Commentary*, 350–52.
12. For a discussion of Jewish practice with regard to food laws, see Keener, *Acts*, 2:1768–71.

agrees to travel with them and enter Cornelius's gentile house. As Peter enters Cornelius's home, he "meets the representative of Rome—from a typical Judean or Galilean perspective, a representative of the occupying power."[13]

Peter starts the conversation with Cornelius with a reminder of the standard Jew-gentile hostility: "You are well aware that it is against our law for a Jew to associate with or visit a Gentile" (Acts 10:28).[14] Then he adds that God has shown him not to call anyone impure or unclean. As a result, Peter acknowledges, he now realizes that God accepts people from every nation.

Peter then proceeds to tell Cornelius the story of Jesus. And he summarizes Jesus's message as the "gospel of peace"! "You know the message God sent to the people of Israel, announcing the good news of peace through Jesus Christ, who is Lord of all" (Acts 10:36). The text here is the Greek construction that we discussed in the previous section. God (and Peter) is "evangelizing" or "proclaiming the gospel" of peace. Peter can summarize the whole message he brings to Cornelius as the "gospel of peace"! The full implication of this language becomes clear as one remembers not only the intense hostility between Jews and gentiles in general but also that Cornelius, a Roman centurion, represents the national enemy of the Jews. Speaking to a key representative of the hated Roman imperialists, Peter says Jesus's message is a gospel of peace.[15] As Craig Keener notes, in doing that, Peter "is preaching good news of peace to a traditional enemy."[16]

One more thing is especially significant. The pagan Roman emperor claimed to bring the good news of peace to the world. We know from an ancient (9 BC) inscription found in Priene (present-day Turkey) that many people hailed Augustus (emperor from 27 BC to AD 14) as the "divine Son and cosmic Savior." "He who put an end to war and will order peace, Caesar." And they used the Greek word for "gospel" to refer to the good news of the birth of this founder of the Pax Romana.[17] As the bringer of "world peace" (by the sword, of course), Augustus established the worship of the goddess Pax (peace).[18]

Peter tells the Roman centurion that Jesus, not the Roman emperor, is the Lord who brings the gospel of peace! Augustus allegedly brings peace by the sword of his successful legions. Jesus brings peace as persons embrace the cross and resurrection. But they both offer a "gospel of peace." And in

13. Keener, *Acts*, 2:1774.
14. See Keener, *Acts*, 2:1787–92.
15. A. Kreider, E. Kreider, and Widjaja, *Culture of Peace*, 18–27.
16. Keener, *Acts*, 2:1800.
17. Dechow, "'Gospel' and the Emperor Cult," 73.
18. Mauser, *Gospel of Peace*, 86.

neither case is that peace purely personal. Certainly, in the case of Jesus, it includes personal forgiveness of sins (Acts 10:43). But verse 36 explicitly says that the peace Christ brings comes from the one who is "Lord of all." Presumably, therefore, the Lord's peace relates to all reality, not just the hearts of individuals.

Peace between Jews and Gentiles

Ephesians 2:11–22 describes how the peace with God, which both Jews and gentiles enjoy because of the cross, effects a momentous societal peace. To even begin to understand this passage we must realize the depth of hostility between Jews and gentiles in the first century. That is clear from both Jewish and gentile authors.

A Jewish document probably from the first century BC says that Moses surrounded the Jews with "iron walls to prevent our mixing with any of the other peoples in any manner." Moses's teaching hedged the Jews in with strict observances "connected with meat and drink and touch."[19] But the result was hostility toward pagan neighbors on the part of Jews.

And the Jews' gentile neighbors returned the favor. Many Roman writers express strong resentment of Jews, in part because their monotheism led them to reject the Roman gods. Apollonius Molon, a first-century-BC gentile author, "declares Jews to be atheists, misanthropic creatures who have to be held as the most stupid of all the barbarians."[20] Tacitus, a generally fair Roman historian writing at about the same time as the book of Ephesians was written, describes Jewish customs as "base and abominable" and says Jews "feel only hate and enmity" toward all non-Jews.[21]

Not surprisingly, there were many vicious conflicts between Jews and non-Jews in cities, especially in the eastern Roman Empire, in the first century. Josephus reports constant battles in Alexandria, Egypt, between the Jewish community and their neighbors. When one outbreak resulted in three Jews being burned alive, the whole Jewish community threatened to burn their gentile neighbors. And when the Jewish rebels rejected the Roman governor's appeal to calm, the governor ordered his soldiers to destroy the Jewish quarter "until the whole [Jewish] district was deluged with blood and the heaps of corpses numbered fifty thousand" (JW 2.487–98).[22] In another place, Josephus

19. *Letter of Aristeas*; quoted in Mauser, *Gospel of Peace*, 157.
20. Mauser, *Gospel of Peace*, 159.
21. Tacitus, *Histories* 5.3–5; quoted in Mauser, *Gospel of Peace*, 159.
22. See also Josephus's report of the hostility and resulting devastation in Antioch. JW 7.42–64.

describes the "feelings of hatred or fear of their Jewish neighbors" that led to the enslavement or massacre of thousands of Jews in several Syrian cities (*JW* 2.477–80).[23] Clearly the hostility between Jews and gentiles that Ephesians describes was not just theological. The two groups often despised each other, and the result was major, deadly societal violence.

That is the context of the Pauline teaching in Ephesians 2 that Christ brings peace between these two warring communities. Formerly, the gentiles were far from God, but now they "have been brought near by the blood of Christ" (v. 13). The word for "peace" is everywhere in the next five verses:

> For he himself is our peace, who has made the two groups one and has destroyed the barrier, the dividing wall of hostility, by setting aside in his flesh the law with its commands and regulations. His purpose was to create in himself one new humanity out of the two, thus making peace, and in one body to reconcile both of them to God through the cross, by which he put to death their hostility. He came and preached peace to you who were far away and peace to those who were near. For through him we both have access to the Father by one Spirit. (Eph. 2:14–18)

Jesus reconciled both Jews and gentiles to God on exactly the same basis—through the cross. As Paul says in Romans, those who receive forgiveness of sins through Christ's cross "have peace with God" (Rom. 5:1). Since both Jews and gentiles are reconciled to God through the cross (5:10), Jews and gentiles stand equal at the foot of the cross. And the result is peace—within the church—between the two most hostile communities in Paul's day as Jesus's cross produced one new humanity, "thus making peace" (Eph. 2:15).

It is not entirely clear to what "the dividing wall of hostility" in Ephesians 2:14 refers. We saw above that a Jewish writer in the first century BC referred to "iron walls" that prevented the mixing of Jews and gentiles. That may be what the text refers to.[24] But N. T. Wright says that "the image of the dividing wall is, pretty certainly, taken from the Jerusalem temple, with its sign warning Gentiles to come no further."[25]

It is very clear in this passage that Paul understands salvation in Christ to include vastly more than (although certainly not less than!) just the forgiveness of sins and acceptance with our holy God.[26] Salvation also includes the dramatic new social reality in the church where Jews and gentiles overcome their

23. On the slaughter of 10,500 Jews in Damascus see *JW* 2.559–61.
24. So Mauser, *Gospel of Peace*, 157.
25. N. T. Wright, *Justification*, 172.
26. A point made so well by N. T. Wright in his book *Justification*.

ancient hostility. In fact, in chapter 3, Paul goes on to discuss the "mystery" (i.e., God's plan, promised to Abraham in Gen. 12:1–3, to include all people) revealed to him. And this mystery (which Paul preaches as part of the gospel) is that gentiles are now included in God's saving action through Israel: "This mystery is that through the gospel the Gentiles are heirs together with Israel, members together of one body" (Eph. 3:6).[27] And, in fact, this new peace, this social reconciliation of hostile groups, is so important that as the church models this new peace, it is not only visible on earth but is also made known to the "rulers and authorities in the heavenly realms" (3:10)—that is, to the fallen angelic beings, whom Paul believes are interrelated with the distorted socioeconomic, cultural structures of our world.[28]

Ephesians develops much more extensively what Paul says very briefly in Galatians 3:28. In this text, Paul is quite possibly echoing (and correcting) a common prayer probably used by Jewish men in his day where they thanked God they were not gentiles, slaves, or women. But Christ brings a new peace to these social groups. "There is neither Jew nor Gentile, neither slave nor free, nor is there male and female, for you are all one in Christ Jesus."

Clearly, Jews and gentiles were bitter enemies in Paul's day. Just as clearly, Paul announces that central to the gospel is the fact that Christ brings an astonishing new social peace between these ancient enemies. Ephesians does not have any explicit reference to Jesus's command to love our enemies. But it does provide a striking example of how Jesus's new community actually lived that way.

Cosmic Peace

There are clear indications in the New Testament that the peace that Christ brings is not limited to peace with God in forgiveness and peace with other Christians in the new social reality of the church. Colossians says both that God created all things through Christ and that God reconciles all things through him: "For God was pleased to have all his fullness dwell in him, and through him to reconcile to himself all things, whether things on earth or things in heaven, by making peace through his blood, shed on the cross" (Col. 1:19–20). The text says that this reconciliation includes the "thrones or powers or rulers or authorities" (1:16). Those terms refer to the fallen rebellious angels— originally created good—that relate to and influence the socioeconomic and

---

27. See the rather similar statement in Col. 1:26–27.
28. See Sider, *Good News and Good Works*, 150–51 (especially notes 33–34) for a discussion of Paul's understanding of the "rulers and authorities."

cultural structures of our world. And Colossians 2:15 says Christ actually "disarmed" these "powers and authorities" at the cross.[29] That does not mean that they are fully vanquished in this already / not yet era of Christ's dawning kingdom. The text is quite clear that these "powers and authorities" still have power and Christians must do battle with them (e.g., Eph. 6:12). But the victory has begun and will be completed at Christ's return. Meanwhile, the victory of Christ at the cross over these "powers and authorities" has begun to bring cosmic peace—both in heaven and on earth![30]

Roman citizens spoke of their emperor with the same words Christians used for Jesus: "savior," "lord," and "Son of God." The Romans used the word "gospel"—that is, good news—to describe the military victories that ushered in the Pax Romana, the time of widespread peace throughout the Roman Empire.[31] And the Romans worshiped the goddess of peace.[32] "The concept of peace in the book of Acts," according to Mauser, "is engaged in silent dialogue with the ideal of the Roman Peace (Pax Romana)."[33]

The fact that the gospel of peace that Paul preached included much more than personal peace with God and peace in the church helps us understand the story of the riot in Thessalonica when Paul preaches the gospel. Rioters drag Paul's supporters before city officials. The charge: "They are all defying Caesar's decrees, saying that there is another king, one called Jesus" (Acts 17:7). This passage makes sense when we remember the competing claims about the Roman emperors and Jesus.

The angry rioters in Thessalonica are not wrong when they say the Christians announce another king (Jesus) who is a rival to Caesar (Acts 17:5–8). When Peter tells Cornelius, the Roman centurion, that the Christian message is a gospel of peace about "Jesus Christ, who is Lord of all" (10:36) he is implicitly saying that it is Jesus who is in charge and the one who is truly Lord. Obviously, that means that Jesus's peace is much more than personal peace with God. The implicit message is that Jesus is also the way to societal peace.

That is not to say that everyone will be saved. Frequently, the New Testament speaks of final judgment and eternal separation from God. But it does mean that the peace Christ brings extends to the whole created order. In Romans, Paul says the creation (the rivers, trees, air, etc.) has been distorted by sin. But when, at the end, persons experience the resurrection of the body, then

29. See Sider, *Just Politics*, 47–48, 62.
30. "Peace in the Colossian hymn is associated with cosmic concerns." Mauser, *Gospel of Peace*, 152.
31. See above, "Peter and Cornelius."
32. Mauser, *Gospel of Peace*, 86.
33. Mauser, *Gospel of Peace*, 85.

"the creation itself will be liberated from its bondage to decay and brought into the freedom and glory of the children of God" (Rom. 8:21). And Revelation says that in the final consummation the kings of the earth will "bring their splendor" into the new Jerusalem. Human civilization must be purged of its evil, but "the glory and honor of the nations will be brought into it [the new Jerusalem]" (Rev. 21:24–26).[34] Clearly, Christ brings cosmic peace.

Echoes of Jesus

There are no passages outside the Gospels where the rest of the New Testament explicitly refers to Jesus's teaching in the Sermon on the Mount. But there are a number of places where there are echoes of that sermon.

Do not pay back wrong for wrong. At the end of 1 Thessalonians, Paul gives brief instruction on how Christians should live. "Make sure that nobody pays back wrong for wrong, but always strive to do what is good for each other and for everyone else" (5:15). This passage does not use Jesus's specific words, but it seems to be making the same point as Jesus when he rejected the basic legal principle of an eye for an eye (Matt. 5:38–42). And Paul says Christians should live this way both in the church ("for each other") and in the larger society ("for everyone else").

When cursed, bless. "When we are cursed, we bless; when we are persecuted, we endure it; when we are slandered, we answer kindly" (1 Cor. 4:12–13). Here the echo of Jesus's actual words is perhaps more faint. But the content fits very well with Jesus's command not to respond in a hostile way to those who perpetrate abuse (Matt. 5:38–42).

Do not repay evil with evil. The echo in 1 Peter is more clear. "Do not repay evil with evil or insult with insult. On the contrary, repay evil with blessing" (3:9). We cannot know whether the author was consciously summarizing Jesus's rejection of an eye for an eye. But this statement certainly urges the same response to evil commanded by Jesus. Rather than retaliate against evil, act in love.

Do not take revenge. The echoes of Jesus are especially strong in Romans 12:14–21:

> Bless those who persecute you; bless and do not curse. . . . Do not repay anyone evil for evil. Be careful to do what is right in the eyes of everyone. If it is possible, as far as it depends on you, live at peace with everyone. Do not take revenge, my dear friends, but leave room for God's wrath, for it is

34. See further Sider, *Just Politics*, 50–51, and the literature cited in notes 36–42.

written: "It is mine to avenge; I will repay," says the Lord. On the contrary: "If your enemy is hungry, feed him; if he is thirsty, give him something to drink. In doing this, you will heap burning coals on his head." Do not be overcome by evil, but overcome evil with good.

The similarities to the Sermon on the Mount are so striking that a number of scholars believe that Paul knew and was using "Jesus-tradition" handed down in the church.[35] In fact, after careful evaluation of the evidence, British New Testament scholar James Dunn notes that "the Spirit of the Sermon on the Mount breathes through these verses." And he concludes that "the probability that the Pauline parenesis does reflect the exhortation of Jesus must be judged very strong."[36]

Paul is talking about how to respond to enemies ("those who persecute you"; Rom. 12:14). "Do not repay anyone evil for evil" (12:17) is the same kind of restatement of Jesus's rejection of an eye for an eye that we have seen in 1 Thessalonians and 1 Peter. The explicit prohibition against taking revenge (12:19) makes the same point in a slightly different way.

Paul insists that the call for Christians to forgo vengeance does not mean that evil will remain forever unpunished. The infinite God is different from finite human beings and rightly (given God's perfect combination of love and justice) punishes evil. Miroslav Volf notes that "the certainty of God's just judgment at the end of history is the presupposition for the renunciation of violence in the middle of it."[37]

Romans 12:20 (a quotation from Prov. 25:21–22) underlines the fact that Paul is talking about how to treat enemies. His summons to give food and water to the enemy evokes Jesus's parable of the sheep and goats (Matt. 25:35, 42), although there those in need are not described as enemies. Scholars have puzzled over the meaning of "heaping burning coals" on the enemy's head. Some interpreters believe this sentence refers to pangs of shame and remorse and a search for reconciliation by the enemy who is loved. Or it may mean that when an enemy refuses to respond even to loving treatment, that person adds justification for the final condemnation at the hands of a righteous God.[38]

We cannot be certain of Paul's intent. But that does not undermine the explicit command in Romans 12 to love one's enemies, reject eye-for-eye retaliation, and forgo vengeance. That sounds very much like Jesus in the Sermon on the Mount.

---

35. Hays, *Moral Vision*, 330.
36. Dunn, *Romans*, 2:745–51; quoted in Hays, *Moral Vision*, 345n38.
37. Volf, *Exclusion and Embrace*, 302.
38. See Zerbe, "Paul's Ethic of Nonretaliation," 194–202, and the sources cited there. See also Klassen, "Coals of Fire."

Imitating Christ

Again and again, all through the New Testament, the writers insist that Christians must imitate Christ and follow him as faithful disciples.[39] None of these texts speak specifically about whether Christians should ever kill. But if our exegesis of Jesus's teaching is correct, then this vast number of texts calling on Christians to live like Christ reinforces the claim that the rest of the New Testament has not forgotten Jesus's call to love enemies.

Christians must forgive one another "as the Lord forgave you" (Col. 3:13; cf. Eph. 4:32). Living "as Jesus did" is the proof that one is a Christian (1 John 2:6). "We know that we have come to know him if we keep his commands" (2:3). Christians have died to their sinful selves with Christ and now share his risen life and live like him.[40] Christians should serve other Christians as Christ served them.[41] In their economic sharing with other Christians, they should imitate the generosity of Christ, who, "though he was rich, yet for your sake he became poor" (2 Cor. 8:9). Christians should be humble as Christ was humble (Phil. 2:3–14).

The examples seem almost endless. "Walk in the way of love, just as Christ loved us and gave himself up for us" (Eph. 5:2). Christians should suffer even when innocent, "because Christ suffered for you, leaving you an example, that you should follow in his steps" (1 Pet. 2:21). This call to imitate Christ is seen especially clearly in several passages calling Christians to imitate Christ in the home, the church, and socioeconomic life in the world.

Imitating Christ in the home. The recipients of the letter to the Ephesians lived in a male-dominated Hellenistic society. But that does not deter the author from urging husbands to treat their wives with the same self-sacrificing love that Jesus modeled at the cross. "Husbands, love your wives, just as Christ loved the church and gave himself up for her" (Eph. 5:25). That was a deeply radical thing to say in a society where women were considered greatly inferior to men. But think of the quiet agony and the aching unfulfillment that would be avoided if Christian husbands followed the way of the cross in their marriages. The way of the cross is not only a nonviolent way to correct injustice. It is also Christ's way of peace in the persistent struggles that batter every marriage.

The way of the cross in the church. To illustrate the kind of humility and unselfish concern for others that Christians ought to show toward one another,

---

39. Yoder makes this point powerfully in *Politics of Jesus*, chap. 7 (112–31).
40. Rom. 6:6–11; 8:11; Gal. 2:20; Eph. 4:20–24; Col. 2:12–3:1.
41. John 13:1–17; Rom. 15:1–7; 2 Cor. 5:14–21.

Paul uses a marvelous hymn in Philippians 2:5–8: "In your relationships with one another," Paul writes, "have the same mindset as Christ Jesus":

> Who, being in very nature God,
>> did not consider equality with God something to be used to his own
>>> advantage;
>> rather, he made himself nothing
>>> by taking the very nature of a servant,
>>> being made in human likeness.
> And being found in appearance as a man,
>> he humbled himself
>> by becoming obedient to death—
>>> even death on a cross!

Paul's command is clear. The way to peace in the church is for Christians to allow Christ's example at the cross to be the model for their treatment of other Christians. First John teaches the same point with equal power: "Jesus Christ laid down his life for us. And we ought to lay down our lives for our brothers and sisters" (1 John 3:16). That statement perfectly reflects Jesus's command to his disciples as he approached the cross: "As I have loved you, so you must love one another" (John 13:34; cf. 15:12). Imitating Christ at the cross is the way to peace in the church.

The way of the cross in socioeconomic life in the world. First Peter 2 calls on Christian slaves to obey not just kind owners but cruel masters.[42] Christ, who suffered unjustly, is the example to imitate: "To this you were called, because Christ suffered for you, leaving you an example, that you should follow in his steps. 'He committed no sin, and no deceit was found in his mouth.' When they hurled their insults at him, he did not retaliate; when he suffered, he made no threats. Instead, he entrusted himself to him who judges justly. 'He himself bore our sins' in his body on the cross, so that we might die to sins and live for righteousness; 'by his wounds you have been healed'" (1 Pet. 2:21–24).

By pondering the example of Jesus at the cross, Christians learn how to live in their socioeconomic relationships with non-Christians—and that includes even unjust oppressors. That does not mean that oppressed slaves or contemporary victims of systemic injustice should acquiesce in their oppression. We saw in the discussion of Jesus's teaching and example that he clearly, but nonviolently, challenged and condemned evil.[43] But this passage

---

42. But notice, as Richard Hays points out (*Moral Vision*, 345n40), that the norms 1 Peter presents for Christian slaves are about the same as those for all Christians (1 Pet. 3:17–18).

43. See chap. 3, "Eye for an Eye" (under "Six Antitheses"). And see Sider, *Nonviolent Action*, for many contemporary examples of nonviolent challenge to evil.

in 1 Peter clearly shows that if we obey the biblical command to follow in Christ's steps, we will refuse to regard oppressors as enemies to be reviled, hated, and destroyed. Instead, as we remember that Christ died for our sins even while we were enemies of God, we will imitate Christ's love for enemies demonstrated at the cross.

To say that the New Testament constantly calls Christians to imitate Christ is not to say that we are called to imitate every part of Christ's life. His once-for-all sacrifice for the sins of the world can never be repeated. Loraine Boettner is quite correct in insisting that "Christ's expiatory death is no more an object for our imitation than is the creation of the world."[44]

In fact, the New Testament calls on Christians to imitate Christ at just one point: the cross. Even when Paul expresses a preference for celibacy, it never occurs to him to cite the fact that Jesus never married. Never does the New Testament urge Christians to become carpenters like Jesus—or even imitate Jesus's example of spending several years training a small circle of disciples. "There is then but one realm in which the concept of imitation holds—but there it holds in every strand of the New Testament literature and all the more strikingly by virtue of the absence of parallels in other realms. This is at the point of the concrete social meaning of the cross in its relation to enmity and power. Servanthood replaces dominion, forgiveness absorbs hostility."[45]

God's Love for Enemies

We saw in the discussion of Matthew 5 that Jesus grounded his call to love one's enemies, not in a naive hope that it would always produce an instant loving response, but rather in the very nature of God (see chap. 3). "Love your enemies . . . that you may be children of your Father in heaven" (Matt. 5:44–45; also 5:9).

Probably the clearest theological expression of Jesus's teaching on loving enemies appears in the writings of Paul. "God demonstrates his own love for us in this: While we were still sinners, Christ died for us. . . . If, while we were God's *enemies*, we were reconciled to him through the death of his Son, how much more, having been reconciled, shall we be saved through his life!" (Rom. 5:8, 10). This Pauline passage clearly teaches that Jesus's death on the cross shows that God loves God's enemies.

Richard Hays puts it well. "How does God treat enemies? Rather than killing them, Paul declares, he gives his Son to die for them. This has profound

44. Boettner, *Atonement*, 32.
45. Yoder, *Politics of Jesus*, 131.

implications for the subsequent behavior of those who are reconciled to God through Jesus's death. . . . The imitation of Christ in his self-emptying service for the sake of others is a central ethical motif in Paul (e.g., Phil. 2:1–13). It is evident, then, that those whose lives are shaped in Christ must deal with enemies in the same way God in Christ dealt with enemies."[46]

This chapter provides abundant evidence that the earliest church that we see in the New Testament did not forget or neglect Jesus's message of peace. A strong concern for peace—not just in the home and the church but also in heaven and earth (Col. 1:20)—is pervasive in Paul's letters. Hays concludes that "there is not a syllable in the Pauline letters that can be cited in support of Christians employing violence."[47]

Christ brings peace to the worst ethnic hostility in the first century—that between Jews and gentiles. There are echoes of the Sermon on the Mount in several different places. Again and again, the New Testament calls Christians to imitate Christ—precisely at the cross. And in faithfulness to Jesus's teaching that his disciples must love their enemies in order to be children of our heavenly Father, Paul states clearly that at the cross, God loves God's enemies. "Thus, from Matthew to Revelation we find a consistent witness against violence and a calling to the community to follow the example of Jesus in accepting suffering rather than *inflicting* it."[48]

46. Hays, *Moral Vision*, 330.
47. Hays, *Moral Vision*, 331.
48. Hays, *Moral Vision*, 332 (italics original). For a discussion of passages some Christians say do support violence, see the next chapter.

6

But What About . . . ?

Thus far, many critics would charge, this book has ignored a number of things in the New Testament that seem to support the use of violence. What about Jesus's statement that he came to bring a sword? Or the fact that there are several stories about devout soldiers and none were told to stop being soldiers? Jesus used a whip to cleanse the temple. He even told his disciples to buy a sword. In places, the New Testament seems to praise Israelite warriors and endorse the destruction of the Canaanites. Does not the use of military symbols endorse military action? Jesus warned about wars and rumors of wars. Does Matthew 15:4 mean Jesus endorses capital punishment? Romans 13 certainly says that government uses the sword to execute divine vengeance on evildoers. In fact, the New Testament says that God punishes evil, and the book of Revelation uses violent, bloody imagery to describe the final victory over evil.

Do not all these things add up to a clear endorsement of the legitimate use of killing to overcome evil? Paul Copan and Matthew Flannagan put it bluntly: "To proclaim an absolute pacifism . . . requires dismissing or ignoring Jesus's own authoritative statements, vast tracts of Scripture pertaining to divine judgment . . . and the book of Revelation."[1] Careful examination of each of these texts is essential.

"I Did Not Come to Bring Peace, but a Sword"

In Matthew 10:34, Jesus says bluntly, "I did not come to bring peace, but a sword." A number of Christians have claimed that in this statement Jesus

1. Copan and Flannagan, *Did God Really Command Genocide?*, 44.

endorses the violent use of the sword.[2] But the vast majority of commentators believe that in this statement Jesus uses metaphorical language to warn his disciples that following him will invite sharp conflict in one's family, even deadly persecution.[3]

Analysis of the setting of Jesus's statement in Matthew makes this interpretation highly likely. Richard Hays points out that all of Matthew 10:5–42 is "Matthew's mission discourse."[4] Verses 5–15 describe Jesus's instructions as he sends the Twelve out to proclaim the kingdom and heal. Verses 16–33 warn that his followers will encounter severe persecution. Eduard Schweizer points out that "the sword is not in the hands of the disciples, but of their opponents."[5] The verses immediately following verse 34 continue to prepare his disciples for the way those who accept his message will face harsh persecution from family members (vv. 35–40). The text actually says, "I have come to turn 'a man against his father, a daughter against her mother'" (v. 35). But no one thinks Jesus literally means that the purpose of his coming was to destroy families. Jesus means that his disciples must love him more than father, mother, son, or daughter (vv. 35–36). Thus Hays concludes that the "sword" of verse 34 is a metaphor for the division that will occur between those who proclaim the good news of the kingdom and those who refuse to receive it.

It is clear that Luke understands Jesus's statement this way. In a parallel passage about the way Jesus brings division in families, Luke uses the word "division" instead of "sword": "Do you think I came to bring peace on earth? No, I tell you, but division" (Luke 12:51).[6]

When we read Matthew 10:34 in context, it becomes quite clear that Jesus's words have nothing to do with his disciples using the sword.[7] Rather, Jesus uses metaphorical language to warn that his followers will experience rejection by family and severe persecution from those who reject his message. Hays says bluntly, "To read this verse [Matt. 10:34] as a warrant for the use

2. Matthew Black has a good summary of various interpretations in "'Not Peace but a Sword.'"
3. E.g., Bruner, *Matthew*, 1:487–88; Blomberg, *Matthew*, 180; France, *Gospel of Matthew*, 408; Evans, *Matthew*, 228; Schweizer, *Matthew*, 251; Hays, *Moral Vision*, 332; Black, "'Not Peace but a Sword,'" 288.
4. Hays, *Moral Vision*, 332.
5. Schweizer, *Matthew*, 251.
6. It is quite possible that Jesus's statement that he *came* to bring a sword/division is an example of a Semitic idiom where the consequence of an action is described as the purpose. See, e.g., Hosea 8:4. See Macgregor, *Basis of Pacifism*, 20.
7. I find no evidence, however, to support Richard McSorley's claim that the early church used this text to support its opposition to war; McSorley, *Basis of Peacemaking*, 27. None of the references to Matt. 10:34 that I found in the massive publication *ANF* argue that way; see 3:333; 6:220, 234; 7:345.

of violence by Christians is to commit an act of extraordinary hermeneutical violence against the text."[8]

Soldiers in the New Testament

In four significant places, the New Testament implies or states positive things about soldiers without any suggestion that they should stop being soldiers. When some soldiers respond to John the Baptist's call to repentance and ask what they should do, John responds, "Don't extort money and don't accuse people falsely—be content with your pay" (Luke 3:14). John does not tell them to stop being soldiers. Matthew (8:5–13) and Luke (7:1–10) include the story of the centurion who asks Jesus to heal one of his servants and then says Jesus need not come to his house but should rather simply speak the word of healing. In response, Jesus says in amazement, "I have not found anyone in Israel with such great faith" (Matt. 8:10). Jesus says nothing about the centurion's military profession. At the cross, the Roman centurion supervising Jesus's crucifixion is the first human being in Mark's Gospel to say Jesus is the Son of God (15:39). And in Acts, when Peter agrees to share the gospel with a Roman centurion, the Holy Spirit falls on his household and they are baptized (Acts 10:1–11:18). Again, the text says nothing about Peter telling the new Christian centurion that he must leave the Roman army.

For at least fifteen hundred years, prominent Christians have argued that these stories show that Jesus and the rest of the New Testament writers thought that the military profession was perfectly acceptable. Augustine in the fifth century used these stories to persuade a Christian concerned about his military profession that it was quite possible to please God as a soldier.[9] Martin Luther and John Calvin in the sixteenth century made the same argument.[10]

Today, Oxford scholar Nigel Biggar argues in his book *In Defence of War* that these stories show that the New Testament does not think that the military profession is incompatible with Christian faith. He points out that in notable cases, the New Testament describes how sinners who embrace Christ repent and turn from their sinful practices. In Acts 19:18–20, the sorcerers who become Christians burn their books. But none of the New Testament accounts of soldiers give any indication of that kind of change. Biggar concludes, "If the New Testament . . . regarded participation in the military profession as

8. Hays, *Moral Vision*, 333.
9. Augustine, "To Count Boniface," in Holmes, *War and Christian Ethics*, 61–62.
10. See Holmes, *War and Christian Ethics*, 158, 168.

intrinsically sinful, then *surely* its authors would have taken care to tell us that soldiers who became Christian disciples renounced military service."[11]

But is this argument really substantive?

At first sight, the case of John the Baptist might seem significant. Here the soldiers do ask what they are to do to respond to John's call to repentance. John specifies some things, but he does not say they should stop being soldiers. But surely the precursor of Jesus does not have the same authority as Jesus. Luther labels John the Baptist as a "Christian teacher" and "a godly Christian teacher" in order to justify his argument that John's response to soldiers proves that Christians can be soldiers.[12] But John the Baptist was not a Christian. Jesus himself clearly distinguishes the time of John from the time of Jesus and Jesus's inauguration of the messianic kingdom: "Whoever is least in the kingdom of heaven is greater than he [John the Baptist]" (Matt. 11:11). For Christians, Jesus, not John the Baptist, provides the norms for Christian discipleship.

Second, it is important to note that the argument from the silence of Jesus and Peter about whether the God-fearing centurions they encounter should stop being soldiers is precisely that—an argument from silence. It is just as plausible to argue that Jesus and Peter also told the centurions to stop being soldiers as it is to argue that they conveyed the message that continuing as soldiers was quite ethical. The texts say absolutely nothing about either. Both arguments are arguments from silence and as such carry no weight.[13]

We know from many sources that Roman army life was immersed in pagan religion. The emperor Augustus (died AD 14) standardized army religion. Roman soldiers worshiped the gods of the established Roman state religion: Jupiter, Juno, Minerva, and the war god, Mars. Every year, each soldier took an oath (*sacramentum*) that had religious as well as legal implications.[14]

As a leader of his troops, a Roman centurion would necessarily be involved in the Roman army's pagan religious activity. The accounts of Jesus's and Peter's interactions with the centurions also say nothing about telling them to stop such pagan activity. But surely we should not conclude from this silence that Jesus and Peter thought participating in pagan activities was acceptable. Neither text talks about participating in pagan worship or in the army. And

11. Biggar, *In Defence of War*, 41–42 (italics added). See also K. B. Payne and K. I. Payne, *Just Defense*, 94; Copan and Flannagan, *Did God Really Command Genocide?*, 305.

12. See Holmes, *War and Christian Ethics*, 145, 158.

13. Biggar, who writes one of the most recent, best defenses of the just war stance, admits that this argument about the centurions is an "argument from silence," which Biggar acknowledges has significant weakness. Biggar, *In Defence of War*, 56.

14. Watson, *Roman Soldier*, 128–31; Helgeland, "Roman Army Religion," 1470–505, esp. 1478, 1487.

neither text tells us anything about whether either activity is acceptable for Jesus's disciples.

When one examines the accounts of Jesus's and Peter's encounters with the centurions, it is clear that the focus of both stories is the amazing new reality that Jesus's dawning kingdom includes not only Jews but also gentiles, even national enemies. Immediately after Jesus praises the centurion's faith, he proceeds to say that his kingdom will include many more than just the descendants of Abraham (Matt. 8:10–11). The same point pervades the entire story of Peter and Cornelius. The fact that the gentile centurions are military people is incidental except that their being military representatives of the hated national enemy underlines how all-embracing is Jesus's new kingdom. The fact that both stories affirm the faith of centurions does not mean that Jesus and Peter are endorsing a military career any more than Jesus's praise (21:31) of tax collectors and prostitutes (because they are embracing his kingdom more than many other Jews) means that Jesus affirms extortionate tax-farming and prostitution.[15]

Some have argued that since Jesus and other parts of the New Testament advocate paying Roman taxes, which of course helped fund the Roman army, therefore they affirm the validity of the military. But Roman taxes also funded pagan worship and vicious gladiatorial games, where gladiators fought to the death to amuse vast audiences in the "sports arenas." If the argument that paying taxes that funded soldiers means the New Testament affirms the military profession, the same argument means that the New Testament affirms pagan worship and gladiatorial contests.[16]

The subsequent statements of Christian authors (after the New Testament and before Constantine) further undermine the view that the silence about whether the soldiers who met or believed in Christ should continue as soldiers means that Jesus and the New Testament authors thought that the military profession is legitimate. As the section in chapter 13 titled "Pre-Constantinian Christianity" shows, every single Christian author in this period who raises the question of killing says Christians should not do that. Every Christian author who discusses whether Christians should join the Roman army says they should not. And the *Apostolic Tradition* (a church order probably dating from the mid-second century to the first part of the third) specifically deals with how to treat Roman soldiers who become interested in Christian faith and request preparation for baptism. They can be prepared for baptism—but

15. Hays, *Moral Vision*, 335.

16. The earliest available comments from Christians on gladiatorial contests vigorously condemn them. See the citations in Sider, *Early Church on Killing*, 30–32, 47, 84–85, 110–11, 121, 168.

only if they agree never to kill! And baptized Christians who join the army must be excluded from the church.[17]

"Cleansing the Temple"

All four Gospels describe an incident in which Jesus enters the temple, overturns the money changers' tables, and drives out "all who were buying and selling there" (Matt. 21:12; cf. Mark 11:15–17; Luke 19:45–46; John 2:13–17). Only John mentions a whip that Jesus uses at least on the animals being sold for sacrifice (John 2:15). Some Christians cite this incident as proof that Jesus used violence and conclude that any claim that Jesus taught his disciples never to kill is wrong. This action "most assuredly does not fit the profile of the ideological pacifists, for in truth it qualifies as forceful, even violent, resistance."[18]

If one defines pacifism as pure passivity to evil, then of course Jesus's action in the temple is not that of a pacifist. But as we saw earlier,[19] Jesus repeatedly confronts and challenges evil, but never in a way that physically injures or kills people—unless this incident is an exception. But nothing in these texts says that Jesus injures or kills anyone. Below, I will show that the Greek wording in John 2:15 indicates that Jesus uses the whip on the animals, not the people.

There are very strong reasons for thinking that Jesus's "cleansing" of the temple is a brief action of dramatic symbolism, not a violent attempt to take over the temple by force.[20] For one thing, there were two armed forces in the immediate vicinity of the temple that would have quickly intervened if Jesus had initiated a violent attempt to seize the temple.[21] The Jewish authorities controlled the temple police (who would arrest Jesus at night a few days later). And connected to the temple by a broad staircase was the Fortress Antonia, where a Roman cohort of five hundred to six hundred soldiers was stationed.[22] Josephus tells us that additional soldiers were posted there during important festivities. Any substantial tumult would have certainly led to prompt intervention by one or both of those armed groups. In fact, that is exactly what happened a couple decades later when Paul's presence in the temple led to a violent mob (Acts 21:30–32).

17. Sider, *Early Church on Killing*, 169–77, 119–21 (on the *Apostolic Tradition*). For a more detailed description, see chap. 13, "Pre-Constantinian Christianity."
18. Charles and Demy, *War, Peace, and Christianity*, 370. See also Copan and Flannagan, *Did God Really Command Genocide?*, 302.
19. See chap. 3, "Eye for an Eye."
20. So Hays, *Moral Vision*, 334.
21. About thirty-three years later, that did happen when Jewish zealots seized the temple and murdered the chief priest. See Klassen, *Love of Enemies*, 98.
22. Hengel, *Was Jesus a Revolutionist?*, 16; Keener, *Gospel of Matthew*, 498.

It is clear in all three Synoptic Gospels that Jesus continues to teach in the temple courts for several days after this incident without anyone arresting him. The texts show that the chief priests are furious (Mark 11:18). But apparently they feel they have no legitimate basis for arresting Jesus, because the Jewish leaders send several different groups to try to trap Jesus and trick him into saying things that would justify his arrest (Mark 11:27–33; 12:13–27; Matt. 21:23–27; 22:15–32; Luke 20:1–8, 20–39). Furthermore, the delegations that come to confront Jesus do not accuse him of acting violently. Rather, they ask him by what authority he is acting (Mark 11:28).

All four Gospels use the same Greek verb (*ekballō*) to describe what Jesus does. The *Greek-English Lexicon of the New Testament* shows that this word can mean "throw out more or less forcibly" or "send out without the connotation of force."[23] Mark uses this word to describe Jesus's dismissing the mourners before he heals the little girl who has died (Mark 5:40). In Matthew 9:38, the word is used to speak of the Lord sending more workers into the harvest. In Mark 1:12 the same word is used to say that the Spirit has "sent" Jesus into the wilderness to be tempted. Obviously, this word does not necessarily carry any connotation of violence.

But John 2:15 uses this word in connection with Jesus using a whip. Some translations of the Greek suggest that Jesus uses the whip on the money changers as well as the animals. The New King James translates the text as: "He drove them all out of the temple, with the sheep and the oxen." That translation clearly implies that Jesus uses the whip to drive out the people as well as the sheep and oxen. The problem is that the Greek text does not say that.[24] The Good News Translation has the proper translation of the Greek: "[Jesus] drove all the animals out of the Temple, both the sheep and the cattle [or oxen]."[25]

In all accounts, especially that of the Gospel of John, Jesus is far from being passive. He scatters the coins of the money changers and overturns their tables in addition to using his whip on the animals (John 2:15). But nothing in the text says he uses the whip on the people.[26]

23. Arndt and Gingrich, *Greek-English Lexicon*, 236–37.
24. The Greek is: *pantas exebalen ek tou hierou ta te probata kai tous boas*. A careful study of the *te . . . kai* usage in the New Testament shows that in virtually all of the more than ninety instances, the particles *te . . . kai* are used to subdivide a subject or object previously mentioned (here *pantas* [all]) into its component parts (here *ta probata* [sheep] and *tous boas* [oxen]). See Yoder, *Politics of Jesus*, 43n38. And the Greek word *pantas* (all) is rightly masculine because when one adjective qualifies two nouns of different genders it will agree with the masculine or feminine noun (here *tous boas* [oxen]), not the neuter noun (*ta probata* [sheep]). See Macgregor, *Basis of Pacifism*, 17n2.
25. See Yoder, *Politics of Jesus*, 43.
26. See Stassen and Gushee, *Kingdom Ethics*, 157.

In all the accounts, Jesus's words help explain his actions. After overturning the tables of the money changers, Jesus teaches them, saying, "Is it not written: 'My house will be called a house of prayer for all nations'? But you have made it 'a den of robbers'" (Mark 11:17). The first quotation of Jesus comes from Isaiah 56:7 in a passage that foresees a time when peace will prevail and the gentiles will also be a part of God's people. And the second reference is to Jeremiah 7:11, where the prophet denounces the fact that the temple has become a den of robbers.[27] Commentators believe that the incident occurs in the outer part of the temple court reserved for gentiles. A partition with warning signs excluded gentiles from entering the inner court of the temple. It is probable that commercial use of the court of the gentiles for money changers (so pilgrims with many different coins could exchange them for coins they could use in the temple) began shortly before the time of Jesus.[28] It is quite possible that Jesus feels this commercial use of the area for the gentiles violates the fact that the dawning kingdom will be for gentiles as well as Jews. He may also want to "denounce the monopoly in monetary exchange and trade enjoyed by the high-priestly families in the temple."[29]

In any case, Jesus's actions constitute a dramatic act of prophetic protest designed to challenge conduct Jesus rejects. But it is not a sustained effort to take over the temple or even permanently end the activity of the money changers. That would require Jesus to have a large number of troops and provoke a riot—which the Roman soldiers would promptly squelch. It is the moral authority of Jesus, not the size of his following, that leads to a temporary acquiescence to his actions. Apparently Jesus engages in a short symbolic, nonviolent action and then returns to his teaching. Hays is right: "None of the evangelists present this incident as a coup attempt to seize power over the religious or political establishment in Jerusalem. It is, rather, an act of symbolic 'street theater' in line with precedent well established in Israel's prophetic tradition (e.g., Jer. 27:1–22)."[30] This story demonstrates the coercive power of moral authority. But it in no way supports the use of violence, much less killing.

"Buy a Sword"

Luke (and only Luke) includes a conversation between Jesus and his disciples after the Last Supper and before their arrival at the garden of Gethsemane.

27. Hays, *Moral Vision*, 334.
28. Keener, *Historical Jesus*, 292–93; Keener, *Gospel of Matthew*, 500.
29. Hengel, *Christ and Power*, 18.
30. Hays, *Moral Vision*, 334.

After reminding the disciples that earlier he sent them out without purse or sandals, Jesus says:

> "But now if you have a purse, take it, and also a bag; and if you don't have a sword, sell your cloak and buy one. It is written: 'And he was numbered with the transgressors'; and I tell you that this must be fulfilled in me. Yes, what is written about me is reaching its fulfillment."
>
> The disciples said, "See, Lord, here are two swords."
>
> "That's enough!" he replied. (Luke 22:36–38)

Some Christians argue that this passage shows decisively that Jesus was not a pacifist. In preparing the disciples for their future dangerous missionary journeys, Jesus tells them to arm themselves with swords for self-defense. They should even sell their cloaks to buy a sword.[31] The disciples apparently understand Jesus literally, and Jesus expresses no surprise that they have two swords. "If pacifism was the rule, does not Peter's being armed seem quite out of order?"[32]

This literal understanding of the incident, however, is puzzling at several points. If Jesus intends to order his disciples to prepare themselves for self-defense on their future missionary journeys, then it is absurd for Jesus to say two swords are enough. How could two swords be adequate for even twelve disciples?

Furthermore, just a few hours later, after Peter actually uses a sword in a futile attempt to prevent Jesus's arrest, Jesus promptly rebukes Peter. And Jesus's condemnation of Peter, as we saw in chapter 4,[33] was based not only on the fact that Jesus needed to die but also on a general statement that all who take the sword die by the sword. Within hours of this puzzling statement about buying a sword, Jesus vigorously rebukes Peter for using a sword (Luke 22:50–51; cf. John 18:10–11). And a few hours after that, Jesus explicitly tells Pilate that his followers do not fight (John 18:36). These actions make

31. Boettner, *Christian Attitude toward War*, 23–24.
32. K. B. Payne and K. I. Payne, *Just Defense*, 96. The fact that the disciples had two swords (*machaira* [a long dagger]) does not prove that Jesus approved of violent self-defense. This long dagger or short sword was the standard instrument for Jewish travelers to carry for protection against wild animals and robbers (Hengel, *Was Jesus a Revolutionist?*, 21–22). There is plenty of evidence that Peter did not grasp or approve of Jesus's nonviolent messianic understanding. (Immediately after confessing that Jesus is the Messiah, Peter rebukes Jesus for announcing that he will die, and Jesus rebukes Peter as Satan [Mark 8:29–33]). Peter could have carried a sword without Jesus's approval or knowledge. Or Jesus could have approved of Peter's carrying his long dagger as a protection against wild animals, knowing that he would rebuke Peter (as he did at his arrest) if Peter tried to use it on people.
33. See chap. 4, "'All Who Draw the Sword Will Die by the Sword.'"

it highly doubtful that Jesus intends his words about buying a sword to be taken literally as a general affirmation of violent self-defense.[34]

There are two different credible explanations of this passage proposed by a number of scholars. The first involves a literal understanding with a very narrow specific application. The second, more common, view sees Jesus's words as figurative. But in neither case does the incident mean that Jesus wants his disciples to arm themselves for self-defense.

Immediately after telling the disciples to buy a sword, Jesus cites a passage from Isaiah as an apparent explanation for his command: "It is written: 'And he was numbered with the transgressors'; and I tell you that this must be fulfilled in me. Yes, what is written about me is reaching its fulfillment" (Luke 22:37). Here Jesus explicitly quotes Isaiah 53:12: "[He] was numbered with the transgressors." This passage in Isaiah comes at the end of a long depiction of a nonviolent, peaceful suffering servant who dies for the sin of the people. To some extent, Jesus seems to understand his calling in light of this passage.[35] He understands his death as a central part of his mission and has repeatedly predicted his death on a cross. But the Romans were the only ones with the authority to crucify people. And they regularly did it to those who threatened their rule. Jesus would know that possessing swords would make it more likely that the Roman authorities would perceive him as a likely revolutionary.[36] Perhaps, therefore, Jesus wants to have his disciples carry swords at his arrest. Two swords would be ridiculously inadequate for actual armed defense, but they would be enough for conviction as a revolutionary. On this reading, Jesus literally means that two swords will be enough.

Most commentators, however, think Jesus's command about buying a sword is intended as a figurative way to tell his disciples that a time of severe persecution is about to descend on them. Jesus wants to warn his disciples of impending disaster, but the disciples misunderstand his words. So he abruptly ends the conversation with "it is enough," meaning, "Enough of this conversation, because you don't understand." Even John Calvin thought the disciples misunderstood Jesus. Calvin writes that Jesus uses the "analogy of war" to warn the disciples of spiritual battles to come. Of the disciples' misunderstanding, Calvin says bluntly, "Here is another example of dull and most shameful ignorance on the part of the disciples, that after being warned

34. It is important to remember the basic principle that we should interpret obscure texts in light of other clearer passages.

35. See N. T. Wright, *Jesus and the Victory of God*, for an extended discussion of how Isa. 52:13–53:12 contributed to Jesus's understanding of his role (597–611).

36. Sprinkle, *Fight*, 239; Murphy, "Yoder's Systematic Defense," 67.

and admonished so often to bear the cross, they nevertheless think they will have to fight with swords of steel. . . . They were so stupid they never thought of the spiritual enemy."[37]

Preston Sprinkle has examined ten highly respected commentators on this passage. Many were not pacifists, but nine of the ten understood Jesus's words in a figurative way, not a call to armed defense.[38] Darrell Bock says Jesus's words about buying a sword are to be understood in a symbolic way.[39] Reformed commentator William Hendriksen says clearly, "The term *sword* must be interpreted figuratively."[40] British New Testament scholar I. Howard Marshall comments, "The saying can be regarded only as grimly ironical, expressing the intensity of the opposition which Jesus and the disciples will experience."[41] Most commentators agree with Hays that in this passage, "the reference to a sword has a figurative purpose."[42]

Praise of Military Leaders

Stephen, Paul, and the author of Hebrews all refer positively to Old Testament military events or leaders. In his long recitation of Israel's history before he is stoned, Stephen reminds his listeners that their ancestors "took the land from the nations God drove out before them" (Acts 7:45). In his missionary travel in Pisidian Antioch, Paul preaches in a synagogue and talks of the way God has chosen their ancestors. God led them out of Egypt with "mighty power" and "overthrew seven nations in Canaan, giving their land to his people" (13:17–19). And in Hebrews 11, sometimes called the biblical Hall of Fame, the author mentions a long list of Old Testament figures who lived by faith in God. The list includes a number of military leaders, such as Gideon, Samson, and David, who "through faith . . . routed foreign armies" (vv. 32–34). Some writers argue that these texts prove that the New Testament authors believe that killing in battle is legitimate for Christians.[43]

But that is to claim much more than the texts say. The whole focus of Hebrews 11 is on faith in God, not the legitimacy of Christians fighting military

37. Calvin, *Commentaries*, 1:660–61; quoted in Lasserre, *War and the Gospel*, 43.
38. Sprinkle, *Fight*, 238.
39. Bock, *Luke 9:51–24:53*, 747.
40. Hendriksen, *Luke*, 976.
41. I. Marshall, *Commentary on Luke*, 823; quoted in Hays, *Moral Vision*, 333.
42. Hays, *Moral Vision*, 333. So too Caird, *Gospel of St. Luke*, 241; Green, *Gospel of Luke*, 774–75; and Morris, *Gospel according to St. Luke*, 310. See other scholars making the same argument in Macgregor, *Basis of Pacifism*, 24.
43. E.g., Copan and Flannagan, *Did God Really Command Genocide?*, 43; K. B. Payne and K. I. Payne, *Just Defense*, 94.

battles. The list of heroes of faith also includes the "prostitute Rehab" (11:31). The text says nothing about whether being a prostitute is good or evil. The same is true of the mention of the military leaders. In every case, it is their faith that is affirmed. Praising the faith of military leaders does not show that the author approves of their lethal violence any more than praising the faith of the prostitute means that the writer endorses prostitution.

Furthermore, the writer of Hebrews goes on in the next chapter to urge Christians to be encouraged by the faith of earlier persons so that they can persevere in the face of severe persecution. They should follow Christ, who endured the cross. There is absolutely nothing in the text that suggests that persecuted Christians should defend themselves. Rather, Christ, the "mediator of a new covenant" (12:24), is the model to follow. In fact, the text says to "make every effort to live in peace with everyone" (12:14). Furthermore, the author says the Christians have "joyfully accepted the confiscation" of their property (10:34).

Stephen and Paul are Jews. Like Jesus, they believed that God has acted to select the descendants of Abraham as his special chosen people and gave them a land so they could be God's special instruments of revelation—a history of revelation that would culminate in Jesus's dawning messianic kingdom. In neither text do Stephen or Paul discuss whether Christians should kill or even how Christians should understand the Israelites' killing of the Canaanite men, women, and children.[44] To argue that Stephen's and Paul's sermons justify Christian participation in war is simply to read into the text what the text does not say.

Military Symbols in the New Testament

Paul urges Christians to "wage war" (2 Cor. 10:3–4) and put on "the full armor of God" (Eph. 6:11)—helmet, shield, sword (6:14–16). He urges Timothy to "fight the good fight of the faith" (1 Tim. 6:12).[45] And Paul announces toward the end of his life, "I have fought the good fight" (2 Tim. 4:7). Some Christians conclude that the New Testament's use of military symbols suggests that Christian participation in war is legitimate. "It's hardly conceivable that the Scriptures should present the Christian life under a symbolism having to do so distinctively with soldiering and warfare and at the same time repudiate the reality for which that symbolism stands as always and everywhere wrong. We cannot imagine the different aspects of the Christian

44. See chap. 10, "The Violent Texts," for a lengthy discussion of that issue.
45. See also Phil. 1:27–30.

life being set forth through symbolism borrowed from the liquor traffic or the vice rackets."[46]

As a matter of fact, Paul draws an analogy between being drunk with wine and being filled with the Spirit (Eph. 5:18). Likewise, Jesus draws an analogy between himself and a thief in the night (Matt. 24:43), and between God and an unjust judge (Luke 18:1–8). No one would suppose, however, that Jesus is recommending nocturnal thieving or judicial corruption.

A quick explanation of Paul's use of military symbols shows that he explicitly says that Christians do not fight the way the world does. "For though we live in the world, we do not wage war as the world does. The weapons we fight with are not the weapons of the world" (2 Cor. 10:3–4). And in the extended discussion of the Christian's armor, Paul says, "For our struggle is not against flesh and blood" but against the devil and demonic powers (Eph. 6:11–12). Christians are shod with "the gospel of peace," and their sword is "the sword of the Spirit, which is the word of God" (vv. 15, 17). Rather than legitimizing military action, these military metaphors point away from violence and affirm nonviolent struggle. To attempt to justify war on the basis of military metaphors is to ignore the rules of literary interpretation.

Wars and Rumors of Wars

Jesus predicts "wars and rumors of wars" and then adds, "But the end is still to come" (Matt. 24:6; Mark 13:7; cf. Luke 21:9). The text does not actually say that wars will persist until the Lord's return. But human selfishness may very well mean that they will. Does that harsh reality mean, as some have argued, that Christians dare not oppose war?[47] Jesus also predicts terrible persecution and martyrdom for his disciples. Children, he says, will betray parents and brothers will betray brothers (Luke 21:16–17). No one supposes that Christians should not oppose these awful evils with their prayers and actions. The same is true of war.

Until Christ's return, selfish persons and communities will unjustly impose their will on others. But that does not mean we cannot make any progress in substituting nonviolent action for lethal violence in combatting injustice. It does mean that societal violence will persist until the shalom of Jesus's new kingdom comes in its fullness. Until then, we should obey Jesus's command to love our enemies.

46. Boettner, *Christian Attitude toward War*, 33; so too K. B. Payne and K. I. Payne, *Just Defense*, 93.
47. See an example of that argument cited in Rutenber, *Dagger and the Cross*, 31.

Did Jesus Endorse Capital Punishment?

In Matthew 15, Jesus responds to Pharisees who accuse him of breaking the tradition of the elders. In response, Jesus accuses his critics of devising legal technicalities to circumvent the clear teaching of the commandment: "For God said, 'Honor your father and mother' and 'Anyone who curses their father or mother is to be put to death'" (Matt. 15:4). Some argue that this passage demonstrates that "Jesus clearly believes in the appropriateness of . . . the Mosaic death penalty."[48]

Two comments are important. First, Jesus cites the commandment to honor parents, not to comment on the validity of executing children who curse their parents. Jesus's concern is to critique the Pharisees for devising technicalities that allowed children to ignore their financial obligations to their parents (Matt. 15:5–6). Jesus's comments say nothing about whether he supports capital punishment for children who curse their parents.

Second, in the one case in the Gospels where Jesus deals with a situation where the Mosaic law prescribes capital punishment, Jesus very clearly does not support that action. The Pharisees bring to Jesus a woman caught in the act of adultery (John 7:53–8:11).[49] Jesus suggests that those without sin cast the first stone, and the accusers all slink away. Then Jesus asks the woman, "Has no one condemned you?" When she says, "No one, sir," Jesus replies, "Then neither do I condemn you" (8:10–11). In spite of the clear penalty of the Mosaic law, Jesus does not recommend capital punishment.[50]

Romans 13

Romans 13:1–7 is probably the most widely used text to argue that God wants Christians to participate in justly authorized governmental killing.

> Let everyone be subject to the governing authorities, for there is no author-
> ity except that which God has established. The authorities that exist have
> been established by God. Consequently, whoever rebels against the authority
> is rebelling against what God has instituted, and those who do so will bring
> judgment on themselves. For rulers hold no terror for those who do right,
> but for those who do wrong. Do you want to be free from fear of the one in

48. Copan and Flannagan, *Did God Really Command Genocide?*, 42.

49. This passage is not in the earliest manuscripts. But many scholars believe it is a true story about Jesus. See Keener, *Gospel of John*, 1:736: "Many, perhaps most scholars" think the story represents an authentic tradition about Jesus. B. M. Metzger also says this passage has "all the earmarks of historical veracity." Metzger, *Textual Commentary*, 220.

50. See the excellent discussion in C. Marshall, *Beyond Retribution*, 230–34.

authority? Then do what is right and you will be commended. For the one in authority is God's servant for your good. But if you do wrong, be afraid, for rulers do not bear the sword for no reason. They are God's servants, agents of wrath to bring punishment on the wrongdoer. Therefore, it is necessary to submit to the authorities, not only because of possible punishment but also as a matter of conscience. This is also why you pay taxes, for the authorities are God's servants, who give their full time to governing. Give to everyone what you owe them: If you owe taxes, pay taxes; if revenue, then revenue; if respect, then respect; if honor, then honor.

In the immediately preceding verses, Paul has told the Roman Christians, in words that seem to echo Matthew 5, that they should "bless those who persecute you. . . . Do not repay anyone evil for evil. . . . Do not take revenge" (Rom. 12:14–19). But then in chapter 13, Paul says that God has ordained government to punish evildoers. Many Christians argue that the two sets of statements taken together mean that in their personal life Christians should never use lethal violence but in their role as public officials they rightly participate in justly authorized killing.[51] Sometimes, it is argued that Paul purposely wrote Romans 13:1–7 immediately after chapter 12 to make sure that readers would not misunderstand his strong statements in chapter 12 about leaving vengeance to God to mean that government (and Christians in government) should refuse to use lethal violence. The Old Testament condemns individuals taking vengeance into their own hands but clearly authorizes governmental killing in capital punishment and war. Paul, it is said, assumes the same distinction and clearly intends to authorize Christian participation in justly authorized killing by government.

How valid is this argument? Almost all scholars today recognize that Romans 12:14–13:10 is one extended argument.[52] It is also widely recognized that Romans 12, in its strong statements about Christians rejecting revenge and vengeance, contains "reminiscences of the sayings of Jesus."[53] Paul commands Christians to "bless those who persecute you" (12:14) and tells them, "Do not repay anyone evil for evil" (12:17). He continues, "Do not take revenge, my dear friends, but leave room for God's wrath, for it is written: 'It is mine to avenge; I will repay,' says the Lord. On the contrary: 'If your enemy is hungry, feed him.' . . . Overcome evil with good" (12:19–21).

But in the very next verse Paul says that every person should "be subject" to the governing authorities. Since he is writing to Roman Christians, Paul is

51. See Charles, *Between Pacifism and Jihad*, 84–87; Skillen, *With or Against the World?*, 118; Copan and Flannagan, *Did God Really Command Genocide?*, 303–4; Biggar, *In Defence of War*, 42–44.

52. E.g., Biggar, *In Defence of War*, 42–44.

53. Dodd, *Romans*, 214; Hays, *Moral Vision*, 330.

thinking first of all of them, although he may also intend to refer to everyone. It is crucial to understand the meaning of the verb (*hypotassō*) used in 13:1 and 13:5. It is often wrongly translated as "obey." There are three perfectly good Greek words used in the New Testament that mean "obey," but Paul does not use them.[54] The word Paul does use means "to be subject." One can be subject and still refuse to obey evil commands. The early Christians are quite clear that when government commands evil things, they have to obey God rather than human authorities (Acts 4:18–20; 5:29).

Paul goes on to list a number of things that being subject to government involves. It means not rebelling against government.[55] It means paying taxes and offering respect and honor (Rom. 13:6–7). But nowhere does Paul say anything about the responsibility of his readers to participate in the government's punishment of wrongdoers. Paul recognizes that government does that and when it does, it is a servant of God (13:4). But nowhere does the text say that Paul's readers are to do that. Immediately after the section on government, Paul returns to the theme of love, insisting that "love does no harm" to a neighbor (13:8–10).

A comparison of the Greek words in Romans 12:19 and 13:4 demonstrates that government does precisely the things Paul has just commanded Christians never to do. In chapter 12, Paul says that seeking to live at peace with everyone means, "Do not take revenge [*ekdikountes*] but leave room for God's wrath [*orgē*]." Then he quotes Deuteronomy 32:35, where God says, "It is mine to avenge [*emoi ekdikēsis*]; I will repay." Christians must forsake vengeance, knowing that a just God is in charge of the world and will have the final word in the end. Then in 13:4, Paul employs exactly the same words (just used to describe what Christians should *not* do) to speak about what the state does! The state as God's servant is an agent "of wrath [*ekdikos eis orgēn*; lit., an avenger for the purpose of wrath] to bring punishment on the wrongdoer." Paul uses exactly the same words for "vengeance" and "wrath" in both places. The comment by evangelical scholar F. F. Bruce seems correct:

---

54. Cranfield, *Epistle to the Romans*, 2:660; Cranfield, "Observations on Romans XIII:1–7," 242.

55. This is very likely Paul's primary concern. In AD 49, a few years before Paul wrote this letter, the emperor Claudius expelled Jews (and probably Jewish Christians) from Rome because of tumult—perhaps emerging in the Jewish community because of conflict over Christian preaching. The Roman historian Tacitus reports resistance to taxes in Rome in the 50s, so perhaps Paul wanted to be sure Christians in Rome did not join this resistance. See Moo, *Epistle to the Romans*, 792–93. About five years (AD 64) after Paul wrote this letter, the emperor Nero blamed a fire in Rome on Christians and killed a number of them. Furthermore, since many Christians were also Jews, there may have been some sympathy among Jewish Christians in Rome with the Jewish revolutionary fervor that was heating up and led to the Jewish War breaking out in AD 66. See Dodd, *Romans*, 209.

"The state thus is charged with a function which has been *explicitly forbidden* to the Christian."[56]

Yoder's argument is convincing:

> If the statements of 12:19 and 13:4 were not in the same passage, we might not necessarily cross-refer from one to the other. Then we might not have to conclude that the prohibition of vengeance in the one verse excludes the sharing of Christians in the outworking of vengeance as described in the other. One could then say that the contexts are sufficiently different that the terms need not have exactly the same meaning. But within the sustained reasoning of one passage, with the same words being used in the midst of the same text, certainly it is a most likely interpretation that the "vengeance" or "wrath" that is recognized as being within providential control is the same as that which Christians are told not to exercise.[57]

Evangelical scholar Ben Witherington concludes that Romans 13 "says absolutely nothing about Christians' participating in government activities such as war or police actions. . . . This text is about pagan rulers and their right to govern and bear the sword for some purposes. The text says nothing about a Christian's right, much less duty, to bear arms."[58] Richard Hays agrees and concludes: "There is not a syllable in the Pauline letters that can be cited in support of Christians engaging in violence."[59]

One further point about Romans 13 is important. The text clearly says that God uses government to restrain evil. But the text never says God wants government to do all the things it does or that God approves of all the things government does.

Paul embraces the typical Jewish understanding that all governmental power comes ultimately from God, who works in history to achieve God's purposes. But that does not mean that God wills or approves of all that political rulers do. Jesus told Pilate that Pilate's power comes from God (John 19:11), but that does not mean that God approves of Pilate's unjust decision about Jesus. Again and again the Old Testament says God uses pagan rulers (e.g., Isa. 10:5–11; 13:3–5), but God clearly disapproves of some of their actions (10:12).[60] Nor does Paul think God approves when the Roman authorities

---

56. Bruce, *Romans*, 238 (italics added). So too Dodd, *Romans*, 210–11. F. F. Bruce, however, says the idea of a Christian state is beyond the range of Paul's thought and suggests that perhaps the Christian statesman legitimately uses lethal violence.

57. Yoder, *Politics of Jesus*, 198.

58. Witherington, *Paul Quest*, 178.

59. Hays, *Moral Vision*, 331.

60. See Eller, *War and Peace*, 76–77; Sprinkle, *Fight*, 168–69; Yoder, *Politics of Jesus*, 198.

persecute Christians.[61] Nothing in the text suggests that Paul means that God approves of all the actions of the governing authorities that God somehow "establishes." The text does not even say God wants government to execute vengeance via the sword. It simply says that government does that and God uses that to restrain evil.

Since God Kills God's Enemies . . .

Some Christians argue that since God punishes and ultimately in some sense kills sinners, the claim that Christians should never kill collapses.[62] Jesus speaks of a final judgment, after which some people will depart eternally from God. Even if that separation results from persons persisting in their freedom to refuse to accept God's offer of forgiveness, God is ultimately responsible for setting up the universe in a way that results in the eternal separation of some people from God.[63] Since God "kills" evildoers, Christians at times should do the same.

It is clearly the case that the teaching about final judgment and the eternal departure of sinners from God appears frequently in the New Testament.[64] Paul speaks of it repeatedly (e.g., Acts 17:30–31; Rom. 2:5–8; 2 Cor. 5:10–11).[65] Jesus himself, the teacher of love, says as much or more about eternal separation from God as any other part of the New Testament (e.g., Matt. 13:41–42; 18:8; 25:41).[66] Miroslav Volf is right that neither the Old Testament nor the New Testament talks about a "nonindignant God."[67]

But does the fact that God punishes sinners mean that Christians are authorized to kill? Romans 12:14–21 says both that Christians should not seek revenge or repay evil for evil and also that God does that. "Do not take revenge,

61. The verb in Rom. 13:1 translated "established" (*tassō*; participle *tetagmenos*) can mean "appoint to an office" or "order, fix, determine, appoint" (Arndt and Gingrich, *Greek-English Lexicon*, 813). The *Theological Dictionary of the New Testament* says the word means to "appoint" or "order" (hence "to arrange," e.g., religious festivals; "τάσσω," *TDNT* 8:27). John Howard Yoder (*Politics of Jesus*, 201) argues that in Rom. 13:2, the verb does not mean to "create" or "institute" but means to "order," as a librarian orders her books without approving of their content. Unfortunately, he offers no supporting evidence.

62. See Copan and Flannagan, *Did God Really Command Genocide?*, 42–45; Biggar, *In Defence of War*, 50–55.

63. Biggar, *In Defence of War*, 54. Biggar argues that therefore Richard Hays's use of God's love for enemies at the cross (Rom. 5:8–10) as a support for his argument about killing (Hays, *Moral Vision*, 330) fails because "God kills incorrigible sinners." Biggar, *In Defence of War*, 55.

64. C. Marshall, *Beyond Retribution*, 180–97.

65. See also 1 Cor. 6:9–10; Gal. 5:21.

66. See my discussion in Sider, *Good News and Good Works*, 128–33.

67. Volf, *Exclusion and Embrace*, 298.

my dear friends, but leave room for God's wrath, for it is written: 'It is mine to avenge; I will repay,' says the Lord" (v. 19). Paul clearly tells Christians not to seek revenge or pay evil for evil but rather to feed their enemies and bless their persecutors. But Paul says in this same passage that Christians can act this way because they know that the just Lord of the universe will eventually deal with evil.[68] Paul is clearly teaching that God will do what Christians should not do.

God is different from human beings. It is true that the Bible often commands believers to imitate God. But not at every point. Human beings do not create *ex nihilo* or die for the sins of the world. It is crucial to remember, as Volf says, that "humans are not God. There is a duty prior to the duty of imitating God and that is the duty of *not wanting to be God*, of letting God be God and humans be humans."[69] And the New Testament explicitly teaches that Christians should not imitate God in God's exercise of vengeance and killing. Only the One who is the perfect combination of love and justice, mercy and holiness, knows enough to do that rightly.

Therefore, to point out that Jesus seems to recognize and approve of God's destruction of Sodom or the flood in Noah's day says nothing about whether Christians should kill.[70] The same is true of the death of Ananias and Sapphira in Acts 5:1–11.[71] The text does not say that Peter kills them for lying.[72] The clear, although unstated, implication is that God chooses to punish them immediately. The New Testament explicitly tells Christians not to do some things that the all-knowing God rightly does.

Both theodicy and nonviolence require God's ultimate suppression of evil. "The biblical conception of God as all-powerful, all-knowing, and perfectly good requires ultimate vindication in the face of present sickness, sin, suffering, and death. The doctrine of the Last Judgment offers the hope that the results of human wrongdoing will be rectified, that people who have suffered unjustly will be recompensed, and that the wicked who have escaped judgment in this life will face it in the next. Intuitively, most people know that without final judgment, there can be no ultimate justice."[73]

---

68. The same logic appears in 1 Pet. 2:18–23. Christians emulate Christ at the cross, who did not retaliate but instead "entrusted himself to him who judges justly" (v. 23). Also 2 Thess. 1:6.
69. Volf, *Exclusion and Embrace*, 301 (italics original).
70. Copan and Flannagan, *Did God Really Command Genocide?*, 42–44, claim that such passages do warrant Christian use of lethal violence.
71. Copan and Flannagan, *Did God Really Command Genocide?*, 44, make the same unwarranted claim here.
72. Even John Calvin says incorrectly that Peter "then did nothing contrary to his office when he unsheathed in due time the sword which the Holy Spirit had given him." Quoted in Lasserre, *War and the Gospel*, 49.
73. C. Marshall, *Beyond Retribution*, 180–81.

The assurance of a final judgment of evil and evildoers is also a crucial foundation of nonviolence. "Without entrusting oneself to the God who judges justly, it will hardly be possible to follow the crucified Messiah and refuse to retaliate when abused. The certainty of God's just judgment at the end of history is the presupposition for the renunciation of violence in the middle of it. . . . The practice of nonviolence requires a belief in divine vengeance."[74]

To say that in the end some people depart eternally from God is not to claim that God preserves some people in conscious existence in order to punish them eternally. I am inclined to understand eternal separation from God as the result of God taking our freedom so seriously that God (with immeasurable sorrow) allows people to reject God's offer of loving forgiveness so long that they cease to exist.[75] It would be unloving for God to force them to embrace God's love. If some people experience eternal separation from God, it will be "because they have resisted to the end the powerful lure of the open arms of the crucified Messiah."[76]

Revelation's Violent Imagery

The famous nineteenth-century atheist Friedrich Nietzsche called the last book of the Bible "the most rabid outburst of vindictiveness in all recorded history."[77] Some contemporary New Testament scholars share something of Nietzsche's view.[78]

Without question, there is violent imagery in Revelation. It depicts Jesus riding on a white horse with eyes "like blazing fire" as he "wages war" against all who follow the antichrist. "Coming out of his mouth is a sharp sword with which to strike down the nations. 'He will rule them with an iron scepter.' He treads the winepress of the fury of the wrath of God Almighty" (19:11–15). When the kings of the earth and their armies gather to wage war against him, they are killed "with the sword coming out of the mouth of the rider on the horse, and all the birds gorged themselves on their flesh" (19:19–21).[79]

Some Christians conclude that Revelation supports Christian use of violence.[80] Popular evangelical pastor Mark Driscoll has said the book of Reve-

74. Volf, *Exclusion and Embrace*, 302, 304.
75. See my discussion in Sider, *Good News and Good Works*, 130–31.
76. Volf, *Exclusion and Embrace*, 298.
77. Nietzsche, *Birth of Tragedy*, 185; quoted in Hays, *Moral Vision*, 169.
78. E.g., Krister Stendahl and Jack T. Sanders (in Hays, *Moral Vision*, 169); Crossan, *God and Empire*, 224.
79. See also Rev. 14:19–20.
80. E.g., Copan and Flannagan, *Did God Really Command Genocide?*, 43.

lation depicts Jesus as "a prize fighter with a tattoo down his leg, a sword in his hand and the commitment to make someone bleed."[81] But that is to ignore a great deal about this unique book full of strange, powerful imagery.

Modern scholars recognize that the book was probably written around the reign of Emperor Domitian (AD 81–96). The cult of emperor worship flourished at this time, especially in Asia Minor (the location of the seven churches addressed in the book), and Christians were facing the danger of persecution.[82] Babylon is the symbolic name for the exploitative, oppressive Roman Empire,[83] and the prostitute ("drunk with the blood of God's holy people," Rev. 17:6) personifies Rome. The prostitute rides on a beast with seven heads, and the "seven heads are seven hills" (17:9)—a clear reference to the city of Rome, which was built, according to much ancient literature, on seven hills.[84] The book's central message is that Christians should remain faithful to Christ even if they are martyred (2:10), because Christ is now "King of Kings and Lord of Lords" (19:16) and will eventually conquer all evil.

Jesus is the center of Revelation. And the most significant statement about Jesus is that he is the "slaughtered Lamb." That image of Christ appears twenty-eight times in the book.[85] It appears first in chapter 5, where John laments the fact that no one seems able to open the scroll with the seven seals. But one of the elders assures John that the "Lion of the tribe of Judah" (5:5) can open it. Language about the Lion of the tribe of Judah reflects the widespread Jewish expectation for a conquering military messiah. But when the Lion appears, he is "a Lamb, looking as if it had been slain" (5:6). John says this slaughtered Lamb stands at the center of the throne of God. The twenty-four elders standing around the throne sing that the Lamb is worthy to open the seals "because you were slain, and with your blood you purchased for God persons from every tribe and language" (5:9). Everywhere in Revelation Jesus is the slain Lamb. Using this language, Revelation rejects the idea of a militaristic Messiah and explains that the Messiah conquers evil with suffering love.

The message is clear. God is now dealing with the world through the cross of Christ. Jesus is now conquering Rome through his cross as the slain Lamb. Just as clearly, Revelation says that Christians conquer Satan by suffering, not fighting: "They triumphed over him by the blood of the Lamb and by the word of their testimony; they did not love their lives so much as to shrink from death" (12:11). They conquer by dying, just as Christ has done (also 2:10–11).

81. Quoted in Sprinkle, *Fight*, 173–74.
82. Hays, *Moral Vision*, 170.
83. Bauckham, *Revelation*, 89.
84. Morris, *Revelation*, 203.
85. Hays, *Moral Vision*, 174.

"Thus, victory comes not by engaging in armed battle, but by refusing to love one's life so much that one resists martyrdom and through consistent patterning of one's life upon the Lord's sacrifice."[86]

Revelation 13:10 seems to echo Jesus's words of rebuke to Peter when he draws his sword at Jesus's arrest. In chapter 13, John describes how the beast attacks God's people. Then the author interrupts his description of the vision with a clear word to his Christian audience: "Whoever has ears, let them hear. If anyone is to go into captivity, into captivity they will go. If anyone kills with the sword, with the sword they will be killed" (13:9–10 TNIV). Many translations have a different reading for verse 10. The NIV reads, "If anyone is to be killed with the sword, with the sword they will be killed." There is some slight manuscript support for the NIV's translation. But most early Greek manuscripts read, "If anyone kills with the sword, with the sword they will be killed."[87] This better-attested reading sounds very much like Matthew 26:52 ("all who draw the sword will die by the sword"). Thus the probable meaning of Revelation 13:10 is that Christians are not to use the sword to defend themselves against the attacks of the beast.

It is true that the martyred Christians depicted in Revelation long for an end to their suffering. They ask, "How long, Sovereign Lord, holy and true, until you judge the inhabitants of the earth and avenge our blood?" (Rev. 6:10).[88] That question reflects the common New Testament teaching that God will eventually deal with evil. But, as Romans 12:19; 2 Thessalonians 1:6–8; and 1 Peter 2:23 say, it is God who takes vengeance, not people.

The book of Revelation clearly teaches what Jesus also teaches—namely, a final judgment (20:11–15). Before that final judgment, Christ the Lamb powerfully conquers all evil. Some of the imagery used to describe that battle is violent. But one should probably not read those words in a literal way. Revelation is apocalyptic literature, which uses vivid symbols to describe basic truths.[89] And the essential idea is that in the end, God will conquer all evil.

Sometimes even the text suggests that the reality is different from the violent imagery. In the final battle, Christ comes riding on a white horse prepared for battle. His robe is "dipped in blood"—even before the battle begins! This is almost certainly a reference to Calvary, where Christ has conquered by dying.[90] And the text says that he strikes the enemy with a sword in his mouth (19:15).

86. Klassen, "Vengeance," 306.
87. Hays, *Moral Vision*, 178, 185n20.
88. See also Rev. 18:6–7, 20; 19:2.
89. For a discussion of the use of symbolic language in apocalyptic literature, see Boyd, *Crucifixion of the Warrior God*, 1:597–601, and the literature cited there.
90. Morris, *Revelation*, 224. Also Hays, *Moral Vision*, 175.

Some commentators think that means that his weapon for battle is the word of God.[91] And in the final battle with Satan and the nations, the text says only that "fire came down from heaven and devoured them" (20:9). There is no discussion of armies engaged in ferocious conflict. The central point is that God finally conquers evil. We should not try to decipher the symbolic imagery to decide how exactly God in Christ does that.[92]

Even more important is the fact that nowhere does Revelation say that the saints fight in this final battle. The "armies of heaven" that follow the rider on the white horse (19:14) are not human beings.[93] Repeatedly, Revelation says the saints suffer, even up to death. But it never says they fight back. In fact, Revelation 13:10 tells them not to use the sword. Not even in the final battle against evil do human beings participate. At the end, as in the middle of history, vengeance is something that God does, not God's people. As Volf says, "Preserving the fundamental difference between God and non-God, the biblical tradition insists that there are things which only God may do. One of them is to use violence."[94]

Hays is right: "A work that places the Lamb that was slaughtered at the center of its praise and worship can hardly be used to validate violence and coercion. God's ultimate judgment of the wicked is, to be sure, inexorable. Those who destroy the earth will be destroyed (11:18); . . . but these events are in the hands of God; they do not constitute a program for human military action."[95]

Christians over the ages have used the texts and incidents discussed in this chapter to argue that the New Testament teaches that sometimes Christians should kill. But the arguments are often weak and strained. They are never convincing. Careful examination of these passages confirms the view that the New Testament consistently teaches that Christians should never kill.

91. Hays, *Moral Vision*, 175; Sprinkle, *Fight*, 187; Klassen, "Vengeance," 308. In Rev. 2:12, 16, the sword in Christ's mouth seems to be a word of judgment, but Volf, in *Exclusion and Embrace*, 296, disagrees.

92. But Miroslav Volf is probably correct that the picture of violence by the rider on the white horse "is the *symbolic portrayal of the final exclusion of everything that refuses to be redeemed by God's suffering love.*" Volf, *Exclusion and Embrace*, 299 (italics original).

93. Leon Morris (*Revelation*, 224) says the "armies of heaven" are "probably angels rather than the saints." Robert H. Mounce (*Revelation*, 354) thinks the martyrs are part of the "armies of heaven," but he says these "armies take no part in the actual battle."

94. Volf, *Exclusion and Embrace*, 301. I would say "the New Testament tradition" rather than "the biblical tradition."

95. Hays, *Moral Vision*, 175.

7

Foundational Theological Issues

There are crucial theological issues that are relevant to the question of whether Christians should sometimes kill for the sake of peace and justice. Who is Jesus? How is Jesus's resurrection important for the discussion? What are the implications of the fact that the messianic kingdom Christ announced has already begun but is not yet complete? How is the church important to our question? If Jesus did teach a nonviolent ethic, is that only for the church, or even just some Christians?

Who Is Jesus?

John Howard Yoder asks a probing question near the beginning of his famous book *The Politics of Jesus*: "What becomes of the meaning of the incarnation if Jesus is not normatively human? If he is human but not normative, is this not the ancient ebionitic heresy? If he be somehow authoritative but not in his humanness, is this not a new gnosticism?"[1] The early ebionitic heresy claimed that Jesus was truly human but not fully divine. As one human among many, but not truly God, Jesus has no right to imagine that his teaching is normative for everyone. The gnostic heresy taught that Jesus was truly divine

1. Yoder, *Politics of Jesus*, 10.

but not fully human. Therefore, Jesus's human life is not significant enough to be normative for Christians.

If the affirmation of the classical Christian creeds—Jesus is truly God and truly human—is correct, then the incarnate Son of God must be normative for Christians. Christians believe that Jesus lived a sinless life. If he is fully human and fully divine, then his sinless life discloses God's revelation of how humanity should live. Obviously, this does not mean imitating every aspect of Jesus's life (e.g., his singleness or being a Palestinian Jew). But it does mean that Jesus's teaching on how people should live reveals *how* the one God wants persons to live.

Obviously, if Jesus is not true God, then the argument for nonviolence based on his teaching is weak. "If Jesus Christ was not who historic Christianity confesses he was, the revelation in the life of a real man of the very character of God, then this one argument for pacifism collapses."[2]

However, precisely the classical orthodox understanding of Jesus as truly God and truly human demands that Christians seek to submit to his teaching, including his teaching on loving enemies. To do otherwise is to imply that Jesus did not know what he was talking about—that he was mistaken in his teaching—which is a denial of his divinity.

That, it seems to me, is essentially what Reinhold Niebuhr does. He believes that the "ethic of Jesus is an absolute and uncompromising ethic" of pure, totally passive nonresistance to all evil. "The injunctions 'resist all evil,' 'love your enemies' . . . are all uncompromising and absolute." In some sense, Niebuhr claims, Jesus's ethic is finally normative, but it is "not immediately applicable to the task of securing justice in a sinful world."[3] Jesus's teaching on love is an "embarrassment" when one tries to develop a social ethic for societal justice. Jesus's ethic of "pure non-resistance can have no immediate relevance to any political situation."[4] In short, Jesus's ethic does not work in the real world. Responsible Christians should not try to live the ethic of love that Jesus taught.[5]

But that conclusion is simply unacceptable if one believes with the ancient creeds that Jesus is truly God as well as truly human. If the ancient creeds are correct, then orthodox Christians must seek to live what Jesus taught his disciples. Anything less represents theological heresy.

2. Yoder, *Politics of Jesus*, 237. For further evidence of Yoder's "high" Christology, see Carter, *Politics of the Cross*, 27, 65–70.

3. Niebuhr, "Why the Christian Church Is Not Pacifist," 106.

4. Davis and Good, *Niebuhr on Politics*, 137, 140.

5. See chap. 3, "Eye for an Eye," for a discussion showing that Jesus did not teach the pure passivity that Reinhold Niebuhr claims.

That is not to say that every claim that Christians should sometimes kill involves this theological error. As we have seen, many Christians argue that Jesus did not actually teach that Christians should never kill. Rather, he intended his command to love one's enemies to apply only to personal life, not to a Christian's public life as a soldier. I have argued earlier that I think that interpretation fundamentally misunderstands Jesus's teaching.[6] But one can make that argument without falling into theological heresy.

What one cannot do, if one embraces an orthodox Christology, is claim that faithful Christians can set aside Jesus's actual teaching. If he is truly God and truly human, then his teaching is true and normative. If he meant to tell his disciples to love their enemies and not kill them, then orthodox Christians will submit to his teaching and seek to live accordingly. Clarity about who Jesus is must be the starting point for a truly Christian discussion of whether Christians should ever kill.

If Jesus Is Not Risen . . .

The one who taught Jesus's disciples to love their enemies was crucified. The one who commanded his followers to abandon the standard judicial principle of an eye for an eye suffered a most despicable, painful death. The one who claimed to be the long-expected Messiah, the one who announced that the messianic kingdom had broken into history in his person and work, experienced the ultimate human proof that his claims were false.

Every Jew in Jesus's day knew that a self-proclaimed messiah who died was not just a failure. He was also a fraud. Judaism knew how to honor a dead martyr who fought the pagans. But, as N. T. Wright notes pointedly, "The category of failed but still revered Messiah, however, did not exist. A Messiah who died at the hands of the pagans, instead of winning YHWH's battle against them, was a deceiver."[7]

The reason Jesus's disciples still continued to call him Messiah after his crucifixion by the authorities as a false claimant to be the messianic "King of the Jews" was that they found his tomb empty and met the risen Jesus. It was the resurrection that convinced the discouraged disciples that the messianic kingdom Jesus had announced had truly begun and therefore they should make disciples of all nations, teaching them to obey all that Jesus had taught them.[8]

6. See chap. 3, "Sidestepping Jesus's Teaching," and chap. 6, "Romans 13."

7. N. T. Wright, *Jesus and the Victory of God*, 658.

8. For an exhaustive discussion of the historical evidence for Jesus's resurrection, see N. T. Wright, *Resurrection*; Licona, *Resurrection of Jesus*.

Jesus's call to love enemies makes no sense if he is still in the tomb. An empty tomb, a risen Crucified One, is a central, necessary foundation of any claim that followers of Jesus should refuse to kill.[9] "When Jesus rose from the dead on the third day . . . God announced to the world that the power of evil and violence do not have the final word. The resurrection was the vindication of God's ultimate triumph of love over the forces of violence."[10] "None of the New Testament's witness makes any sense unless the nonviolent, enemy-loving community is to be vindicated by the resurrection of the dead."[11]

But the resurrection definitely does not guarantee the immediate success of nonviolent action. Throughout the ages, starting with Stephen, Christian martyrs loved their enemies, but they were killed and they stayed dead. "The resurrection is not the end product of a mechanism which runs through its paces wherever there is a crucifixion."[12] It is only when one grasps the eschatological implications of Jesus's resurrection that it provides the solid foundation for nonviolence. The New Testament says that what happened to Jesus at his resurrection will happen to all who believe in him at his return (Rom. 6:5; 1 Cor. 15:20–23; Phil. 3:21). And at that time, even the groaning creation will be restored to wholeness (Rom. 8:18–23). The New Testament paints a picture of a glorious eschatological future where Christ will abolish all evil, even death itself, and peace will prevail (Rev. 21–22). That eschatological assurance—"the knowledge that the way of the Lamb is what will finally conquer"—demonstrates that the way of nonviolence "is not nonsense."[13] As Paul shows at the end of his lengthy chapter on the resurrection (1 Cor. 15), it is precisely Jesus's resurrection that is the foundation of that glorious hope. Finally, Christians refuse to kill their enemies even when that means their own death because they know where history is going. They know that the resurrected Christ will ultimately prevail.

The last verse of 1 Corinthians 15 clearly states that Christians should begin now living in the assurance of the final resurrection: "Therefore, my dear brothers and sisters, stand firm. . . . Always give yourselves fully to the work of the Lord, because you know that your labor in the Lord is not in vain" (v. 58). Jesus's resurrection assures his followers not only that Christ's

9. In his critique of Niebuhr, Yoder rightly notes that "Niebuhr spoke of the cross repeatedly, of the resurrection of Christ not at all and of the resurrection of the body only as a mythological symbol." Yoder, *Niebuhr and Christian Pacifism*, 20.

10. Roth, *Choosing against War*, 92. See also Ellul, *Violence*, 150; Hauerwas, *Peaceable Kingdom*, 87–91.

11. Hays, *Moral Vision*, 338.

12. Yoder, *Nevertheless*, 126.

13. Yoder, *Original Revolution*, 76; see Yoder's whole pamphlet "Peace without Eschatology?" reprinted here, 55–90.

messianic kingdom has begun—not only that it will reach completion at his return but also that our work now living according to Christ's kingdom teaching is not in vain. N. T. Wright captures these truths wonderfully: "I know that God's new world of justice and joy, of hope for the whole earth, was launched when Jesus came out of the tomb on Easter morning, and I know that he calls his followers to live in him and by the power of his Spirit and so to be new-creation people here and now. . . . The resurrection of Jesus and the gifts of the Spirit mean that we are called to bring real and effective signs of God's renewed creation to birth even in the midst of the present age."[14]

But does that include obeying Christ's call to love, rather than kill, our enemies now in this interim time when vicious enemies still prowl and destroy? That question leads to one of the major divides that separate Christians on the basic question of this book.

The Already / Not Yet Kingdom

One of the most important differences between Christian pacifists and Christian just war advocates is their different assessment of the implications that Christ's kingdom has already begun but is not yet complete. The difference between pacifism and just war thinking, Lisa Cahill argues, "lies, perhaps not exclusively but certainly most characteristically, in their disagreement about how present and accessible in human life the kingdom, by the grace of God, really is."[15] She also states, "Violent action becomes acceptable to the degree that the heavenly kingdom recedes from history and becomes a distant ideal to be fulfilled eschatologically."[16]

Christians have argued in a variety of ways that the kingdom of God has not yet arrived and therefore Christians should sometimes kill.

Classical dispensationalists argued that Jesus did announce the messianic kingdom, but the Jewish people rejected his message. Therefore the messianic kingdom—along with Jesus's ethical teaching—was postponed until the millennium. Therefore Jesus's teaching on loving enemies is not relevant for Christians in this age of the church. Fortunately, contemporary scholars in this tradition now recognize that Jesus's kingdom has begun.

In the twentieth century, many scholars following Albert Schweitzer believed that Jesus's understanding of the kingdom involved an imminent end

---

14. N. T. Wright, *Surprised by Hope*, 209.
15. Cahill, *Love Your Enemies*, 213.
16. Cahill, *Love Your Enemies*, 79.

to space-time history.[17] Jesus's radical ethic was an interim ethic for this short space of time. But since history has continued, Jesus's radical interim ethic is not normative for Christians.[18]

Niebuhr's critique of Christian pacifism relates to this question of Christ's dawning kingdom. Niebuhr rightly criticizes theologically liberal pacifists for having an inadequate understanding of human sin. Their easy call to love overlooks the depth of human sinfulness. But it is also true that Niebuhr largely ignored Jesus's resurrection and its implications for whether Christians can now live in Jesus's dawning kingdom. "If Christian pacifists have an underdeveloped appreciation for human sinfulness, Niebuhr has an underdeveloped confidence in the power of the resurrection."[19] At the very least, if Jesus rose from the dead, we must ask what that means for living his call to love our enemies.

In more recent discussion, however, Christians who argue that sometimes Christians should kill to preserve peace and justice clearly affirm that Jesus's messianic kingdom has begun. In significant ways, Christians now live in that new kingdom. But the old age of evil and injustice remains strong. The kingdom of God is obviously not here in its fullness. That will happen only when Christ returns. And in this interim "already / not yet" period, Christians should sometimes use lethal force.

This widely used argument appears very clearly in the famous pastoral letter *The Challenge of Peace* issued by the US Catholic bishops in 1983. The bishops note that Augustine "was impressed by the fact and the consequences of sin in history—the 'not yet' dimension of the kingdom."[20] They argue that "Christians are called to live the tension between the vision of the reign of God and its concrete realization in history. The tension is often described in terms of 'already but not yet'; i.e., we already live in the grace of the kingdom, but it is not yet the completed kingdom."[21] Therefore, the bishops conclude, Christians must use the just war tradition and sometimes decide to go to war. Many Christians agree with the Catholic bishops.[22]

On the contrary, Christians who believe Jesus's followers should never kill typically place much more emphasis on the fact that Christ's kingdom has dawned powerfully. Therefore, now, with the help of the Holy Spirit,

17. See chap. 1, "Messianic Expectations," for N. T. Wright's refutation of this idea.
18. Ramsey, *Basic Christian Ethics*, 35–40; Cahill, *Love Your Enemies*, 200.
19. Allman, *Who Would Jesus Kill?*, 111.
20. *Challenge of Peace* §81, p. 37.
21. *Challenge of Peace* §58, p. 26.
22. E.g., Clough and Stiltner, *Faith and Force*, 33, 50–52; O'Donovan, *Just War Revisited*, 5–7; and Mouw, "Christianity and Pacifism," 105.

Christians should and can live Jesus's radical kingdom ethics.[23] Stanley Hauerwas rejects the Catholic bishops' argument that Christians must sometimes go to war because the kingdom is not fully present.[24] Jesus's life demonstrated that "living a life of forgiveness and peace is not an impossible ideal but an opportunity now present. . . . The announcement of the reality of this kingdom, of the possibility of living a life of forgiveness and peace with one's enemies, is based on our confidence that that kingdom has become a reality through the life and work of this man, Jesus of Nazareth."[25]

N. T. Wright is surely right to assert that Jesus's gospel of the kingdom "is the story of God's kingdom being launched on earth as in heaven, generally a new state of affairs in which the power of evil has been decisively defeated, the new creation has been decisively launched, and Jesus's followers have been commissioned and equipped to put that victory and that inaugurated new world into practice."[26] He continues, "Christian ethics is the lifestyle that celebrates and embodies that new creation."[27]

But just war advocates might largely embrace Wright's statements and still reject the claim that killing is always wrong for Jesus's disciples. After all, it is painfully obvious that the complete kingdom of peace and justice has not yet arrived. A quick look around our violent world proves that. Until that kingdom arrives in its fullness, they conclude, Christians sometimes must use lethal violence.

Is there any way to adjudicate this disagreement over the implications of the already / not yet kingdom for our topic? What in the New Testament is relevant? Several things are important.

First, in spite of the fact that Jesus clearly teaches that the kingdom was already present but not here yet in its fullness, there is not a hint in Jesus's teachings that that means that his disciples should postpone following his teaching until the kingdom arrives in its fullness. Precisely in the passage on loving enemies, Jesus ends with the command to be "perfect, therefore, as your heavenly Father is perfect" (Matt. 5:48). A bit later, he says that the person who hears his words and practices them is like the wise man who builds his house on a rock (7:24). When Jesus rejects Moses's allowance of divorce and returns to God's intention in creation, he does not say that unfortunately since the old age with its temptations is still present, divorce will sometimes still be

---

23. Cahill, *Love Your Enemies*, ix–xi, 164, 223–28; Hauerwas, *Should War Be Eliminated?*, 49–53; Hauerwas, *Peaceable Kingdom*, esp. 72–95; Yoder, *Original Revolution*, 55–90.

24. Hauerwas, *Should War Be Eliminated?*, 49.

25. Hauerwas, *Peaceable Kingdom*, 85.

26. N. T. Wright, *Surprised by Hope*, 204.

27. N. T. Wright, *Surprised by Hope*, 284.

acceptable. He says that if one's eyes tempt one to adultery, one should take drastic action to avoid that sin (5:29–30). Jesus does not say that sometimes because the old age continues, it will be necessary to lie. He insists that our honesty must be so genuine that we need not, should not, use oaths (5:33–37). Repeatedly Jesus demands that his disciples must live like him: "Whoever wants to be my disciple must deny themselves and take up their cross and follow me" (Mark 8:34). Jesus insists that "anyone who loves me will obey my teaching" (John 14:23). And at the ascension, Jesus commands his disciples to teach new disciples "to obey everything I have commanded you" (Matt. 28:20). There is not the slightest suggestion by Jesus that his disciples should postpone obeying his ethical teaching until the kingdom arrives in its fullness.

Second, the rest of the New Testament, as we have seen, calls Christians to imitate Jesus's self-sacrificial love at the cross—in the home, in the church, and in society.[28] First Peter urges slaves to imitate Jesus's nonretaliating love at the cross *now* in the world of injustice (1 Pet. 2:18–23). With echoes of Jesus's words, Paul urges Roman Christians, who have already faced injustice, to refuse to repay evil for evil, but rather to feed their enemy (Rom. 12:17–20). There is no suggestion that since injustice persists in the world Christians should reluctantly abandon Jesus's teaching for a while.

Third, all the New Testament insists on high ethical standards in Jesus's new messianic community.[29] Paul says adulterers, thieves, and the greedy will not inherit the kingdom.[30] Paul acknowledges that some of the Corinthians were like that before they became Christians, but they are different now because they have been "washed" and "sanctified" (1 Cor. 6:11). The very thought that Christians should continue doing sinful things horrifies Paul (Rom. 6:1–2).

The foundation of Paul's conviction and demand that Christians live ethically faithful lives now is that their faith in Christ has radically transformed them. They have been baptized into Christ's death and raised with him to a new life (Rom. 6:4). Christians must not let sin reign in their lives, because they have been "set free from sin" (6:12, 18). God has acted in such a way in Christ "that the righteous requirement of the law might be fully met in us, who do not live according to the flesh but according to the Spirit" (8:4). Paul tells the Corinthians that "if anyone is in Christ, the new creation has come" (2 Cor. 5:17). Christ is the Messiah, and that means his messianic kingdom has begun. Christians are already living in the new messianic kingdom that

28. See chap. 5, "Imitating Christ."
29. See Sider, *Scandal of the Evangelical Conscience*, 31–53.
30. 1 Cor. 6:9–10; also Gal. 5:19–21.

Christ announced. Therefore, they can and must live radically transformed lives.

Romans 13:11–14 states a clear eschatological reason for rejecting sinful behavior. Christians should not engage in sin, "because our salvation is nearer now than when we first believed" (v. 11). Because the kingdom has already begun and will soon be completed, Christians should "clothe [themselves] with the Lord Jesus Christ, and . . . not think about how to gratify the desires of the flesh" (v. 14). Paul undoubtedly expected a shorter time frame for the completion of the kingdom than we who live two millennia later. But the logic both then and now is the same. Since the kingdom has begun and will surely be completed in God's time, Christians now live the values of the new messianic kingdom.

Perhaps no biblical texts state the radical ethical transformation that genuine Christian faith produces more pointedly than Ephesians and 1 John. The goal in the body of Christ is that all attain "to the whole measure of the fullness of Christ" (Eph. 4:13). What a standard! Christians must "no longer live as the Gentiles do" (4:17). Christians should imitate God's action in Christ, who "gave himself up for us" (5:2). First John is equally blunt: "We know that we have come to know him if we keep his commands. Whoever says, 'I know him,' but does not do what he commands is a liar" (1 John 2:3–4). That does not sound like a suggestion that Jesus's disciples should sometimes choose not to follow his commands because the world is still a wicked, vicious place.

Finally, the New Testament says that Christians should live differently from the world. Jesus bluntly warns his disciples that the world will hate them just as the world has hated him: "If the world hates you, keep in mind that it hated me first" (John 15:18). First Peter addresses Christians as "foreigners and exiles" because they abstain from the evil practices of the world (2:11). Knowing that the kingdom has been revealed "in these last times," Christians should live as "foreigners" in the world (1 Pet. 1:17–20). As Paul switches in Romans 12 to offering comments on how to live the Christian life, he starts with a sweeping call to nonconformity to the world: "Do not conform to the pattern of this world, but be transformed by the renewing of your mind" (v. 2).[31]

Colossians 2:15 gives us reason to hope that even the socioeconomic-political structures of the world can be somewhat improved. Paul often talks about the "powers and authorities," which he understands to be fallen angelic beings who now interact with the socioeconomic-political and cultural structures of our world in a way that produces injustice, violence, and

---

31. See also 2 Cor. 6:14–17.

destruction. But Colossians 2:15 says that at the cross Christ has disarmed these powers.[32] "And having disarmed the powers and authorities, he made a public spectacle of them, triumphing over them by the cross." Paul of course knows very well that these evil powers are not yet totally defeated. But since they were disarmed in some significant way at the cross, it is now possible on this side of the cross (where Christ's kingdom has already broken powerfully into this world) to make progress in moving society somewhat closer to that perfection that will come only at Christ's return. Because the kingdom has begun and the powers have been disarmed, it is now possible to reduce violence in the world.

None of the texts that I have cited in the last few pages speak explicitly to the question of whether Jesus's commands may or should sometimes be temporarily suspended because the kingdom has not yet come in its fullness. And certainly none of them deal with that question with reference to Jesus's command to his disciples to love their enemies. But there is not a hint of this logic in any of what Jesus and the writers of the New Testament say. Again and again Jesus insists that his disciples must keep his commands. Overwhelmingly, the New Testament writers emphasize the radical transformation that happens to Christians with the result that they are no longer conformed to the evil practices of the world. All that evidence weighs strongly against the argument that Christians should, in spite of Jesus's command to love one's enemies, sometimes kill their enemies because the kingdom has not yet fully arrived.

The Importance of the Church

There are many varieties of pacifism—both religious and secular.[33] Not all emphasize the importance of community. But for the kind of biblical pacifism developed here—where Jesus's true humanity, divinity, and bodily resurrection are foundational—Jesus's new messianic community is central.[34]

Following Jesus's radical call to love enemies is not possible for isolated individuals lacking the transforming power of Jesus's gospel.[35] Living like Jesus

32. For a discussion of the "powers and authorities" and their disarmament at the cross, see Sider, *Just Politics*, 47–48.

33. See Yoder, *Nevertheless*.

34. Yoder identifies himself with what he calls "the Pacifism of the Messianic Community": Yoder, *Nevertheless*, 122–27. See also Lisa Cahill's emphasis on Christian community in both Yoder and Stanley Hauerwas: Cahill, *Love Your Enemies*, 224, 227–28.

35. That is not to say that non-Christians (e.g., Gandhi) are incapable of amazing acts of nonviolence. See Sider, *Nonviolent Action*, chaps. 2, 8, 9, 10.

is finally possible only for people who repent of their sins, embrace Christ as Lord and Savior, experience the sanctifying power of the Holy Spirit, and enjoy the social support of Jesus's new kingdom community. "Christian discipleship . . . presupposes the resources of faith: the assurance of forgiveness, the counseling and accepting fellowship of the Christian [community], the presence of the Holy Spirit as source of insight and motivation, a changed attitude of the regenerate will."[36]

Earlier, we saw how dramatically the New Testament sees Jesus's followers as profoundly transformed persons who have "died" to their sinful selves in baptism and risen to a new (albeit not perfect) life empowered by the Holy Spirit. As members of Jesus's one body, they hold one another accountable to live transformed lives.[37] God wants all people to love their enemies. But Christians know that it is the transforming power of personal faith in Christ and the social support of the Christian community that enables Christians to truly live that way.

It is also true that when a community turns away from the sinful practices of the world and lives profoundly different lives, the response of the larger society is not always positive. A new community modeling radical love even for enemies implicitly at least condemns unloving behavior. And people thus rebuked (however lovingly) frequently resent persons who even indirectly point out their sin. That is why Jesus warns his followers that the world will hate them. That is why the early church understood themselves as sojourners and exiles in a foreign land. In order to retain a commitment to Jesus's new messianic community with its countercultural values, Christians must accept the fact that the faithful church will often—perhaps always—be a minority community in a broken world.

The contrast with Niebuhr and his rejection of Christian pacifism is striking. Niebuhr has no place in his thinking for the doctrines of regeneration and sanctification that for Paul make possible radically transformed Christian lifestyles. For Niebuhr, grace is primarily forgiveness of sins, not sanctification. Niebuhr has virtually no doctrine of the Holy Spirit, and he believes that the bodily resurrection of Jesus is mere myth. Not surprisingly, "the church as distinguished from society has no significant place" in Niebuhr's ethical thought.[38] It is not surprising, therefore, that whereas the New Testament

---

36. Yoder, *For the Nations*, 112. See also Yoder, *Nevertheless*, 124–26; Yoder, *Christian Witness to the State*, 78; and Hauerwas, *Peaceable Kingdom*, 97.

37. See the example of church discipline in 1 Cor. 5:1–13; and Jesus's teaching in Matt. 18:15–17.

38. Yoder, *Niebuhr and Christian Pacifism*, 21. See the similar critique of Niebuhr in Friesen, *Christian Peacemaking*, 99; and Macgregor, *Basis of Pacifism*, 136–37.

derives Christian ethics from God's redeeming activity in Christ, Niebuhr
derives his ethics from the fallen condition of sinful humanity. The presence
or absence in one's theology of regeneration, sanctification, the power of
the Holy Spirit, and the church as Jesus's new messianic community living
differently from surrounding society's sin profoundly shapes one's ethics—
including the question of whether Christians can and should love their enemies
and refuse to kill them.

Niebuhr also illustrates a related way that just war and pacifist Christians
tend to differ. For Niebuhr, clearly the decisive reasons for his embrace of
the necessity of war come from human reason and experience, not biblical revelation. In a different but somewhat parallel way, Thomas Aquinas
develops his just war stance primarily using natural law discerned through
human reason, which is available to everyone. For many Christian pacifists,
however, the decisive source for thinking about war is the revelation given
in Jesus Christ. This difference is also connected to still another divergence:
just war thinkers like Aquinas and Niebuhr seek to develop an ethic for
everyone, whereas many Christian pacifists tend not to expect those who lack
the transforming power of Christian faith to be able to love their enemies
as well as those who do have the transforming power of Christian faith.[39]

Yoder and Hauerwas often say that the first task of the church is to be the
church.[40] Some people understand this statement to mean that pacifists like
Yoder and Hauerwas abandon all responsibility for the larger society. Below,
I will argue at length that a rejection of killing does not require abandonment
of responsibility to make society more just and peaceful.[41] What the statement
rightly points to is that the first task of Christians is to live now the message
and ethics of Jesus's new messianic kingdom. When surrounding society says
we should abandon Jesus's teaching for the sake of short-term effectiveness,
we must refuse—precisely because we know that the risen Jesus is now Lord
of history and that his kingdom will finally prevail. If Jesus is truly Lord and
Messiah, then in the long run his way will also be most effective.[42] If it is not,
Jesus is not truly Lord.

As the church models now Jesus's kingdom teaching, it provides a powerful
glimpse of where history is going, what the ultimate future will be. "The

39. See the helpful discussion of these differences in Clough and Stiltner, *Faith and Force*,
13–18.

40. E.g., Hauerwas, *Peaceable Kingdom*, 99; Yoder, *Politics of Jesus*, 150.

41. See chap. 8, "Failure to Take Responsibility for History." Yoder very clearly rejects this
charge; see Yoder, *For the Nations*, 6.

42. Cf. Yoder's comment: "For those who confess the Lamb that was slain as risen Lord
worthy to receive power, there can be no ultimate need to choose between suffering love and
social effectiveness." Yoder, *Nonviolence*, 38.

people of God is called to be today what the world is called to be ultimately."[43] The church is the "new world on the way."[44] As Karl Barth says, "The decisive contribution which the Christian community" can make to the civil society is its witness given by "the form of the order of its own upbuilding and constitution." The very life of the church in the world is a "reminder of the law of the kingdom of God already set up on earth in Jesus Christ. . . . It should demonstrate . . . that there are other possibilities, not only on heaven but earth, not merely one day but already, than those to which [the world] thinks it must confine itself."[45] As the church demonstrates new possibilities for community grounded in Jesus's teaching, the church models a new reality that historically has profoundly shaped surrounding society.[46] Perhaps it is not an overstatement to say that "only a continuing community dedicated to a deviant value system can change the world."[47]

Is Biblical Nonviolence Only for Some Christians?

As we have just seen, truly living like Jesus is possible only for those who embrace Christ as Lord and Savior and receive the transforming power of the Holy Spirit. We should not expect that non-Christians can and will live the way Spirit-filled Christians can and should live. But that is not to say that God has two ethics: one for faithful Christians and another for others.

Historically, Christians have sometimes advocated two different ethics. Some medieval Catholics distinguished between the "counsels of perfection" (e.g., loving enemies), which apply only to a special class of Christians, and the normal ethical demands that apply to everyone. Aquinas agreed that "some biblical counsels are meant for some classes of persons only." Aquinas said that "the clergy have a special vocation to imitate the nonviolence of Christ, one not obligatory for the laity."[48]

The early Anabaptist Schleitheim Confession (1527) seems also to embrace a double ethic: "The sword is an ordering of God outside the perfection of Christ. It punishes and kills the wicked, and guards and protects the good. In the law, the sword is established over the wicked for punishment and for death, and the secular rulers are established to wield the same. But within the perfection of Christ only the ban is used for the admonition and

43. Yoder, *Body Politics*, ix.
44. The title of Yoder's Stone Lectures at Princeton, 1980; see Carter, *Politics of the Cross*, 204.
45. Barth, *Church Dogmatics*, IV/2, 721; quoted in Yoder, *For the Nations*, 27.
46. See Yoder's discussion of this in *Body Politics*.
47. Yoder, *Nevertheless*, 125.
48. Cahill, *Love Your Enemies*, 87.

exclusion of the one who has sinned."[49] This confession seems to say God does not want Christians to use the sword but that God does want secular rulers to do so. Such an argument, however, is fundamentally problematic. First, such a position would mean that God would never want all people in a society to become Christians because then there would be nobody to use the sword, which God desires. That position contradicts Peter's teaching that God wants "everyone to come to repentance" (2 Pet. 3:9). And it seems to imply that God's salvation is not for the real world. Second, to claim that God wills an ethical norm for society different from that revealed by Christ for Christians implies that there is some ethical standard that can be known outside of Christ. But if Jesus is fully human as well as fully divine, then his life and teaching provide the one norm for how God desires human beings to live.[50] Third, the New Testament consistently teaches that the crucified Lamb who has been resurrected is now the Lord of history, the "ruler of the kings of the earth" (Rev. 1:5). Christians know both that Christ is now Lord of the world and that his will and way will ultimately prevail throughout the universe. And finally, all people ought to live according to Jesus's messianic teaching precisely because "all people have been called to be part of the kingdom initiated by Jesus."[51]

The New Testament does not say that it is God's will for the world to continue in its fallen state. Rather, the New Testament constantly invites non-Christians to embrace Christ and begin living according to Christ's kingdom norms.[52] "Because the risen Messiah is at once head of the Church and *kyrios* of the *kosmos*, sovereign of the universe, what is given to the church through him is in substance no different from what is offered to the world. The believing community is the new world on the way."[53] The fact that Jesus is both Creator of the universe as preexistent Son and Redeemer of the world as incarnate Son contradicts the idea of a dual ethic. "One set of principles" underlies "the natural order . . . and the redemptive order."[54] Reformed thinker David A. Hoekema makes the same point, noting that "Jesus Christ is the Lord not just of the church, nor of a special sphere of religious activity, but of all of the natural and human world." He concludes that if Jesus did call his followers to renounce all killing, that norm applies to everyone.[55] Finally,

49. Loewen, *One Lord, One Church*, 80.
50. For this and the next point, see Yoder's discussion in *Christian Witness to the State*, 71.
51. Hauerwas, "Pacifism," 102.
52. Yoder, *For the Nations*, 158–59.
53. Yoder, *For the Nations*, 50.
54. Schertz, "Partners in God's Passion," 172.
55. Hoekema, "Practical Christian Pacifism," 918.

rejecting all killing even for the sake of trying to promote societal peace and justice is God's will for all Christians, indeed all people, or it is not God's will for anyone.[56]

Biblical pacifism rests on several central theological affirmations. If the historic creeds are correct that Jesus is truly God and truly human, then rejecting Jesus's teaching on loving enemies involves fundamental christological heresy. Only if Jesus rose bodily from the dead does it make sense to claim that we should still believe that his messianic kingdom has truly begun and his followers should and can live the ethics of his dawning kingdom. It is true that the New Testament teaches that Christ's kingdom is not yet here in its fullness. But nowhere does the New Testament conclude that therefore Christians should postpone living Jesus's kingdom ethics until the returning Christ brings the completion of the kingdom. On the contrary, the New Testament repeatedly insists that Christians should not be conformed to the patterns of the fallen world (Rom. 12:1–2). To do that, to be sure, we need the loving support of the church, Jesus's new messianic community. Lacking that communal support and the empowering presence of the Holy Spirit, non-Christians will frequently not succeed in living Jesus's ethic, including his call to love enemies. But they should.

56. See Yoder's vigorous argument at the beginning of *The Priestly Kingdom* that his arguments "do not describe a Mennonite vision. They describe a biblically rooted call to faith, addressed to Mennonites or Zwinglians, to Lutherans or Catholics, to unbelievers or other-believers" (8).

8

Problems with Pacifism

Many people, indeed many Christians, have sharply criticized Christians who claim that Jesus did not ever want his disciples to kill. Pacifists, it is charged, have no love for neighbor. They take no responsibility for history, ignoring their obligation to move society toward justice and peace. They have an unrealistic, optimistic view of human nature. In short, they are naive idealists, selfish cowards, and reprehensible free riders benefiting from social order that they refuse to help create.

Failing to Love the Neighbor

In the introduction, I noted C. S. Lewis's famous question, "Does anyone suppose . . . that if a homicidal maniac, attempting to murder a third party, tried to knock me out of the way, I must stand aside and let him get his victim?"[1] Or as Jean Bethke Elshtain asks, "If our neighbor is being slaughtered, do we stand by and do nothing?"[2] The prominent fourth-century Christian leader Ambrose of Milan insisted that "he who does not keep harm off a friend, if he can, is as much in fault as he who causes it."[3]

Pacifists, it is claimed, turn their neighbor's cheek to the oppressor.[4] They are selfish cowards afraid to defend a neighbor under attack. In fact, they are

1. Lewis, *Weight of Glory*, 86.
2. Elshtain, *Just War*, 51.
3. Ambrose, *Of the Duties of Clergy* 1.36.179; quoted in Johnson, *Quest for Peace*, 55. Cf. K. B. Payne and K. I. Payne, *Just Defense*, 70.
4. Cromartie, *Peace Betrayed?*, 147.

"free riders." They benefit from the peace and social order that others (e.g., the police and military) provide but make no positive contribution to that order.[5] Pacifists let others "do the dirty work." "Why should we assume that *someone else* will protect our homes and bank accounts, offer security to our public buildings, guard our cities and borders . . . ?"[6] Daryl Charles is surely right: "We may not in good conscience expect that *others* be required to officiate, adjudicate, protect or provide for social benefits and privileges in a free society in which we are not willing to participate and yet from which we expect to receive privileges."[7]

This is clearly a serious charge. Pacifist ethicist John Howard Yoder has said that this is "the one serious argument . . . to justify participation in war."[8] But I think there are significant, decisive things to say in reply.

First and perhaps most important, this argument assumes that there are only two options: do nothing to defend the neighbor or use lethal weapons. Gandhi famously remarked that if those are the only two options, then of course one should kill to resist evil.

In reality, however, it is simply false to suggest that there are only two options. Always, in every situation, there is a third option: vigorous nonviolent resistance to the aggressor. As in the case of war, there is no guarantee that nonviolent resistance will succeed in the short run. But the history of the past one hundred, and especially the past fifty, years demonstrates clearly that nonviolent resistance often does succeed in defeating injustice and increasing societal shalom.[9] Martin Luther King Jr.'s nonviolent civil rights movement dramatically reduced structural racism in the United States. Gandhi's nonviolent campaign for Indian independence eventually prevailed against the British Empire.

Nor is it the case that nonviolent resistance works only in democracies and with "humane" imperialists like the British (the British actually mercilessly slaughtered hundreds of Gandhi's nonviolent marchers). A massive nonviolent campaign successfully overthrew the longtime Filipino dictator Ferdinand Marcos—a result many thought only a devastating, decade-long civil war could achieve. In 1989, Solidarity in Poland and the "revolution of the candles" in East Germany successfully used nonviolent action to bring an end to communist dictators. A daring nonviolent campaign of Christian and Muslim women eventually forced the vicious dictator President Charles Taylor

5. Allman, *Who Would Jesus Kill?*, 97.
6. Charles and Demy, *War, Peace, and Christianity*, 274 (italics original).
7. Charles, *Between Pacifism and Jihad*, 92 (italics original).
8. Yoder, *Original Revolution*, 80.
9. See the numerous examples cited in Sider, *Nonviolent Action*, and the literature cited there.

of Liberia to step aside. In the "Arab Spring" of 2011, nonviolent campaigns in Tunisia and Egypt forced long-serving, violent dictators to step down.[10]

It is simply contrary to historical fact to say that "Gandhi's method is powerless and inefficacious against tyranny as we have known it in the last century."[11] Numerous historical examples disprove the claim that "there are no cases" in which nonviolent action has caused "a tyrant to cease and desist from his oppressive deeds."[12] A recent scholarly volume by Erica Chenoweth and Maria J. Stephan explores all the known cases (323) of major *armed* and *unarmed* insurrections from 1900 to 2006. The conclusion? "Nonviolent resistance campaigns were nearly twice as likely to achieve full or partial success as their violent counterparts."[13] Furthermore, nonviolent campaigns were far more likely to lead to democratic results and avoid future societal conflict than violent campaigns. Chenoweth and Stephan have discovered that "the probability that a country will be a democracy five years after a campaign ends is 57 percent among successful nonviolent campaigns but less than 6 percent for successful violent campaigns."[14]

A comparison of the casualties in Algeria's violent campaign for independence and India's nonviolent campaign reveals a striking difference. India's nonviolent struggle for independence from the British took longer (twenty-eight years, 1919–47) than Algeria's violent victory over French colonialism (eight years, 1954–62). But only eight thousand Indians died, whereas a million Algerians lost their lives. Even more staggering is the comparison of the numbers of dead with total population figures. Of India's three hundred million, only one in four hundred thousand died. Of Algeria's ten million, one in ten was sacrificed.[15]

Recent history demonstrates that nonviolent resistance to tyranny and injustice often succeeds and also that more and more Christians (and others) are exploring new nonviolent ways to resist evil. In addition, major church bodies have recently called for more use of nonviolent methods. The official public policy document of the National Association of Evangelicals says, "As followers of Jesus, we should, in our civic capacity, work to reduce conflict by promoting international understanding and engaging in nonviolent

10. See Sider, *Nonviolent Action*, chaps. 2, 5, 6, 7, 8, 9.
11. Charles, *Between Pacifism and Jihad*, 102.
12. Charles, *Between Pacifism and Jihad*, 99.
13. Chenoweth and Stephan, *Why Civil Resistance Works*, 7.
14. Chenoweth and Stephan, *Why Civil Resistance Works*, 213–14. See further the support of other similar studies cited in Sider, *Nonviolent Action*, 160n8.
15. Wink, *Violence and Nonviolence*, 41–42. In *A History of Warfare*, John Keegan notes that today the Algerian government says that one million people died, out of a prewar Muslim population of nine million (55). That would mean the ratio is 1:9, not 1:10.

conflict resolution." A joint statement by the Vatican's Pontifical Council for Promoting Christian Unity and the Mennonite World Conference sought to promote more use of nonviolence in the resolution of domestic and international disputes.[16]

C. S. Lewis, Bishop Ambrose, and others are right. It is immoral to stand aside and do nothing when evil people oppress and destroy our neighbors (near and far). People who believe that Jesus calls them to refuse to kill must take the lead in developing new, better, and more vigorous forms of nonviolent resistance to evil. Unless they are ready to risk death as soldiers do in nonviolent campaigns against injustice and oppression, their claim to follow Jesus's way of peacemaking is a farce. But as they do embrace nonviolent resistance to evil, they demonstrate that in every historical injustice, there are not just two options, but three. One can do nothing, kill, or resist nonviolently. The first option is immoral. The second, I believe, is not what Jesus taught. And the third is both faithful to Jesus and (as history shows) often successful.[17]

A second response to the charge that pacifists fail to love their neighbor is that the argument seems to move within the logic of general human thinking rather than the logic of Jesus's dawning messianic kingdom. There is nothing specifically Christian about the argument.[18] But we have seen that the basic logic of Christian ethics is that Jesus's messianic kingdom has already begun and Jesus's disciples are called and empowered by the Holy Spirit to live *now* the norms of Jesus's new kingdom. And that includes loving even enemies. That in no way means ignoring one's responsibility to nurture peace and justice in society. But it does mean that one should refuse to use methods that Jesus forbids to seek to improve society or prevent evil. It also means that one has a clear distinction between the church and the world. The church transformed by divine grace can and should follow Jesus's kingdom norms even though the sinful world regularly does not.

A third response to the charge that pacifists fail to love their neighbor is that too often, people making this charge forget that, according to Jesus, the neighbor Christians must love includes the enemy. Both the evil person attacking my neighbor and the neighbor under attack are neighbors Jesus calls me to love.[19] That is not to ignore the moral distinction between an evil aggressor and a relatively innocent neighbor under attack. But both are

16. For the sources, see Sider, *Nonviolent Action*, 164 (and all of 162–66).

17. I do not, however, mean to argue that the primary reason for using nonviolence is the evidence that it often succeeds. I advocate the use of nonviolence first of all because it is faithful to Jesus's teaching.

18. See Yoder, *Original Revolution*, 80–84.

19. See Hauerwas, "Pacifism," 100.

persons whom God loves and calls me to love. It is true that just war proponents like Augustine argue that one can love enemies even as one kills them.
But that argument sounds highly questionable at best.[20] And it is certainly
not the case that one can call on "enemies" to repent and accept Christ as
one kills them. However, one can certainly do that when one uses vigorous
nonviolent resistance. In nonviolent resistance, one can at the same time both
resist the evil person and love that person as neighbor.

Failure to Take Responsibility for History

In a variety of ways, many people accuse pacifists of abandoning their obligation to shape history in ways that promote peace and justice. Nigel Biggar
charges that prominent Christian pacifists John Howard Yoder and Stanley
Hauerwas abandon any attempt to control history and give the impression
that they do not care about what happens in society.[21] Reinhold Niebuhr
charges pacifists with a "tendency toward social irresponsibility."[22] Oxford
ethicist and just war advocate Oliver O'Donovan says that "non-violence,
non-resistance and all the other great watchwords of pacifism evoke a set of
limits which circumscribe the possibility of action in the world."[23] Pacifism,
it is charged, pays no attention to consequences.[24] Christian pacifism, James
Turner Johnson asserts, is grounded in the view that "only in separation
from the affairs of the secular world could Christianity be true to itself."[25]
Daryl Charles and Timothy J. Demy claim that Anabaptist pacifists "not
only abstain from political involvement and embrace nonviolence, but also
abstain from all forms of civil service and most forms of public service."[26]
And that includes, they say, vocations like economics, social service, law, and
legal theory.[27]

It is certainly correct that faithful Christians dare not withdraw from society. Precisely because their Lord commands them to love *all* their neighbors,

20. Especially when Augustine argues that what really matters is one's inner attitude. See
chap. 9, "Can We Truly Love Our Enemies and Kill Them at the Same Time?"

21. Biggar, *In Defence of War*, 330. Jeffrey Stout charges that Stanley Hauerwas fails to
promote American democracy. Grimsrud, "Anabaptist Faith and 'National Security,'" 317–18.

22. Davis and Good, *Niebuhr on Politics*, 142.

23. O'Donovan, *Just War Revisited*, 10. Below we will see that Oliver O'Donovan's own just
war position sets "limits which circumscribe . . . action in the world."

24. Weigel, *Tranquillitas Ordinis*, 247.

25. Johnson, *Quest for Peace*, 51. See also Shannon, *War or Peace?*, 33.

26. Charles and Demy, *War, Peace, and Christianity*, 145.

27. Charles and Demy, *War, Peace, and Christianity*, 145n179. See below for evidence that
this charge is plainly false.

they must seek to promote the societal well-being of everyone. Paul insists that Christians must "do good to all people," not just Christians (Gal. 6:10). Jesus did not withdraw from society. He challenged religious leaders (Matt. 23:1–39) and political leaders (Luke 13:31–33). And it was precisely his public act of nonviolent civil disobedience in overthrowing the money changers' tables in the temple that, according to Mark's Gospel, moved the religious leaders to look for a way to kill him (Mark 11:15–18). Jesus ended up on the cross precisely because he challenged the societal rulers of his day.[28] "If God is the kind of God-active-in-history of whom the Bible speaks, then concern for the cause of history is itself not an illegitimate or an irrelevant concern."[29] Catholic just war ethicist George Weigel is right: a rejection of killing "without a parallel commitment to civic responsibility—without a concrete expression of one's commitment to work for the peace of the political community—is not pacifism, but anarchism."[30]

The crucial question, however, is this: Do Jesus's kingdom teaching and ethics provide the norms for *how* one exercises social responsibility, or does one look elsewhere for those norms? If one believes, as the early Christians did, that Jesus is Lord of history, that his messianic kingdom has already begun, and that Jesus's disciples are now called to live according to the norms of that dawning kingdom, which will eventually prevail throughout the universe, then faithful Christians dare not abandon Jesus's teaching in order to exercise "responsible" concern for society. They dare not, with Niebuhr, say "yes, Jesus, you teach unconditional love, but that does not work in the real world, so we must ignore and abandon what you taught." Faithful Christians will work for societal well-being in every way that is faithful to Jesus's teaching, but they will insist that there are some things that they simply will not do. Human calculation of short-term effectiveness dare not overrule Jesus's ethical norms.

Nor are pacifists the only people who make this point. Just war theorists also argue that there are some things Christian morals forbid them from doing, even if that means military defeat. O'Donovan insists that following just war principles means that there are some things one must not do (e.g., intentionally targeting civilians), even if that means accepting defeat. O'Donovan says that "when self-defense, of state, community or individual, has the last word, paganism is restored." Just war criteria "cannot possibly issue a license to

---

28. Friesen, "In Search of Security," 49.

29. Yoder, *Politics of Jesus*, 232. By the title *For the Nations*, and repeatedly in that book, Yoder insists on the importance of pacifist Christians working for peace and justice in society. Yoder, *For the Nations*, 1–6, 20–36, and elsewhere.

30. Weigel, *Tranquillitas Ordinis*, 345.

avoid defeat by all possible means."[31] Similarly, Daniel M. Bell Jr. argues that
the just war criteria sometimes justify Christian participation in warfare but
at other times demand refusing "to fight in the first place or to surrender once
the fighting is under way."[32] Although careful application of the just war criteria will sometimes lead faithful Christians to fight, Bell insists that "the first
and overriding concern with regard to matters of war is the Church's faithful
following of Jesus Christ."[33] Both pacifists and just war Christians agree that
there are some things Jesus's teaching forbids, and this means that they will
not do those things, even if that means defeat, even martyrdom at the hands
of a vicious foe.[34] So for both groups, the crucial question is not short-term
"effectiveness" or survival but rather what Jesus taught.

Prominent just war ethicist Paul Ramsey has argued that people like himself
and Niebuhr should withdraw the charge that pacifists are "irresponsible"
and "ineffective." He acknowledges that *the future is radically unpredictable*, for pacifist and just warrior alike."[35] Neither can adequately predict the
consequences of their actions. And Ramsey recognizes that pacifists do many
things that promote societal well-being.

Thus both those who embrace pacifism and those who affirm just war
criteria (at least all who like O'Donovan refuse to lapse into "paganism")
agree that short-term calculations of effectiveness dare not be the ultimate
norm.[36] Obedience to Jesus's teaching must be all Christians' first ethical
obligation. Second, of course, pacifists insist that careful analysis of effectiveness is entirely appropriate. Yoder insists that "to follow Jesus does not
mean renouncing effectiveness."[37] Because faithfulness to Jesus must be our
highest priority, Christians refuse to do everything that a human calculation
of short-term effectiveness might demand. But the Christian who knows that
Jesus is truly Lord of history does not therefore conclude that "we don't care
about planning, thinking, analyzing. . . . No! We do need to think about

31. O'Donovan, *Just War Revisited*, 7–8.
32. Bell, *Just War as Christian Discipleship*, 241.
33. Bell, *Just War as Christian Discipleship*, 20.
34. See also Yoder's discussion of this point and his citation of Paul Ramsey and John Court-
ney Murray in Yoder, *When War Is Unjust*, 64–67.
35. Ramsey and Hauerwas, *Speak Up*, 120–23 (italics original). Yoder makes the same point,
using Reinhold Niebuhr's work on the "irony" of history, noting that "when people try to
manage history, it almost always turns out to have taken another direction." Yoder, *Politics
of Jesus*, 230.
36. See Koontz's comments in "Response: Pacifism, Just War, and Realism," 223–25.
37. Yoder, *Politics of Jesus*, 246. On occasion, however, Yoder seems to question a concern for
effectiveness (230). See Friesen, "Power," 88–90. But Mark Thiessen Nation argues persuasively
that Yoder never rejected a concern for effectiveness. Nation, *John Howard Yoder*, 145–88.

mechanisms, causality, probabilities."[38] But we do all that within the larger framework of the knowledge that since Jesus is truly Lord of the universe, following his ethical demands will also be effective in the long run because they fit with the nature of reality. "For those who confess the Lamb that was slain as risen Lord worthy to receive power, there can be no ultimate need to choose between suffering love and social effectiveness."[39]

Furthermore, even in the short run, nonviolence is often effective. One can point to Gandhi in India, King in the United States, and Walesa's Solidarity in Poland to show that nonviolence often works.[40] King, Gandhi, the nonviolent protestors who overthrew the Filipino dictator Ferdinand Marcos, and many others have been politically relevant and very successful.[41] In fact, as we saw earlier, a careful study of the most important violent and nonviolent movements in the past one hundred years shows that nonviolent campaigns succeeded more often than violent ones.[42] Yoder concludes that nonviolent campaigns "can be effective politically; i.e., they can work even when their bearers do not avow their historic derivation from Jesus" because they fit with "the grain of the universe."[43] Sometimes, of course, nonviolent struggles fail in the short run. But "in the long run faithfulness and effectiveness ultimately converge"—precisely because Jesus is truly Lord of history.[44] If faithfulness and effectiveness do not ultimately converge, then our Christian conviction that Jesus is truly Lord is false.

Another aspect of the charge that pacifists abandon the attempt to shape society is that they simply withdraw into their little sectarian community and ignore the larger world. It is true that sometimes pacifists have done this—often, alas, in response to severe societal persecution. But the historical record flatly contradicts any suggestion that pacifists always do this. All social scientists know that one changes society not only from the top down but also from the bottom up.[45] Simply living wholesome family life contributes to society. So does creating new economic enterprises and educational institutions.

Mennonites (who often have been pointed to as examples of pacifists who neglect their obligation to shape the larger society) have contributed to societal well-being in numerous ways.[46] Mennonite doctors and mental health

38. Yoder, *For the Nations*, 150.
39. Yoder, *Nonviolence*, 38.
40. Yoder, *War of the Lamb*, 178.
41. See the many examples in Sider, *Nonviolent Action*.
42. See in this chap. under "Failing to Love the Neighbor."
43. Yoder, *War of the Lamb*, 178–79.
44. Friesen, "In Search of Security," 50.
45. Friesen, "In Search of Security," 53.
46. See all of Friesen and Schlabach, *At Peace and Unafraid*, esp. 84–87.

workers have helped improve mental health practices. Mennonite Central Committee's excellent programs in relief and community development have saved and improved the lives of millions around the world. Mennonite specialists in conflict resolution, like Notre Dame professor John Paul Lederach, have pioneered new ways of resolving societal conflict.[47] Mennonite-initiated Christian Peacemaker Teams have pioneered methods of nonviolent accompaniment in situations of violent conflict.[48] Mennonites have pioneered Victim-Offender Reconciliation Programs that go beyond legal procedures to bring deeper reconciliation between offender and victim.[49] Thousands of Mennonite doctors, lawyers, educators, and agricultural specialists contribute daily to societal well-being.[50]

Undoubtedly, the most striking Anabaptist contribution to the larger society has been their pioneering of religious freedom and their contribution to democracy.[51] They died by the hundreds in the sixteenth century for their insistence that the church should be able to run its own affairs free from control by the state. Slowly their demand for religious freedom prevailed—first in Holland, then England and the new United States. Today all (non-Muslim) countries at least theoretically embrace religious freedom for all citizens.

The Anabaptists' championing of religious freedom illustrates the fact that simply creating an alternative society can have a profound political impact. Karl Barth argues that the common life of the church is "the decisive contribution which the Christian community can make to the upbuilding and work and maintenance of the civil [order]."[52] In several places, Yoder argues that the common life of the church has contributed enormously to societal well-being. The early Christian inclusion of Jews *and* gentiles, men *and* women, slaves *and* free in Christ's one body promoted an egalitarian perspective. Jesus's radical call to forgiveness points to what Hannah Arendt recognizes as an essential element of societal wholeness.[53] The dramatic economic sharing in the early church modeled a new concern for economic well-being for everyone. And the worship practice of the early church, where everyone was allowed to speak, provided the egalitarian idea that everyone has gifts to share.[54]

"Hospitals" and schools for the poor emerged out of the work of the church. In the Middle Ages, Christians, especially in the monasteries, took the

47. Lederach, *Building Peace*.
48. See Sider, *Nonviolent Action*, 146–51.
49. Zehr, *Changing Lenses*. See also introduction to chap. 11 in the present book.
50. See Friesen, *Artists, Citizens, Philosophers*; Sampson and Lederach, *From the Ground Up*.
51. Grimsrud, "Anabaptist Faith and 'National Security,'" 315.
52. Barth, *Church Dogmatics*, IV/2, 721; quoted in Yoder, *For the Nations*, 27.
53. Arendt, *Human Condition*, 238–43.
54. Yoder, *For the Nations*, 29–33, 43–50. See also Arendt, *On Violence*.

lead in caring for the sick. The first "Sunday schools" in England developed when Christians decided that even uneducated poor children working six days a week should receive some basic education in reading and arithmetic on Sunday. Slowly, the larger society came to embrace universal health care and education as a right.[55]

One of the more important contributions to recent thinking about peace-making has been made by a group of Christian ethicists—both pacifists and just war advocates—in a book called *Just Peacemaking: The New Paradigm for the Ethics of Peace and War*.[56] In spite of ongoing disagreement about whether war is sometimes necessary, they agree that the ten nonviolent practices they outline have and can promote a more peaceful world. Many pacifist scholars contributed to this significant development.

The evidence is clear. Not only should Christians who oppose all killing work for the well-being of society. They do. They should also seek to take responsibility for history in every way that is faithful to Jesus.

Is Pacifism Based on a Naive View of Human Nature?

Many Christians claim that pacifism is based on a naive view of human nature. It is a central argument in Niebuhr's famous essay "Why the Christian Church Is Not Pacifist." "Most modern forms of Christian pacifism are heretical. . . . They have really absorbed the Renaissance faith in the goodness of man, [and] have rejected the Christian doctrine of original sin as an outmoded bit of pessimism."[57] Weigel says that religious pacifists tend to "minimize the abiding fact of sin and brokenness in the world."[58] So too J. Daryl Charles: "Pacifists tend to underestimate—if not disavow—the extent to which sin introduces conflict into the world."[59] And even more sweepingly Loraine Boettner says, "Most pacifists ignore completely the Scripture's teaching that we enter this world members of a fallen race. They assume rather that human nature is inherently good."[60]

The first thing to say about this charge is that it is true of some pacifists. Mahatma Gandhi, Leo Tolstoy, and some Quakers have embraced an un-biblically optimistic view of human nature. The famous nineteenth-century

55. Larsen, "When Did Sunday Schools Start?"
56. Stassen, *Just Peacemaking*.
57. Reprinted in Holmes, *War and Christian Ethics*, 303.
58. Weigel, "Five Theses for a Pacifist Reformation," 74. Also Allman, *Who Would Jesus Kill?*, 254.
59. Charles, *Between Pacifism and Jihad*, 105.
60. Boettner, *Christian Attitude toward War*, 41.

Unitarian pacifist William Ellery Channing naively claimed that the world is progressing, year by year, closer and closer to blissful shalom.[61] Niebuhr rightly charged the theologically liberal pacifists of his day with embracing a naive, optimistic view of human nature.[62]

But there are many other pacifists who embrace a biblical understanding of the depth and persistence of human sin. Prominent pacifists like Hauerwas and Yoder do not ground their thinking in a naive view of human goodness. The pacifism promoted in this book is based on the center of historic Christian orthodoxy, including the theological conviction that since the fall, all persons have a pervasive inclination to selfishness. Only the liberating power of the Holy Spirit can transform self-centered sinners into persons capable of beginning to truly love their enemies. Biblical pacifism is grounded in supernatural grace, not natural human goodness.

Even while enjoying the presence of the Holy Spirit, Christians never achieve perfection in this life. But they know that they have been called *and empowered* to begin to live now the ethics of Jesus's dawning kingdom. With Paul, they know that sin still lurks within them, but they also know that Paul never argued that because sin still lingers in the Christian, it is acceptable to fornicate, lie, and steal. Why, then, should we argue that the persistence of sin even in Christians would justify ignoring Jesus's clear call to love our enemies?

Another aspect of human sinfulness is relevant here. There is a questionable logic in the suggestion that since all persons are deeply sinful, war is inevitable.

> The generalization from sin to war as a necessary and permanent component of the fabric of human history fails to ask whether the general condition of sinfulness must express itself in war. For example, crime and physical violence are expressions of human sinfulness. Although theologically we would say all humans are sinners, most persons do not express their sinfulness in a life of crime or physical violence. These expressions of sinfulness occur *under certain conditions*. The key question, then, is, what are the conditions under which human sinfulness expresses itself in the institution of warfare? Slavery, dueling, lynching, vigilantism, and war are expressions of human sin under certain conditions. . . . If war is resorted to only under certain conditions within the international system, then we ought to determine what those conditions are and seek to create such conditions that war cannot or will not occur.[63]

61. Channing, *Discourses on War*, 45–71; see Hershberger, *War, Peace, and Nonresistance*, 177.
62. Even a recent book by Catholic ethicist Joseph J. Fahey lists as number one (in his summary of the key points of the pacifist model): "Human beings are naturally peaceful." Fahey, *War and the Christian Conscience*, 66.
63. Friesen, *Christian Peacemaking*, 42 (italics original).

This is not to claim that it will be possible to eliminate all war. But it does mean that the mere fact that all persons are sinners does not mean that warfare happens everywhere constantly. It is more likely to happen in certain circumstances rather than others, and sinful persons have the freedom to make choices that reduce the likelihood of it happening.

For centuries, people assumed that slavery was a necessary part of sinful human civilization. Then economics and societal thinking changed, and most societies outlawed slavery. Two centuries ago, dueling was an accepted way for (sinful) gentlemen to resolve a dispute. Today the same sinners normally resolve disputes nonviolently through the courts. That is not to claim that people today are less sinful than persons of earlier centuries. But the form that sinfulness takes has changed. The right kind of societal changes might very well dramatically reduce the amount of warfare in the world. At the very least, it is simply the case that the fact of universal sinfulness does not mean that the level of warfare in the twentieth or early twenty-first century is inevitable.

In an interesting essay, David A. Hoekema, a philosopher in the Christian Reformed tradition, shows how the issue of pervasive human sinfulness might also support a pacifist position.

> Realism about human nature cuts two ways: if it undermines a pacifism based on optimism, it also undermines the assumption that weapons of destruction and violence intended to restrain evil will be used only for that purpose. The reality of human sinfulness means that the instruments we intend to use for good are certain to be turned to evil purposes as well. There is therefore a strong presumption for using those means of justice that are least likely to be abused and least likely to cause irrevocable harm when they are abused. An army trained and equipped for national defense can quickly become an army of conquest or a tool of repression in the hands of an unprincipled leader. But a nonviolent national defense force, or a peacekeeping force bringing together citizens of a dozen nations, is of little use except for its intended purpose.[64]

History is full of evidence that very frequently—probably almost always— tribal or nationalistic fervor sweeps vast numbers of people into joining every war that their leaders declare. Very seldom have Christians been able to apply the just war criteria in ways that have led them to refuse to fight their tribe's or nation's wars.[65] Unthinking sinful tribalism and nationalism overwhelm thoughtful moral analysis. Given this almost universal way that sinful persons

64. Hoekema, "Practical Christian Pacifism," 918.
65. See chap. 9, "Have the Just War Criteria Prevented or Stopped Wars?," for a more detailed discussion of this point.

irrationally and enthusiastically join their group's wars, it may very well be that a general moral teaching against all killing would be a more realistic fit with sinful human nature.

Biblical pacifists remember that Christ said there will be wars and rumors of wars until his return. And they also know that ongoing pervasive human sinfulness is the ultimate explanation. But they know as well that sinfulness does not make inevitable a particular frequency of warfare. The right human action could reduce it dramatically. And the most important action would be for Christians to decide to follow Christ's command not to kill and instead engage in persistent nonviolent challenge to all injustice. If all Christians chose to do that, many would suffer. But the amount of killing and warfare in the world would almost certainly decrease dramatically.

Biblical pacifists love their neighbors—even engaging in daring acts of nonviolent intervention to protect their neighbors from injustice and harm. Biblical pacifists eagerly seek to move toward greater shalom, but they refuse to use methods that Jesus prohibited. And biblical pacifists take sin very seriously, but they also know that the transforming presence of the risen Lord in their lives enables them to love their enemies.

9

Problems with Just War Thinking

Along with the challenges posed to pacifism, which we discussed in the prior chapter, difficult challenges have also been posed to those who embrace the just war stance. How can one kill a person and at the same time fulfill Christ's mandate to invite that person to accept Christ? How can one obey Christ's command to love one's enemies while one is killing them? Have the just war criteria actually been applied to real life in a way that has prevented or ended war? And since it cannot be the case that both sides in a battle are fighting a just war, why have almost no Christians not only refused to fight for their nation but instead also have chosen to fight on the other side when their nation fought unjustly? And since Christian just war theorists argue that Christians should refuse to fight unjust wars, why have they not established structures to help Christians make that determination and not made it a priority to demand legal protection for conscientious objectors to particular wars? What should one conclude from the fact that for centuries, just war Christians have regularly fought and killed other Christians?

Many charge that pacifists ignore the Old Testament. But do not key just war criteria (e.g., noncombatant immunity) also contradict clear Old Testament commands to destroy all men, women, and children? And given the historical fact that human sinfulness and uncritical nationalism almost always lead Christians to embrace whatever war their nation declares, does the just war framework depend on a naively optimistic view of human goodness?

131

Finally, is it really possible to predict the outcome of going to war with enough accuracy to meet the just war criterion that the good results of going to war outweigh the bad results?

Can One Evangelize and Kill a Person at the Same Time?

Jesus's last command to all his followers is to go and make disciples of "all nations" (Matt. 28:19). Christ calls all Christians to seek in appropriate loving ways to share the gospel with all persons they meet and invite them to accept Christ.[1] Can one really do that while one is killing another person? Hans-Werner Bartsch says, "The question whether waging war against an enemy can be proclamation of the gospel to that enemy is the most urgent question for any Christian before and during a war."[2]

I do not see how it is possible to seek to kill people and at the same time be engaged in inviting them to accept Christ. One can constrain another person physically, one can boycott another person's unjust activity, one can confront another person in vigorous nonviolent action and at the same time express genuine love for the person and invite them to accept the gospel. But seeking to kill the other person is not compatible with demonstrating Christ's love for them as one invites them to accept the gospel. In addition, killing that person ends that person's historical opportunity to accept Christ.[3] In an article in *Christianity Today*, Myron Augsburger says that "from an evangelical perspective, it may be said that whenever a Christian participates in war, he has abdicated his responsibility to the greater calling of . . . evangelism."[4]

Can We Truly Love Our Enemies and Kill Them at the Same Time?

Augustine and Ambrose (late fourth century, early fifth century)—the earliest Christian theologians to somewhat systematically develop the just war tradition—sought to argue that it is possible to love enemies as one kills them. It is a measure of their attempt to be faithful to Jesus's teaching that both Augustine and Ambrose start their defense of Christian participation in warfare

---

1. That is not to say that one must include a verbal sharing of the gospel in every personal encounter. But it does mean a stance that hopes and prays that everyone one meets will become a Christian and that prays for the right (Spirit-prompted) time to speak of the gospel.
2. Bartsch, "Foundation and Meaning of Christian Pacifism," 192.
3. See Yoder, *What Would You Do?*, 39–40.
4. Augsburger, "Swords into Plowshares," 197. I would not call evangelism a "greater" or more important task than other missional obligations. See Sider, *Good News and Good Works*, chaps. 9, 10.

with Jesus's command to love one's enemies. Unlike Thomas Aquinas, who starts his thinking about just war with natural law, Augustine believes that Christians must and can love their enemies even as they sometimes kill them.[5] Out of love for a neighbor being attacked, out of loving concern to preserve or restore peace in society, Christians should sometimes kill. Jesus's command not to "resist evil" forbids killing an attacker in personal self-defense.[6] But one may kill to protect others. Augustine insists that it is an act of love to restore peace by using violence. It is even an act of love toward the aggressor. By this "kind harshness" an unjust aggressor may be helped to repent.[7]

It is interesting, however, that Augustine feels compelled to argue that Christians obey Christ's command to love their enemies even as they kill them, not as an outward act but as an "inward disposition." "If it is supposed that God could not enjoin warfare, because, in after times, it was said by the Lord Jesus Christ, 'I say unto you, that ye resist not evil, but if anyone strike thee on the right cheek, turn to him the left also,' the answer is that what is here required is *not a bodily action, but an inward disposition.*"[8] Daniel Bell says Augustine's principal example is Christ, who does not turn the other cheek when struck at his trial (John 18:22–23).[9] But Jesus at his trial is challenging an unjust action in a verbal, nonviolent way. That one can do that and still love the person hardly proves that one can love a person while one kills that person!

In a letter to Marcellinus, a Christian political leader who asked Augustine whether Jesus's teaching was compatible with being a good Roman citizen, Augustine replies that Jesus's teaching about loving enemies and turning the other cheek "ought to be always retained in the habitual discipline of the heart" and "fully cherished in the disposition." But that does not mean that Christians should not fight wars.[10]

To restrict Jesus's call to love enemies to the inner disposition of the heart seems to ignore the context of Jesus's teaching. Jesus is rejecting the violent action of devout Jewish revolutionaries who are calling on their fellow Jews to kill the Roman imperialists. Jesus, on the contrary, commands his disciples

---

5. See Cahill, *Love Your Enemies*, 14, 83.

6. Both Augustine and Ambrose insist on this; see Cahill, *Love Your Enemies*, 58–60.

7. Bell, *Just War as Christian Discipleship*, 31. Many other Christian just war theorists seek to ground justified war in Jesus's command to love enemies: Bell, *Just War as Christian Discipleship*, 31, 237; Biggar, *In Defence of War*, chap. 2; and Ramsey, *Basic Christian Ethics*, 12, 17–27, and elsewhere.

8. Augustine, *Reply to Faustus* 22.76 (see also 22.79); NPNF[1] 4:301 (italics added).

9. Bell, *Just War as Christian Discipleship*, 29 (see Augustine, *Letter 138 to Marcellinus* 2.13; NPNF[1] 1:485).

10. Augustine, *Letter 138 to Marcellinus* 2.14; NPNF[1] 1:485.

to love them—even to carry their bags a second mile. That is an external act, not just an inward disposition! In fact, all of Jesus's illustrations of what it means to love enemies rather than seek an eye for an eye involve external acts, not just inward dispositions. And all the Christian writers of the first three centuries who discuss killing say that following Christ means not just some loving inward disposition but refusing to kill anyone.[11]

Have the Just War Criteria Prevented or Stopped Wars?

The historical record demonstrates with painful clarity that the just war tradition has been very ineffective in preventing unjust warfare. There are very few historical instances where nations chose not to go to war because Christians in the government and/or army argued that the proposed war did not meet the criteria of the just war tradition. Christians have, with painfully few exceptions, defended their own nation's wars. They have condemned and then accepted every new escalation of military technology. And they have developed no mechanism independent of the state to evaluate the justice of specific wars. Obviously, failure to implement a theory does not necessarily invalidate it. But consistent, widespread failure should raise serious questions about its usefulness and prompt further consideration of its validity.[12]

History shows that the just war criteria are especially vulnerable to societal pressures of tribalism and jingoistic nationalism. This becomes clear when we look at the various ways just war theory has been applied in the past.

On the basis of the just war tradition, it would seem that at least one side in each conflict is fighting for an unjust cause. Yet in both world wars and in the hundreds of European battles in previous centuries, Christians fought on both sides. If the just war tradition had functioned effectively, the Christians fighting on the wrong side should frequently have realized their country's injustice and opposed their nation's military activities.[13] The acid test of be-

11. See chap. 13, "Pre-Constantinian Christianity." Nigel Biggar (*In Defence of War*, chap. 2) seeks to support the claim that soldiers can love enemies even while they kill them. He cites a number of stories of soldiers who restrain their passions and remember that the enemy also has value. These cases, he concludes, provide empirical evidence that soldiers can love their enemies even as they seek to kill them.

12. Even ardent just war advocates like J. Daryl Charles and Timothy J. Demy acknowledge that Christians have often (e.g. in the crusades, Wars of Religion) not applied the just war criteria properly; Charles and Demy, *War, Peace, and Christianity*, 20.

13. I find Oliver O'Donovan's response to this argument puzzling. He says the just war tradition was never intended to tell people whether their own side was in the right. And he adds that "war can be ostensibly just on both sides." Sider and O'Donovan, *Peace and War*, 12. See also O'Donovan's rejection of the idea that just war theory was supposed to "*validate* or *invalidate*

lief in the just war tradition would seem to be a willingness to fight *against* one's country when it fights unjust wars.[14] Apart from isolated individuals, however, there are very few examples of even effective verbal opposition, much less enlistment in the army of the enemy.

The German church's response to Hitler underlines this failure. If allied opposition to Hitler is the classic example of a just war, then Hitler's attacks provide the classic example of an unjust war. What did German Christians do? Only a tiny minority opposed Hitler.

After a careful study of the German Catholic response to Hitler, Gordon Zahn shows that "German Catholics with but the rarest of exceptions did support the Hitler war effort."[15] At the very beginning of the war (September 1939), the German Catholic bishops said at their national meeting that they intended "to encourage and exhort our Catholic soldiers to do their duty in obedience to the Führer, ready for sacrifice and with the commitment of the whole being."[16] In 1941 the combined South German (Bavarian) hierarchy urged each Catholic "to fulfill his duty fully and willingly and loyally" and "to devote your full efforts to the service of the *Vaterland* [fatherland] and the precious *Heimat* [homeland]."[17] A prominent German Catholic theologian wrote a pamphlet urging Catholics *not* to raise the question of the just war. The question of the justice of the war, he argued, could only be answered "scientifically" after the war when all documents were available. Therefore, each individual should "do his best with faith in the cause of his *Volk* [nation]."[18]

Christians at other times and places have not been much more discerning in the heat of national conflict. In *The Origin and Development of the Moral Ideas*, Edward Westermarck says of Protestants: "It would be impossible to find a single instance of a war waged by a Protestant country from any motive,

---

particular wars." O'Donovan, *Just War Revisited*, 13 (italics original). That disagreements between nations are complex and that honest people sometimes come to contradictory conclusions are obviously true. But if this complexity means that it is regularly impossible to apply the just war criteria in a way that truly helps Christians decide whether proposed or actual wars are just and therefore whether they should support or oppose them, then I fail to see how the just war tradition is useful.

14. Kirk, *Theology Encounters Revolution*, 152.

15. Zahn, "Case for Christian Dissent," 120.

16. Quoted in Zahn, *German Catholics*, 64.

17. Zahn, "Case for Christian Dissent," 121.

18. Zahn, "Case for Christian Dissent," 128. In spite of the small confessing church and individuals like Dietrich Bonhoeffer, German Protestants did little better. See, e.g., the statements of support for Hitler made by a leading Protestant bishop quoted in Duchrow, *Lutheran Churches*, 266.

to which the bulk of its clergy have not given their sanction and support."[19]
The historian W. E. H. Lecky, in his *History of European Morals*, likewise
observes, "We may look in vain for any period since Constantine in which
the clergy, as a body, exerted themselves . . . to prevent or abridge a particular
war."[20] Perhaps the substantial Christian opposition to the American war in
Vietnam and to the American invasion of Iraq in 2003 are exceptions.

Even in the case of the classic illustration (World War II) of an unjust war,
the overwhelming majority of Christians did not faithfully apply the criteria
of the just war tradition. That raises serious questions about the usefulness
of the entire approach. Perhaps this consistent pattern of nationalistic ratio-
nalization suggests that the hope of faithfully applying just war criteria rests
on a naive view of human nature. Might consistent nonviolence be a more
realistic response to this essential human sinfulness?[21]

The church has also throughout history denounced and then accepted
each new advance in the methods of warfare. In the tenth to twelfth centuries, the more deadly crossbow gradually replaced the short bow. In
1139, the Second Lateran Council condemned the crossbow,[22] but Christians continued to use it. Christian opposition to gunpowder apparently
delayed its development in the West—but only for a time. When the first
submarine successfully torpedoed and drowned twenty-five hundred men,
people denounced it as a terrible crime—and "immediately set out to improve on it."[23]

When Germany first attacked the British civilian population in aerial raids,
British Christians denounced this gross immorality and vowed not to retaliate in kind. A prominent British churchman, Dr. J. H. Oldham, said in 1940,
"The deliberate killing of non-combatants is murder. If war degenerates into
willful slaughter of the innocent, Christians must either become pacifists or
give up their religion."[24] Three years later, he concluded that the line "between
attacks on military targets, on the one hand, and indiscriminate slaughter
and wanton destruction on the other" was of "secondary importance." The
government could choose whatever military necessity demanded.[25] Christian pilots participated in the allied firebombing of German cities, including
Dresden, where over one hundred thousand noncombatants perished in one

19. Cited in Rutenber, *Dagger and the Cross*, 90.
20. Cited in Rutenber, *Dagger and the Cross*, 90.
21. Kirk, *Theology Encounters Revolution*, 154.
22. Clark, *Does the Bible Teach Pacifism?*, 49.
23. Rutenber, *Dagger and the Cross*, 46.
24. Quoted in Macgregor, *Basis of Pacifism*, 95.
25. Quoted in Macgregor, *Basis of Pacifism*, 96.

day in a huge firestorm. Just war criteria about just means for fighting have often produced verbal objections to the development of new weapons. But they have almost never prevented either the development or use of whatever was technologically feasible.[26]

The widespread failure of just war Christians to embrace and implement selective conscientious objection is another aspect of the weakness of that tradition. The just war tradition assumes that at least some wars declared by rulers will be unjust. In those cases, Christians who follow the just war tradition should refuse to fight.[27] But only in more recent decades have just war theorists begun to have even a modest conversation about selective conscientious objection. Many democracies have laws allowing "conscientious objectors" (those who oppose *all* war) to choose alternative service. But hardly any nation has laws recognizing *selective* conscientious objection to particular wars. And just war Christians have invested very few resources to persuade governments to pass such laws—even though the just war criteria, if applied with any seriousness, would require frequent conscientious objection to particular wars.[28]

Nor is it enough for churches in the just war tradition to begin supporting selective conscientious objection to particular wars on the part of individual Christians. Surely this approach is too individualistic. The individual Christian needs the help and insight of other Christians in such complex issues. Within those churches that still accept the just war tradition, there ought to be a specific, well-developed mechanism for assembling the insight of ethicists, theologians, social scientists, and so on, to examine carefully the validity of possible wars that the nation might plausibly consider fighting.[29] Individual Christians, of course, would still need to reach their own personal conclusions. But decisions as weighty as war and peace require the collective wisdom of the corporate body of believers.

26. See also Yoder's discussion of how the modifications of the just war tradition (especially in the past fifty years) "have hollowed out the tradition to little more than a shell." Yoder, *When War Is Unjust*, 41.

27. See Bell's forceful argument for this in *Just War as Christian Discipleship*, 116–18.

28. Some churches did make some effort in 1971, testifying in favor of a proposed bill legalizing selective conscientious objection (Yoder, *When War Is Unjust*, 92). See also *National Services and the Military Profession*, a statement made in October 1970 by the American Lutheran Church. In 1968, the US Catholic bishops asked for selective conscientious objection to the draft. See Hunt, "Selective Conscientious Objection," 221. In their 1983 *The Challenge of Peace*, the US Catholic bishops called for legislation to respect selective conscientious objection (§233). For a recent discussion of selective conscientious objection, see Ellner, Robinson, and Whetham, *When Soldiers Say No*; and Clifford, "Legalizing Selective Conscientious Objection."

29. See the pointed comments in this regard by G. Schlabach, "Just Policing," 412–13.

The isolated individual needs help to understand complex issues and withstand nationalistic propaganda. Secular governments will always rationalize current plans and narrow national self-interest. Only if churches in the just war tradition develop sophisticated, functioning mechanisms for evaluating the validity of the wars their members may be called to fight will the just war tradition maintain credibility. The absence of such mechanisms is one measure of the failure of that tradition.

Just war ethicists argue that failure to successfully apply the just war criteria does not prove that the ethical stance is wrong.[30] Paul Ramsey has insisted that "failure to make just war *effective* in national policy formation, as well as failure to make a pacifism of nonviolence effective in national policy, is no argument against either."[31] It is certainly correct that human failure to faithfully apply an ethical position does not prove that the stance is a mistake. But the just war tradition has been the mainstream teaching of Christian thinkers for more than fifteen hundred years.[32] It has been the official way that most Christian leaders have argued that faithful Christians should think about war and violence and act to avoid engagement in unjust, misguided war. If that tradition has almost always failed to do that,[33] surely that raises serious questions about whether the just war tradition is really a helpful, useful approach. Donald W. Shriver Jr., former president of Union Theological Seminary, says that "*there has been so colossal an accumulation of injustice in the conduct of twentieth-century wars . . . that only a very brazen moralist will think serenely of commending the just war theory to the political thinking of the twenty-first century.*"[34]

While Ramsey is technically correct, that the failure of the just war tradition to prevent unjust wars does not logically prove that the stance is wrong, nevertheless its widespread failure surely raises a serious question about its

30. Bell, *Just War as Christian Discipleship*, 64–65.
31. Ramsey and Hauerwas, *Speak Up*, 107.
32. Yoder is probably correct in arguing that in actual practice, most Christians since Constantine have actually operated on the basis of the thinking of the crusade ("this is God's Holy War") or national interest ("my nation right or wrong"). In theory, the just war tradition represented the best insight from the Christian intellectual elites (and in that sense it can be called the "official" position), but in actual practice most Christians operated with a "crusade" or "national-interest" approach. Yoder, *When War Is Unjust*, 71–72. Lutheran ethicist Charles P. Lutz (who wrote an introduction to Yoder's book) agrees with Yoder. Yoder, *When War Is Unjust*, 10.
33. That is not to deny that just war thinking has had some effect, e.g., on many rules on treatment of war prisoners. See O'Donovan's comments on this in Sider and O'Donovan, *Peace and War*, 13. See also Yoder's recognition of some ways that just war thinkers have sought to apply the tradition: Yoder, *When War Is Unjust*, 42–55.
34. Shriver, *Ethic for Enemies*, 65 (italics original).

usefulness. If almost every time nonviolent activists sought to apply their theory to concrete situations, the result was failure to reduce violence and injustice, I would agree with those who question its usefulness. As we have seen, however, the historical record demonstrates that nonviolence actually often works better than violence to promote peace and justice. The fact that history discloses very few instances where just war thinking has actually been used to avoid unjust violence surely must raise the question of whether it is a useful, effective way for the Christian church to think about war.

Christians Killing Christians

With the just war tradition as their basic theoretical framework, Christians have gone to war to slaughter other Christians by the tens of thousands, hundreds of thousands, indeed millions. Before the United States entered World War I, forty-six million Protestants and sixty-two million Catholics were trying to kill forty-five million Protestants and sixty-three million Catholics on the other side. In that war, Christians succeeded in killing millions of other Christians. Reflecting back on the war in 1925, one Christian said, "Christian nations engaged in the most frightful carnage of history. No human device of cruelty and murder was too terrible to use. No human ingenuity was inappropriate for the purpose of destroying life. Nominal and real Christians fought other nominal and real Christians. Pulpits behind both trenches preached the crusade, held the cross before armed regiments and called down upon the carnage the blessing of God."[35] And the inability of the Christian church to prevent this war between Christian nations led many to develop deep doubts about Christianity itself.

Nor was the slaughter of Christians by Christians in the two great world wars of the twentieth century anything new—except in the numbers killed. Catholics and Protestants fought numerous bloody battles in the almost 150 years of the Wars of Religion that devastated "Christian" Europe after Luther sparked the Protestant Reformation.

Surely Christians killing Christians violates the New Testament teaching about the one body of Christ. "There is neither Jew nor Gentile, neither slave nor free, nor is there male and female, for you are all one in Christ" (Gal. 3:28). In Christ there is neither British nor German. In begging the Ephesian Christians to peace and unity, Paul reminds them that "there is one body . . . ; one Lord, one faith, one baptism" (Eph. 4:1–6). And Jesus makes it clear that commitment to him is a higher allegiance even than one's commitment

35. R. C. Hutchinson, quoted in Showalter, *End of a Crusade*, 173; for statistics on Christians on both sides, see p. 31.

to natural mother or father: "Anyone who loves their father or mother more than me is not worthy of me" (Matt. 10:37).

If New Testament teaching means anything, every Christian's commitment to Christ must be a higher commitment than to one's biological family, political party, or nation. As the official public policy document of the National Association of Evangelicals says, "commitment to the Lordship of Christ and his one body far transcends all political commitments."[36] When Christians embrace a nationalism that places loyalty to their nation above loyalty to the one global body of Christ, they engage in idolatry and violate the biblical teaching about Christ's one body.[37]

Yoder is right:

> No doctrine of Christian unity has yet explained why it should be more serious for Christians to disagree about the relative merits of episcopal, synodical, or congregational polity than for them to accept, under formal protest but with no real intention to object effectively to prepare for, and to carry out if necessary mass killing of other Christians at the call of their respective governments. . . . None of the arguments that justify morally the participation of Christians in war can justify their participation *on both sides* of a war. . . . If Christians in the allied nations were right in accepting war because the defeat of Hitler was necessary for the defense of order, then for the same reason all Christians in Germany should have been conscientious objectors."[38]

Tragically, Christians have consistently failed to do that. Again and again Christians in "Christian" nations have placed loyalty to their nation above loyalty to the one global body of Christ. As a result, Christians claiming the just war tradition as their framework have slaughtered other Christians in warfare by the millions. Surely that raises serious questions about the usefulness of the just war tradition.

The Just War Tradition and the Old Testament

The just war tradition forbids what the Old Testament commands and encourages what the Old Testament condemns. The just war tradition unequivocally condemns targeting noncombatants and captured soldiers. The Old

36. See "For the Health of the Nations" in Sider and Knippers, *Evangelical Public Policy*, 367.
37. Mennonite Central Committee (located in Akron, PA) circulated a postcard with the words "a modest proposal for peace: Let the Christians of the world agree that they will not kill each other."
38. Yoder, *Royal Priesthood*, 227 (italics original).

Testament repeatedly commands slaughtering all men, women, and children in a conquered territory. The just war tradition encourages preparing to defend the nation with state-of-the-art weapons. The Old Testament frequently condemns amassing and depending on military might.

Again and again, Old Testament texts command Israel to slaughter every living person in cities captured by Israel—often, the text says, at the explicit command of God. "Do not leave alive anything that breathes. Completely destroy them . . . as the Lord your God has commanded you" (Deut. 20:16–17). When the Israelites spare the captives after defeating the Midianites, Moses is angry and commands the army to "kill all the boys. And kill every woman who has slept with a man" (Num. 31:13–17). After the Israelites have captured Jericho, "they devoted the city to the LORD and destroyed with the sword every living thing in it—men and women, young and old" (Josh. 6:21).

Joshua 10:28–39 describes Joshua leading the people of Israel to defeat city after city. Repeatedly, the text says that Joshua put everyone to the sword and left no survivors there (10:30, 32, 35, 37, 39). The passage concludes by saying that Joshua subdued the whole region: "He left no survivors. He totally destroyed all who breathed, just as the Lord, the God of Israel, had commanded" (10:40). The next chapter describes what the Israelites do after capturing more cities: "The Israelites carried off for themselves all the plunder and livestock of the cities, but all the people they put to the sword until they completely destroyed them, not sparing anyone that breathed. As the LORD commanded his servant Moses, so Moses commanded Joshua, and Joshua did it" (Josh. 11:14–15). And the prophet Samuel declares, "What the LORD Almighty says. . . . 'Now go, attack the Amalekites and totally destroy all that belongs to them. Do not spare them; put to death men and women, children and infants'" (1 Sam. 15:2–3).[39]

Even John Calvin acknowledged that God's command to destroy everything alive inevitably strikes us as an act of "savagery" and "a deed of atrocious and barbaric ferocity."[40] Certainly the repeated Old Testament stories about how Israel (often at the command of God) slaughters men, women, and children after defeating their armies describe activities that the just war tradition explicitly prohibits.[41]

39. See also the following for examples of total destruction of captured towns and cities: Num. 21:1–3; Deut. 2:32–36; 3:1–7; 7:1–2, 16, 24; 20:10–14; Josh. 8:18–24; 10:28–40; 11:10–15; 1 Sam. 15:2–9, 18–20.

40. Quoted in Boyd, *Crucifixion of the Warrior God*, 1:291.

41. David Clough and Brian Stiltner claim to see "the distant origins of the just war tradition" in Amos 1:3–2:3 (*Faith and Force*, 24). It is true that Amos condemns foreign nations for atrocities committed in war. But Amos's main concern is to seek support for his prophecy against Israel by first condemning surrounding enemy nations so that his condemnation of Israel

A second area of conflict with the just war tradition occurs in a number of Old Testament texts that condemn Israel for acquiring the current military equipment (especially chariots and warhorses). "No king is saved by the size of his army; no warrior escapes by his great strength. A horse is a vain hope for deliverance" (Ps. 33:16–17). Isaiah says, "Woe to those who go down to Egypt for help, who rely on [war] horses, who trust in the multitude of their chariots and in the great strength of their horsemen, but do not look to the Holy One of Israel" (Isa. 31:1). Deuteronomy 17 describes a future time when Israel will want a king like the other nations. It was the role of kings to acquire military equipment to defend their nations. But Deuteronomy explicitly says that when Israel gets a king, the king must *not* do that. "The king, moreover, must not acquire great numbers of horses for himself" (17:16). The prophet Hosea predicts national captivity for sins of idolatry, economic injustice, *and trust in its military preparations*: "Because you have depended on your own strength and on your many warriors, the roar of battle will rise against your people" (10:13–14).

The psalmist contrasts trust in a strong military with trust in God: "Some trust in chariots and some in horses, but we trust in the name of the LORD our God" (Ps. 20:7). And Zechariah describes a future time when God will

---

itself has special power. Furthermore, even the worst things condemned here are precisely the things that the many texts we have just examined say God commands Israel to do. One text that perhaps condemns the killing of noncombatants is insignificant in comparison with many texts that describe Israel as doing precisely that—often at God's command. Arthur Holmes also seeks to find hints of the just war's criteria in the Old Testament. Holmes, "Just War," 123. Holmes cites Deut. 2 as evidence, but the only reason this text gives for Israel's not fighting the descendants of Esau and the Moabites is that God has not given Israel their land. And Deut. 2:34 reports that Israel destroyed all "men, women and children" of the Amorites. Nor does Holmes's reference to the fact that David, the man of war, was forbidden to build the temple or that the psalmist says that God destroys the weapons of war say anything about just war criteria. No more convincing are the arguments of Paul Copan and Matthew Flannagan in *Did God Really Command Genocide?*, 58–59, 142. They quote Deut. 20:10–18 and claim that it contains the principle of noncombatant immunity. The evidence? The passage says that when the Israelites capture a city outside the land promised to Israel, they may take the women and children as plunder. But the text also says: "When the LORD your God delivers it [the city] into your hand, put to the sword all the men in it" (v. 13). There is no hint here of treating captured soldiers (who are now noncombatants) humanely. Keith Payne and Karl Payne say that "it is often evident throughout the Old Testament that noncombatants were to be spared" (*Just Defense*, 43), but they provide no evidence! Joseph Fahey finds in Deut. 20:10–12 the principle of last resort (*War and the Christian Conscience*, 75). But the text describes an aggressive war where before attacking, the Israelites are to offer peace terms stating that if the inhabitants of the city surrender, they will "be subject to forced labor and shall work for you" (v. 11). This account describes an aggressive attack, not a defensive war after the Israelites have explored all reasonable alternatives to war. The just war tradition's criterion of last resort does not mean it is morally legitimate for one country to make war on another country unless that other nation agrees to be its slaves.

use a king riding on a donkey, not a warhorse, to restore Jerusalem: "See, your king comes to you, righteous and victorious, lowly and riding on a donkey. . . . I will take away the chariots from Ephraim and the warhorses from Jerusalem" (9:9–10).

The prophetic call to trust in Yahweh rather than state-of-the-art military equipment is certainly not the only theme in the Old Testament. But it appears with some frequency. If just war Christians followed this Old Testament summons, they would urge their nations to trust in God rather than build the strongest, best-equipped military. History provides virtually no examples of just war Christians doing that!

It seems that the Old Testament is almost as problematic for just war Christians as for pacifists. It repeatedly commands activities that they condemn and sometimes urges an approach that they ignore. It is simply not convincing for just war Christians to claim that they are merely embracing what the Old Testament teaches about war.[42]

Is the Just War Tradition More Realistic about Human Nature Than Pacifism Is?

Just war advocates often claim that the Just War tradition is more realistic about human nature than pacifism is. They claim that pacifists assume that people are basically good and can therefore easily persuade people to do what is right. But in fact, the Christian doctrine of sin explains why people regularly do awful things to their neighbors.

As we saw in the last chapter, some pacifists do have a naive view of humans as basically good. But the kind of biblical pacifism advocated in this book fully recognizes the pervasiveness and depth of human sinfulness. Indeed, this sinful reality may explain what we have seen in this chapter, namely, that again and again, indeed probably most of the time, selfish interests, blind tribalism, and jingoistic nationalism have prevented Christians from effectively applying the just war criteria. Instead, they have embraced virtually every war their leaders declared. Perhaps, as we saw in the last chapter, a realistic understanding of this persistent sinfulness should lead to the conclusion that a pacifist stance fits better with our fallen nature than a just war stance. If one believes, before one's nation makes emotional appeals to fight a war, that Jesus calls his followers always to refuse to kill, one is better protected against the ongoing temptation to quickly yield to emotional appeals to narrow self-interest and

42. See Yoder's comment: "Only if wars today were commanded by prophets and won by miracles would the wars of Yahweh be a pertinent example." Yoder, *War of the Lamb*, 70.

excessive nationalism than if one thinks one should carefully and thoughtfully apply the just war criteria. Given the reality of human sinfulness, it is very plausible to argue that the pacifist is more realistic than the just war advocate.

The Impossibility of Accurately Predicting the Outcome of Going to War

Just war ethicist Nigel Biggar has said that the strongest cord in the pacifist's hand is that we cannot know ahead of time that the horrible evils that are inevitable in war will be less than the evils that would result if we chose not to go to war.[43] That fact, of course, makes it difficult to implement the just war criterion of proportionality, which insists that it is wrong to fight a war unless the good results of the war will exceed the horrible evils that always accompany war.

In his development of this argument against the just war tradition, Yoder uses Reinhold Niebuhr's work on the "irony" of history: "When people try to manage history, it almost always turns out to have taken another direction."[44] Biggar acknowledges that "here Yoder presses down on one of the weakest elements of just war reasoning. There is no common currency in terms of which to weigh together the evils caused [by war] . . . and the goods achieved."[45]

I think this argument underlines the importance of starting with Jesus's teaching. We dare not argue that some envisioned evil outcomes are so awful that we should set aside Jesus's ethical commands. But as we saw earlier,[46] both pacifists and just war Christians agree on this point. Pacifists believe Jesus taught his disciples not to kill. Just war Christians believe Jesus's teaching demands that we never target noncombatants. They both agree that there are some things Christians must not do even if our best calculations indicate that the likely result is that we will be conquered by a vicious enemy.

But if one believes as I do, that all Christians should be (secondarily!) concerned with effectiveness, then this inability to accurately predict the outcome of our actions is a problem for both pacifist and just war Christians. I do not believe our first concern should be some short-term calculation of effectiveness. Our first concern should be faithfulness to Jesus. But after one agrees that the starting point must be that we never choose to act in a way contrary to Jesus's teaching, we should proceed to seek to move society in the direction of justice and peace in all the ways we can. And that will require

43. Biggar, *In Defence of War*, 326.
44. Yoder, *Politics of Jesus*, 230.
45. Biggar, *In Defence of War*, 32.
46. See chap. 8, "Failure to Take Responsibility for History."

decisions about effectiveness—that is, about which actions are more likely to produce the best results. And at that point, just war advocates like Biggar and Ramsey are right, that *"the future is radically unpredictable*, for pacifist and just warrior alike."[47] Thus I conclude that although the inability to accurately predict the consequences of our actions makes it difficult to implement one of the just war criteria and thus points to a weakness of that tradition, I do not consider that inability in itself a decisive refutation of the just war tradition.

The cumulative effect, however, of the problems with the just war tradition does lead to serious doubt about the usefulness of that tradition. One cannot invite someone to accept the gospel and simultaneously kill that person. It is very doubtful that one can implement Jesus's command to love one's enemies and kill them at the same time. There is little evidence to show that the just war tradition has prevented war or encouraged significant numbers of just war Christians to refuse to fight their nation's unjust wars. The scandal of Christians killing Christians by the thousands and millions in their nation's wars underlines the fact that Christians repeatedly fail to act on the implications of the just war tradition. At least for anyone who seeks to justify participation in war on the basis of the Old Testament, it is problematic that the just war tradition forbids what the Old Testament frequently commands and encourages what the Old Testament condemns. In light of the failures and problems, it is certainly plausible to argue that pacifism fits better with the Christian understanding of the prevalence of sin than does the just war tradition.

47. Ramsey and Hauerwas, *Speak Up*, 123 (italics original); cf. Biggar, *In Defence of War*, 33.

10

Jesus and Killing in the Old Testament

All Christians agree that the one God of the universe is revealed most fully in Jesus of Nazareth, truly God and truly human. Jesus tells us to love our enemies "that you may be children of your Father in heaven" (Matt. 5:44–45). Did that same God repeatedly command the people of Israel to slaughter every man, woman, and child in city after city? Did that same God command capital punishment for lazy children or those who gathered sticks on the Sabbath?

The Violent Texts

As we saw in the last chapter, the Old Testament again and again says that God commands the Israelites to obliterate every living person in the towns they capture: "Do not leave alive anything that breathes. Completely destroy them" (Deut. 20:16–17). As Joshua 10 describes Joshua conquering city after city, the Bible says, "The city and everyone in it Joshua put to the sword. He left no survivors there" (Josh. 10:30; also vv. 32, 35, 37, 39). And after relating Joshua's victory over the whole region, the Bible declares, "He left no survivors. He totally destroyed all who breathed, just as the LORD, the God of Israel, had commanded" (10:40).

These texts reflect Israel's holy war tradition of *herem* (setting something apart for destruction).[1] A Moabite inscription from the ninth century BC reflects

1. See "חָרַם *ḥāram*," *TDOT* 5:180–99.

147

the same practice of slaughtering all the captives of a city defeated in battle as a sacrifice to one's god for giving victory in battle.[2] This genocidal practice (often commanded by Yahweh) appears thirty-seven times in the Old Testament.[3] Apparently Israel understood slaughtering every man, woman, and child in a defeated Canaanite city as an act of worship to Yahweh.[4] After capturing Jericho, the Israelites "devoted the city to the LORD and destroyed with the sword every living thing in it—men and women, young and old" (Josh. 6:21).

The Old Testament also depicts God as commanding death for a wide range of things: adultery (Lev. 20:10); lighting a fire or gathering sticks on the Sabbath (Exod. 31:14; 35:2–3; Num. 15:32–36); children who are stubborn, lazy, or drunkards (Exod. 21:15, 17; Lev. 20:9; Deut. 21:18–21); cursing God (Lev. 24:16); and sacrificing to an idol (Exod. 22:20). The Bible says Yahweh sends an angel to slaughter seventy thousand Israelites because King David has taken a census (2 Sam. 24:15).

Some psalms portray God and God's people engaged in vicious actions. Saying that God will crush God's enemies, the psalmist says the Lord "will bring them from the depths of the sea, that your feet may wade in the blood of your foes" (Ps. 68:22–23). Predicting the destruction of Babylon (which has destroyed Jerusalem), the psalmist declares, "Happy is the one who seizes your infants and dashes them against the rocks" (137:8–9).

Judges 20 tells the story of how the other tribes go to war against the tribe of Benjamin because of a gross evil committed by some Benjamite men. Several times the other tribes ask God for guidance, and God repeatedly tells them to do battle (Judg. 20:18, 23). They ask, "Shall we go up again to fight against the Benjamites, our fellow Israelites, or not?" The Lord responds, "Go, for tomorrow I will give them into your hands" (20:28). The next day, "the LORD defeated Benjamin before Israel, and on that day the Israelites struck down 25,100 Benjamites" (20:35). In more than one hundred biblical passages, Yahweh commands people to kill other persons.[5]

One of the common titles for God in the Old Testament is "Lord of Hosts." The literal meaning of "hosts" is "armies." God is the Lord of armies. That title appears over two hundred times in the Old Testament.[6] Israel's God is the one who fights in support of Israel's army.

How can all this Old Testament material where God commands killing, war, the slaughtering of every man, woman, and child, indeed genocide,

2. J. Collins, *Does the Bible Justify Violence?*, 5.
3. Boyd, *Crucifixion of the Warrior God*, 1:294.
4. Boyd, *Crucifixion of the Warrior God*, 1:301.
5. Boyd, *Crucifixion of the Warrior God*, 1:305.
6. Craigie, *Problem of War*, 36.

be reconciled with God's final revelation in Jesus that God wants us to love our enemies? Many Jews in Jesus's day longed for another "holy war" when their God would again destroy the national enemy, the Roman conquerors. But Jesus totally rejected that approach.[7] The contrast between Moses's final words to his people and Jesus's final words to his disciples can hardly be more stark.[8] Moses tells his people to enter the land and do to the Canaanites "all that I have commanded you" (Deut. 31:1–5). Jesus's final command is to go into the whole world and make disciples of all nations, teaching them "to obey everything that I have commanded you" (Matt. 28:20). And that includes loving their enemies!

Jesus and the Old Testament

An easy solution, of course, would be to reject all these Old Testament texts as ancient documents reflecting ghastly primitive ideas that have no authoritative relevance for New Testament Christians. But the same Lord Jesus who taught his disciples to love their enemies clearly shared the first-century Jewish and then Christian view that "all Scripture is God-breathed" (2 Tim. 3:16). In the story of his temptation by Satan, Jesus responds to each of Satan's three temptations with the phrase "it is written" and then cites a text from Deuteronomy (Matt. 4:1–11). The phrase "it is written" was a common way in Jewish circles of Jesus's day to introduce the Hebrew Bible.[9] Jesus introduces a quotation from the Psalms with the statement "David himself, speaking by the Holy Spirit . . ." (Mark 12:36). After the resurrection, Jesus explains to his disciples how the "Law of Moses, the Prophets and the Psalms" (the typical way to refer to the Hebrew Bible) all have spoken of him (Luke 24:44). And near the beginning of the Sermon on the Mount, Jesus states his commitment to the "Law" and "the Prophets": "Until heaven and earth disappear, not the smallest letter, not the least stroke of a pen, will by any means disappear from the Law until everything is accomplished" (Matt. 5:17–18).

Clearly Jesus thought and taught that the Law, Psalms, and Prophets were the authoritative word of God. If we confess that Jesus is truly God and truly human, then we dare not dismiss his teaching about the Hebrew Bible.[10]

7. See N. T. Wright's discussion of how prominent was the idea of holy war in Jewish thought in Jesus's day and how Jesus rejected "the whole movement in Jewish life which had embraced exactly this tradition of holy war." N. T. Wright, *Jesus and the Victory of God*, 449.

8. Sparks, *Sacred Word, Broken Word*, 69, makes this point.

9. Keener, *IVP Bible Background Commentary*, 54.

10. One of the many strengths of Greg Boyd's impressive book *Crucifixion of the Warrior God* is that Boyd makes this point central to his thinking (1:3–7, 348–50).

In a variety of ways, many contemporary scholars do something of that sort. In his book *The Violence of Scripture*, Eric Seibert proposes commonly accepted standards of morality "as a good norm for judging what the Bible says." The standard is what "any mentally healthy, rationally functioning human being should quickly and easily recognize" as right or wrong.[11] But it is not obvious that Jesus's command to love our enemies would fare much better with this standard than Old Testament texts on violence. For those who confess Jesus as Lord, some widely accepted (modern!) ethical norms dare not provide our fundamental ethical criteria.

Proposed Solutions

There have been a number of attempts to justify or at least soften the texts that describe the slaughter of everything that breathes in the Canaanite cities that the Israelites reportedly conquered. First of all, some argue, it never happened. But even if it did, God promised the land to Israel. Also, the Canaanites were wicked and would have corrupted the people of Israel had they remained in the land. The command to kill them was only an occasional command. All Near Eastern nations of that day did the same thing. Perhaps the language about killing everything that breathes represents a widely used literary form that greatly exaggerates the amount of killing. Since God chose to reveal Godself to a nation and warfare was essential to the survival of any nation, warfare was necessary.

It never happened. Many Old Testament scholars argue that the massive destruction of Canaanite cities by Joshua and his troops simply never took place. Archaeologists have done extensive excavations in the area of the cities allegedly totally destroyed according to Joshua 6–11. Only seven of the twelve cities reportedly destroyed by Joshua were even occupied at the time, and only three show signs of destruction at the time of the alleged conquest. So in response to the question of how God could have all those Canaanites put to death, Peter Enns has a simple answer: God didn't. It never happened, Enns says.[12]

I am not an Old Testament scholar, and this is not the place to try to assess this conclusion of many modern scholars.[13] But even if they are right, it does not remove the theological problem: the biblical text that is part of the God-breathed, authoritative Scripture according to Jesus says that God ordered the annihilation of all that breathed.[14]

11. Seibert, *Violence of Scripture*, 86.
12. Enns, *Bible Tells Me So*, 58–60.
13. See the parallel but less sweeping conclusion of Stone, "Early Israel."
14. So rightly Craigie, *Problem of War*, 50.

God promised the land to Abraham's descendants. It is true that the Bible repeatedly says that God promised the land to Abraham. In Genesis 17:8, God declares to Abraham, "The whole land of Canaan, where you now reside as a foreigner, I will give you as an everlasting possession to you and your descendants."[15] One can accept the fact that God wanted Abraham's descendants to live in the land of Canaan and be a special people through whom God would work to bless all nations (Gen. 12:1–3). And God did accomplish that plan when Jesus, the son of Abraham and David, came as the Savior of the world. But surely that does not mean that the only way Almighty God could have accomplished this plan was to slaughter every Canaanite living there. Surely our powerful, wise God could have used some means other than genocide to achieve this goal.

The Canaanites were wicked. It is true that the Canaanites were wicked. They worshiped idols, sacrificed their children to their gods, and practiced cult prostitution. "It is on account of the wickedness of these nations that the LORD is going to drive them out before you" (Deut. 9:4).[16] The biblical text also frequently says that God does not want these idol-worshiping Canaanites to live among the chosen people and seduce them into idol worship. Among the laws given to Israel by God through Moses is the command not to allow the Canaanites to live with the people of Israel: "Do not let them live in your land or they will cause you to sin against me, because the worship of their gods will certainly be a snare to you" (Exod. 23:33).[17] And Moses warns them that Israel must not imitate the Canaanites' abominable practices or God will also destroy them (Lev. 18:27–28).

But again, we must ask: Is genocide the only way to punish such sinners? And is it the only way to protect the Israelites from idolatry? It is true, of course, that finite human beings do not know enough to say that something God does is wrong.[18] God's right to do whatever God chooses does not, however, change the fact that it seems very hard to see how the God revealed in Jesus, the only Son of God, would order genocide.

The command was an "occasional command." Nor does it help much to argue, as Paul Copan and Matthew Flannagan do, that since the command to slaughter all that breathes is only an "occasional command," it is therefore

15. See also Gen. 13:14–17; 26:3; 28:13. But it is certainly special pleading to argue that since Abraham bought a plot of land from the Canaanites to bury his wife (Gen. 23:17–20) and Jacob bought a little plot from Canaanites (Gen. 33:19–20), the land already belonged to the people of Israel and the Canaanites were "strictly speaking, trespassers." See Copan and Flannagan, *Did God Really Command Genocide?*, 63–64.

16. See also Lev. 18:1–2, 24–25, 27, 30; Deut. 9:5; 12:29–31.

17. See also Exod. 34:15–16; Deut. 7:4, 16; 20:18.

18. Nugent, *Politics of Yahweh*, 111–15.

not so problematic. They point out that Deuteronomy 20 says that when Israel conquers cities "that are at a distance from you" (i.e., not part of the land promised to Abraham and his descendants), they are not to kill anyone other than the men (20:10–18). But in the case of cities in the land promised to them, Israel is commanded, "Do not leave alive anything that breathes" (20:16).[19] The fact that God does not tell the people of Israel to slaughter all that breathes in every city they conquer hardly lessens the problem that the biblical text repeatedly says God orders them to do that in all the Canaanite cities.

Other Near Eastern nations did it. We know from extrabiblical documents that slaughtering all the inhabitants of a defeated city was not uncommon at this time in history. An inscription from an Assyrian temple depicts the Assyrian King Ashurnasirpal mutilating and burning people, including children, from a captured city.[20] And as we saw above, a ninth-century-BC inscription depicts a Moabite king slaughtering everyone in an Israelite city he captured. But I fail to see any validity in the argument by some evangelical scholars[21] that somehow this widespread practice by pagans justifies God's alleged command to Israel to do the same.

The language is hyperbolic. Copan and Flannagan, however, advance another argument based on the evidence from the ninth-century-BC Moabite inscription and many other Near Eastern documents of this period. These documents show that the kings of the day regularly used widely hyperbolic language to vastly overstate the extent of killing resulting from their military campaigns. The language in Joshua where everything that breathes is wiped out is strikingly similar to other ancient accounts of military victories. In other contemporary Near Eastern documents, "Victories are narrated in an exaggerated hyperbolic fashion in terms of total conquest, complete annihilation and destruction of the enemy, killing *everyone*, leaving *no* survivors."[22] So the killing reported in some biblical texts was probably not intended to be taken literally and was not really as extensive as the texts seem to imply. To strengthen the argument that Joshua's account should be understood as hyperbole, not literal history, Copan and Flannagan also note that the book of Judges frequently describes battles against the Canaanites that the book of Joshua says have already been obliterated.[23] Their conclusion is that the final

19. See Copan and Flannagan, *Did God Really Command Genocide?*, 58–59.
20. See Grayson, *Assyrian Rulers*, 201, cited in Lamb, *God Behaving Badly*, 79, 192.
21. See Lamb, *God Behaving Badly*, 77.
22. Copan and Flannagan, *Did God Really Command Genocide?*, 97 (italics original).
23. Copan and Flannagan, *Did God Really Command Genocide?*, 85–93. Cf. Josh. 10–11; Judg. 1:1–2:5.

editor of the books of Joshua and Judges was not intending to imply that Joshua literally slaughtered all that breathed.[24] Therefore, the final biblical text does not intend to command or describe genocide. Copan and Flannagan conclude that neither Moses nor God commanded the slaughtering of all that breathes.[25]

How much does this argument help? Perhaps a little. We can at least say there was probably much less slaughter of Canaanites than some texts seem to suggest. Perhaps, too, the final editor knew that the language of slaughtering all that breathed was typical hyperbolic language, not a description of what actually happened. But if the final editor did not think that God or Moses commanded the slaughter of all that breathes, then it is very strange that that editor repeatedly included language that explicitly states that God and Moses *do command exactly that*.[26] So we are still left with the fact that the biblical texts repeatedly say that God commands genocide. I find it very difficult to think that the Father of our Lord Jesus would actually do that.

A nation-state must defend itself. Peter Craigie offers a vigorous statement of the argument that since God chose to reveal Godself through a particular historical nation, war was a necessity. "As a nation state in the real world of that time, Israel could not exist without war."[27] The argument sounds reasonable. Since God chose to reveal Godself through a nation of Abraham's descendants, that nation would have to fight to establish and defend itself like every other nation.

One problem with this argument, however, is that there is repeated evidence in the Old Testament text that God does *not* want God's chosen people to act militarily like other nations. In the accounts of the exodus from Egypt, Israel does nothing to defend itself against Pharaoh's pursuing army. One text suggests that God intends to use hornets to displace the Canaanites (Exod. 23:27–28).[28] God is opposed to Israel's desire for a king to lead them in battle like all the other nations. And when God finally agrees, God warns Israel's king not to amass chariots and horses like other nations. Repeatedly, later prophets condemn Israel for trusting in military forces rather than in God (Isa. 31:1).[29] There are repeated indications in the Old Testament that God wants Israel

24. Copan and Flannagan, *Did God Really Command Genocide?*, 90.
25. Copan and Flannagan, *Did God Really Command Genocide?*, 104.
26. See the extensive critique of Copan and Flannagan in Boyd, *Crucifixion of the Warrior God*, 2:946–60. Among other things, Boyd points to several biblical texts where it is very difficult to consider the *herem* command as hyperbolic (2:951–59).
27. Craigie, *Problem of War*, 71.
28. See Boyd's attempt to argue from a number of texts that God's original plan was to drive out the Canaanites nonviolently. Boyd, *Crucifixion of the Warrior God*, 2:964–72.
29. See also chap. 9, "The Just War Tradition and the Old Testament."

to be very different from the surrounding nations—and that includes where they look for defense. The Old Testament itself warns us against arguing that since God chose Israel to be a nation to use as God's special instrument of revelation, therefore, God wanted that nation to defend itself with the normal nation-state's state-of-the-art military weapons.

John Howard Yoder's Explanation

The fact that Yoder advocated a canonical approach that sought to accept the full canon as an authoritative word of God means that his thinking on this topic merits special attention.[30]

Yoder rejects several common approaches.[31] Dispensationalists say a sovereign God commands different things in different dispensations. That approach seems to compromise Jesus's teaching that he is the fulfillment of Israelite faith. Is war in the Old Testament perhaps a concession to disobedience, in the way Moses allows divorce because of the hardness of people's hearts? Yoder rejects this approach because the idea of concession to disobedience is not in the texts on holy war. Nor does Yoder accept the idea that the texts on killing in the Old Testament come from a "primitive moral immaturity" that our more civilized culture rightly rejects. It is problematic, Yoder insists, because this position seems to derive from "an evolutionist liberal theological perspective" that he does not share. And Yoder also rejects the widespread view that the Old Testament description of private and public responsibility (the individual should not kill on one's own initiative but the state rightly does so) also applies in the New Testament. Yoder rejects this approach, which claims that Jesus's rejection of killing applies only to one's private life, not one's public life as citizen and soldier.

Yoder's *canonical-directional* approach seeks to embrace what the biblical text says in its story of the history of Israel. And within that history, he finds a progressive direction where the sacredness of human life is increasingly protected. "It is therefore more proper, on reading the Old Testament story, to ask not how it is different from what came later, but rather how it differs from what went *before*, or what prevailed at the time, and how it moves toward what was to come later."[32]

---

30. See John Nugent's recent book-length analysis of John Howard Yoder's understanding of the Old Testament: *Politics of Yahweh*. Nugent describes Yoder's approach as "canonical-directional" (11).

31. See Yoder, *Original Revolution*, 91–100.

32. Yoder, *Original Revolution*, 100–101 (italics original).

God calls Abram out of a violent culture, promising to make of his descendants a great nation that will bless the whole world (Gen. 12:1–3). Yoder does not deny the violence in the exodus story but emphasizes that "the Israelites did nothing to bring about the destruction of the Egyptians."[33] In his discussion of holy war and its prominence during the conquest of Canaan and the time of the judges, Yoder emphasizes the fact that often the Israelites do little or no killing.[34] Yahweh does that. The texts clearly call on the people of Israel to depend on God's miraculous intervention, not on their military prowess and preparation. But Yoder accepts the slaughter of all that breathes as a "bloody sacrifice to the God who had given the enemy into our hands."[35] He also says, "We can affirm that in these events there was, as the story says, a real word from the true Yahweh of hosts, speaking to His people in historically relevant terms."[36]

In his discussion of the period of the monarchy, Yoder stresses the texts that say God strongly opposes Israel when they ask for a king like the surrounding nations. Even as God acquiesces to their demand for a king to lead them into battle, God warns the people of Israel about how a king will oppress them and rely on military prowess rather than trust in Yahweh (1 Sam. 8:1–21; cf. Deut. 17:16). And the prophets often condemn the kings for trusting in military preparedness rather than in Yahweh's protection.[37] After the Babylonians capture Jerusalem and take captives to Babylon, Jeremiah urges the Israelites to settle down and seek the peace of that city (Jer. 29:7). And since they are no longer a nation needing defense, they do not need to fight military battles.[38]

The prophets also point to an expansion of the people of God beyond the children of Abraham. Yoder perceives an ever-broadening expansion of the understanding of the people of God—which culminates in Jesus's gospel to all nations. "The identification of the people of Israel with the state of Israel was progressively loosened. . . . It was loosened in a positive way by the development of an increasing vision for the concern of Yahweh for *all* peoples and by the promise of a time when *all* peoples would come to Jerusalem to learn the law. . . . Once all [people] are seen as potential partakers of the covenant, then the outsider can no longer be perceived as less human or as an object for sacrificing."[39] Thus God's people rightly use military weapons

33. Quoted in Nugent, *Politics of Yahweh*, 46.
34. Especially in his discussion of holy war, Yoder relies significantly on the work of his Old Testament colleague: Lind, *Yahweh Is a Warrior*.
35. Yoder, *Original Revolution*, 104–5.
36. Yoder, *Original Revolution*, 107.
37. Isa. 31:1; Hosea 10:13–14; Zech. 9:9–10. See also Deut. 17:16; Pss. 20:7; 146:3–5.
38. Jer. 29:4–7. See Nugent, *Politics of Yahweh*, 75–80.
39. Yoder, *Original Revolution*, 108 (italics original).

in the time of Moses and Joshua but no longer do that in Jesus's dawning kingdom, because God's original design to use Abraham's descendants to bless all nations is reaching its fulfillment in Christ's church, where there is neither Jew nor gentile.[40]

There is obvious merit in Yoder's argument. He accepts the Old Testament as part of God's authoritative revelation. Jesus is the fulfillment of God's promise to bless all nations through Abraham's descendants. There is a development within the Old Testament.

But Yoder's argument still seems to affirm that God does command the people of Israel to slaughter everything that breathes in the conquered Canaanite cities. That means that God commands genocide. Must we accept that the Father of our Lord Jesus would command something so utterly contradictory to what our Lord Jesus taught?

It is true, as John Nugent argues in his exposition of Yoder's understanding of the Old Testament, that Jesus's teaching on loving enemies does not represent "an exhaustive representation of God's response to evil." The New Testament explicitly teaches that God does some things that Christians must not (Rom. 12:19). Furthermore, as Yoder argues, finite human beings have no adequate way to judge whether the actions of the infinite God are morally justified. Since there is an "infinite qualitative distinction" between God and human beings, we have no criteria for judging what would be right for God to do. "We cannot be certain that divine sanction of genocide is a contradiction unless we have a firm grasp on the nature of divinity which we lack."[41]

But that still seems profoundly inadequate. It is true that it is a mistake to argue that Jesus *totally* reveals everything about God.[42] And Jesus repeatedly teaches that God punishes evil. God properly does some things that Jesus's disciples are commanded not to do.[43] But Jesus does tell us that when we love our enemies, we act like God, who sends the rain on the just and unjust. Is genocide compatible with the loving God Jesus describes?

Greg Boyd's Explanation

Greg Boyd believes we must answer no to the question of whether genocide is compatible with the loving God Jesus describes. And in his recent massive,

40. Nugent, *Politics of Yahweh*, 189.

41. Nugent, *Politics of Yahweh*, 112–13.

42. Boyd, it seems to me, makes this mistake. He writes, "Jesus is the *total* content of the Father's revelation to us." Boyd, *Crucifixion of the Warrior God*, 1:40 (italics original).

43. See further the paragraphs about J. Denny Weaver in chap. 12, under "Challenges to Traditional Understandings of the Atonement."

two-volume work, *Crucifixion of the Warrior God*, he develops a way to reconcile Jesus's call to nonviolence with Jesus's belief in the Old Testament as the authoritative word of God.

We must start with Jesus. In many different places and ways, the New Testament says what is very clear in Hebrews.[44] In the past God spoke through the prophets, but now God has spoken through the Son, who is "the exact representation of his being" (Heb. 1:1–3). The Law and Prophets are inferior to Jesus in the way a shadow is inferior to the substance (Heb. 8:5; 10:1; cf. Col. 2:17). The New Testament authors read the Old Testament in light of Jesus, and we must do the same.[45] Jesus is the center of the Bible, and the cross is the center of Jesus.

The cross is the interpretive key that unlocks everything about Jesus. "The thread that weaves together everything Jesus was about is the nonviolent, self-sacrificial, enemy embracing love of God revealed on the cross."[46] God's essence is love. God is not wrath in the way that God is love. "The fury of God's 'wrath' against sin, injustice, violence and everything else that destroys people is nothing other than the fury of his love for people."[47] And at the cross, God shows the extent of that love. At the cross, God's love is so great that God becomes sin and a curse for us (2 Cor. 5:21; Gal. 3:13), dying in our place. The seemingly God-forsaken criminal on the cross, who is in fact also true God, reveals the power and wisdom of God (1 Cor. 1:18–24). The cross reveals how "God gets things done"—"'not by a conventional human use of power, by displays of force' but by the kind of self-giving love expressed on Calvary."[48] The cross, therefore, is the "unsurpassable revelation of God."[49]

So how does Boyd propose that we understand the Old Testament where God does or commands violence? The cross is the key. At the cross, God refused to coerce people, suffering instead as God allowed sinful people to choose to do what was wrong. Something analogous happens in the writing of the Scriptures. God does not coercively override the human authors, forcing them to write only what is true and right. In love, God allows the human authors of Scripture to choose to say things about God that are false. The God revealed at the cross is always the key for interpreting the Old Testament. Boyd concludes:

44. Boyd, *Crucifixion of the Warrior God*, 1:37–59.
45. Boyd, *Crucifixion of the Warrior God*, 1:97–110.
46. Boyd, *Crucifixion of the Warrior God*, 1:142.
47. Boyd, *Crucifixion of the Warrior God*, 1:146.
48. Boyd, *Crucifixion of the Warrior God*, 1:195.
49. Boyd, *Crucifixion of the Warrior God*, 1:155.

> To the degree that any portrait of God [in the Old Testament] reflects the
> cruciform character of God revealed on the cross, I submit that we should
> consider it a direct revelation that bears witness to God's historic faithful-
> ness in continually acting toward his people to reveal as much of his true
> character as possible. . . . But to the degree that any portrait of God [in
> the Old Testament] reflects a character that is antithetical to the cruciform
> character of God revealed on the cross, I submit that we must consider it
> an indirect revelation that bears witness to God's historic faithfulness in
> continually stooping to allow the fallen and culturally conditioned state of
> his people to act on him.[50]

Whenever an Old Testament text depicts God in a way that corresponds to
God revealed at the cross, it is a direct revelation that we must accept. But when
an Old Testament passage describes a violent God who does not conform to
the nonviolent God revealed at the cross, it is the human author expressing
wrong, sinful ideas that we must reject.

How adequate is Boyd's solution? I find many commendable things in his
massive, fourteen-hundred-page magnum opus.[51] He is right to start with
Jesus as God's fullest revelation to us. He is right to show the numerous ways
Jesus and the New Testament fulfill the Law and the Prophets by modify-
ing or setting aside numerous Old Testament demands—whether food laws,
the Sabbath, circumcision, and so on. But in the end, it is not clear that his
position differs substantively from those modern authors who say we must
simply say the Old Testament is wrong and must be rejected at crucial points.
Boyd's approach is certainly vastly more complex than many others. But in
the end, he says that whenever the Old Testament depicts a violent God, we
are dealing with sinful, misguided human authors. We should respect their
attempt to understand God, but they are wrong.

Other Old Testament Texts

It is simply not the case that the Old Testament texts that depict God commanding or doing violence provide the only picture of who God is. There are
many texts, perhaps even more texts, that describe God's overflowing love. In
Exodus, God describes Godself as "the compassionate and gracious God, slow
to anger, abounding in love and faithfulness, . . . forgiving wickedness, rebellion

---

50. Boyd, *Crucifixion of the Warrior God*, 1:502.
51. It is impossible to adequately summarize Boyd's many extensive exegetical and theological arguments in a few paragraphs!

and sin" (34:6–7).[52] The description of God as "slow to anger, abounding in love" appears again and again in the Old Testament.[53] One of the most common words applied to Yahweh in the Old Testament is *hesed*, which means "steadfast love." Forty-two times, the Old Testament declares that God's steadfast love "endures forever."[54] Some Old Testament passages, especially in the Prophets, describe God as hating violence and bringing peace in the future (Isa. 11:6–9; Mic. 4:3). Love is central to the Old Testament depiction of who God is.[55]

These many texts, however, do not change the fact that the Old Testament repeatedly depicts God as commanding and doing violence, even genocide. So the problem remains: How do we reconcile these texts with what Jesus tells us about God?

I am not satisfied with any of the attempts just explored to understand how Old Testament passages that depict a violent God fit with Jesus's revelation of a God who calls us to love even our enemies. Perhaps, this side of eternity, no answer will seem adequate. I certainly do not have a solution that leaves me fully satisfied. But I do think some things are clear. We should start with Jesus. And Jesus and the New Testament fulfill—by transcending and replacing—many central Old Testament things.

Darrell Cole is certainly correct to insist that the New Testament presupposes the theological and moral foundation of the Old Testament. But does that mean, as he claims, that "we cannot interpret the character of Jesus in a way that conflicts with God's eternal and unchanging moral character as it is revealed in the Old Testament"? Is Cole right to insist that "the character of Jesus must harmonize with the portrayal of God in the Old Testament"?[56] Surely since the New Testament repeatedly says that Jesus is the clear, decisive revelation of which the Old Testament is but a shadow (Heb. 10:1), our starting point must be Jesus, not the Old Testament. Pope Benedict puts it well: "Christ is the key to all things. . . . Only by walking with Christ, by reinterpreting all things in this light, with him, crucified and risen, do we enter into the riches and beauty of sacred scripture."[57] And that includes seeing the numerous ways that Jesus and the New Testament say that the new covenant transcends the old, setting aside many central aspects of the Old Testament.

52. It is also true that the rest of v. 7 talks of God's punishment of sinners. See chap. 12, "God's Wrath" where I affirm this part of biblical teaching.
53. Num. 14:18; Neh. 9:17; Pss. 86:15; 103:8; 145:8; Joel 2:13; Jonah 4:2.
54. Lamb, *God Behaving Badly*, 39; the phrase appears twenty-six times in Ps. 136.
55. See Boyd's long footnote of many modern authors who emphasize this aspect of God in the Old Testament; Boyd, *Crucifixion of the Warrior God*, 1:281–82nn5–6.
56. Cole, *When God Says*, 32.
57. Quoted in Sparks, *Sacred Word, Broken Word*, 107.

The Shadow and the Reality

Hebrews declares that the Old Testament law is but a shadow of the genuine reality disclosed in Jesus Christ (10:1–10). Now that Christ, the "exact representation" of God, has come (1:3), the old is set aside. In the new covenant, many things central to the old covenant—the law, the temple, circumcision, the Sabbath, oaths, an eye for an eye—are no longer normative for God's people.

Both in the teaching of the Old Testament and the belief of first-century Jews, the law and the temple were at the center of Jewish faith. Keeping the details of the law scrupulously was the way to obey Yahweh and demonstrate that one was a faithful Jew. The temple was the place where God was uniquely present and where daily sacrifices for sin were made. The early church set all that aside, believing that Jesus, not the law and the temple, was the way to God.

Keeping Torah, the law given by Moses, was a central feature of Jewish faith and life in Jesus's day. "The temple cult, and the observance of Sabbaths, of food taboos, and of circumcision were the key things which marked out Jew from Gentile."[58]

Keeping the Sabbath is unnecessary. The Sabbath is firmly established in the Ten Commandments (Exod. 20:8) as a central feature of Jewish life. The Old Testament repeatedly emphasizes the importance of observing it (e.g., Exod. 34:21). Numbers 15 contains a story about a man who "was found gathering wood on the Sabbath day" (v. 33). When the people ask Moses what to do, the Lord says to Moses, "The man must die. The whole assembly must stone him outside the camp" (v. 35). Even lighting a fire in one's home on the Sabbath merits death (Exod. 35:2–3).

Jesus has repeated conflicts with the Pharisees about the Sabbath. He defends his disciples when the Pharisees criticize them for picking heads of grain to eat on the Sabbath (Matt. 12:1–8). He denounces the Pharisees for objecting when he heals on the Sabbath (12:9–14). He even claims to be "Lord of the Sabbath" (12:8), insisting that the "sabbath was made for humankind, and not humankind for the sabbath" (Mark 2:27 NRSV).

There is no evidence that Jesus specifically rejected Sabbath observance. But the early church clearly considered it unnecessary. Paul surely has the Sabbath in mind when he says that "one person considers one day more sacred than another; another considers every day alike" (Rom. 14:5). Paul believes both views are acceptable for Christians. And Colossians 2 declares the Sabbath as "a shadow of the things that were to come; the reality, however, is found

---

58. N. T. Wright, *Jesus and the Victory of God*, 384.

in Christ" (vv. 16–17)—a view, as we will see, that Paul applies to the entire Torah.

Food laws are set aside. Food laws were also an important part of the Torah. The entire chapter of Leviticus 11 specifies in great detail which foods are clean (e.g., cows, fish with fins and scales) and unclean (e.g., rabbits, pigs, fish without fins and scales). The Torah commands God's people to eat only clean food. And the story of Peter's vision before he goes to Cornelius's house shows that devout Jews of Jesus's day observed the food laws scrupulously. When he sees a vision of all kinds of animals and a voice commands him to kill and eat, Peter insists on keeping the Torah's food laws: "'Surely not, Lord!' Peter replied. 'I have never eaten anything impure or unclean'" (Acts 10:11–14).

Jesus, however, teaches that nothing that enters the body from outside can defile a person. The Gospel of Mark adds, "In saying this, Jesus declared all foods clean" (Mark 7:17–19). Other parts of the New Testament demonstrate that keeping the Torah's food laws is no longer an obligation for God's people. At the great council in Jerusalem, the question is whether "the Gentiles must be circumcised and required to keep the law of Moses" (Acts 15:5). The decision is that the gentiles should not eat food sacrificed to idols, blood, or the meat of strangled animals, but gentile Christians do not need to keep the other food laws of the Torah. And in Romans 14, Paul has a long discussion of how to treat Christians who have different views of what is permissible to eat. Paul's starting point is clear: "All food is clean" (v. 20)—a clear rejection of the Old Testament's food laws. Jesus's followers, Paul taught, are free to "eat anything sold in the meat market" (1 Cor. 10:25).[59]

The observance of the Torah's strict food laws was one important reason many devout Jews did not eat with or even visit gentiles. One of the first things Peter tells Cornelius is, "You are well aware that it is against our law for a Jew to associate with or visit a Gentile" (Acts 10:28). But Peter remembers the vision that has declared all food clean (10:11–16), and he therefore tells Cornelius that he now realizes he should "not call anyone impure or unclean" (10:28). Unfortunately, Peter seems to have relapsed to earlier Jewish thinking when he later visits the multiracial Christian community in Antioch. At first Peter eats with gentile Christians; but, when Christian Jews from the "circumcision group" arrive from Jerusalem, Peter stops eating with gentile believers. Paul denounces Peter to his face, insisting that the very heart of the gospel is at stake. All followers of Jesus know, Paul insists, that everyone, both Jew and gentile, "is not justified by the works of the law, but by faith in Jesus

59. See also Col. 2:16.

Christ" (Gal. 2:16). The Torah's food laws are irrelevant for both Jewish and gentile followers of Jesus.

A bleeding woman is accepted. Also striking is Jesus's response to a woman with a bleeding disorder who touches him. The Torah not only specifies that a woman is regularly unclean for seven days because of her monthly period and therefore must not be touched (Lev. 15:19–24). It also states that a woman with an extended discharge of blood is unclean and that anyone who touches her must wash and be unclean until evening (15:25–27). Luke reports that a woman with a bleeding disorder for ten years touches Jesus in a crowd. According to the law, Jesus is supposed to bathe and remain unclean until evening. Instead, Jesus calls her "daughter," commends her faith, and continues on his journey (Luke 8:42–48).

Circumcision is nothing. Male circumcision was a central part of the Mosaic law and an important practice for first-century Jews. It was a crucial way that Jews distinguished themselves from gentiles. Genesis 17 specifies circumcision for Abraham's descendants as an essential sign of God's covenant. Any uncircumcised descendant must be cut off from God's people because "he has broken my covenant" (17:14). At the Jerusalem Council, the early church clearly rejects the idea that gentile Christians must be circumcised to be part of the people of God (Act 15). Paul is very clear in Romans 4 that both Jewish Christians (who are circumcised) and gentile Christians (who are not) are equally children of Abraham (4:9–17). Circumcision has no significance. It is as both circumcised and uncircumcised followers of Jesus share Abraham's faith, which was "credited to him as righteousness" (4:9), that they are Abraham's children. "Circumcision is nothing and uncircumcision is nothing" (1 Cor. 7:19). "In Christ Jesus neither circumcision nor uncircumcision has any value" (Gal. 5:6; also 6:15). Circumcision, so central to Old Testament faith, is irrelevant for God's new multiethnic people. Enns is right: "Because of Jesus, the physical marker commanded by God to be an everlasting command to mark off the people of God had met its expiration date."[60]

Torah is abolished. The New Testament does not merely set aside important parts of the law such as circumcision, Sabbath, and food laws. Ephesians says that the law itself has been "set aside," abolished, in Christ (Eph. 2:15). One grasps how radical this teaching is only when one remembers how important the law is to Old Testament life.

Deuteronomy says that as Moses prepares to give the "decrees and laws" to Israel, he says, "Follow them so that you may live" (Deut. 4:1). In another place, God commands the people, "Keep my decrees and laws, for the person

60. Enns, *Bible Tells Me So,* 225.

who obeys them will live by them" (Lev. 18:5; also Ezek. 20:11). At the end of Deuteronomy, Moses orders a copy of the law to be placed in the ark of the covenant and read to the people at the festival every seven years so the people will "follow carefully all the words of this law" (Deut. 31:12). But just a few verses later, Moses predicts that the people will disobey the law and disaster will result (31:24–29). Keeping the law brings life. Disobeying the law brings divine punishment.

That was still the belief of devout Jews in Jesus's day. Failure to keep God's law had resulted in national destruction and exile (Deut. 31:24–29). But they waited expectantly for a return from exile and the freeing of Israel from its pagan masters. There was widespread belief that "those who are faithful to the covenant God and [God's] Torah will be rescued from their enemies."[61] Some Jewish teachers taught that repentance and keeping the law would hasten the coming of the Messiah.[62]

Why then does Paul teach that "all who rely on the works of the law are under a curse" (Gal. 3:10)? Why does he insist that "you who are trying to be justified by the law have been alienated from Christ" (5:4)?

In Christ, people are justified by faith. But the law, Paul insists, "is not based on faith; on the contrary, it says [quoting Lev. 18:5], 'The person who does these things will live by them'" (Gal. 3:12). According to the law, life comes through obeying its provisions.

Paul, of course, believes that the law itself is good but that the effect of its demands is to reveal the extent and power of sin (Rom. 7:7–12). Thus the result of the law is to disclose our powerlessness and lead us to the solution in Christ. In fact, Paul understands the law as a "guardian" (needed only until the minor reaches adulthood). "We were held in custody under the law, locked up until the faith that was to come [in Christ] would be revealed. So the law was our guardian until Christ came that we might be justified by faith. Now that this faith has come, we are no longer under a guardian" (Gal. 3:23–25). Paul is very clear. Believers in Christ—both Jew and gentile—are "not under the law" (5:18). The law is a mere "shadow" of what is present in Christ (Col. 2:17). Paul is setting aside not this or that minor provision of the Old Testament but the Torah itself, which is at the very center of Old Testament faith.

The temple is replaced. Along with the Torah, the temple in Jerusalem was at the core of Jewish life in Jesus's day. Yahweh was uniquely present there. In the sacrificial system at the temple, Yahweh offered forgiveness and cleansing. N. T. Wright says, "Forgiveness, and consequent reintegration into the

---

61. N. T. Wright, *New Testament and the People of God*, 221.
62. Keener, *Acts*, 2:1106–8.

community of Israel, was attained by visiting the temple and taking part in the appropriate forms of ritual and worship."[63] He continues, "The Temple thus formed in principle the heart of Judaism."[64] But Jesus somewhat indirectly and the later New Testament explicitly say that Jesus replaces the temple.

Matthew, Mark, and Luke all tell the story of the lame man carried to Jesus by his friends (Matt. 9:2–8; Mark 2:1–12; Luke 5:17–26). But when Jesus says, "Son, your sins are forgiven" (Mark 2:5), the religious leaders are horrified and denounce Jesus's action as blasphemy. "He's blaspheming! Who can forgive sins but God alone?" (Mark 2:7). Every good Jew knew that God forgave sins "through the officially established and authorized channels of Temple and priesthood."[65] Jesus is implying here, as N. T. Wright points out, that "all that the Temple had stood for was now available through Jesus."[66]

Jesus's "cleansing" of the temple is an even more explicit claim to have authority over the temple. Jewish belief in Jesus's day understood the true, expected Davidic king to be the true ruler of the temple.[67] Jesus has just ridden into Jerusalem in the "triumphal entry," making a clear claim to be the expected Messiah. Now he claims the authority to "cleanse" the temple. If N. T. Wright is correct, Jesus's action in the temple is not only a judgment on the temple but also by implication a claim that he himself is the new temple.[68] Perhaps that is part of the implication in the statement attributed to Jesus, that he will destroy the temple and rebuild it in three days (Matt. 26:61; Mark 14:58; 15:29; John 2:19). In Matthew 12:6, Jesus says, in his dispute over the Sabbath and his claim to be Lord of the Sabbath, that "something greater than the temple is here."

Whether or not Jesus himself claims that he is replacing the temple, the New Testament certainly does. Hebrews 7–10 has a long discussion of Jesus as both priest (7:11–12; 9:11) and sacrifice (9:26). The true temple is in heaven, not in Jerusalem. The Jerusalem temple is only a "copy and shadow of what is in heaven" (8:5). The old sacrificial system had to be constantly repeated to cover sins. But Jesus has offered himself in the true heavenly temple "once for all by his own blood, thus obtaining eternal redemption" (9:12).

Jesus establishes a better covenant. Hebrews makes it quite clear that Jesus has replaced everything that the temple stood for and accomplished. The old covenant, which prescribes regular sacrifices in the temple in Jerusalem, is now

63. N. T. Wright, *New Testament and the People of God*, 225.
64. N. T. Wright, *New Testament and the People of God*, 226.
65. N. T. Wright, *Jesus and the Victory of God*, 435.
66. N. T. Wright, *Jesus and the Victory of God*, 436.
67. N. T. Wright, *Jesus and the Victory of God*, 490.
68. N. T. Wright, *Jesus and the Victory of God*, 423, 426.

"obsolete; and what is obsolete and outdated will soon disappear" (8:13). Jesus has established a "new" and "better" covenant, which is "superior to the old one" (7:22; 8:6). In fact, in some sense, even though the law prescribes regular sacrifices, God does not really desire that (10:8). Jesus therefore rightly "sets aside the first to establish the second" (10:9). The law, the temple in Jerusalem with its sacrifice, and the old covenant are all only a "shadow" (10:1) of what we have in Christ.[69]

Paul is at least as stark in describing the difference between the old and new covenants (2 Cor. 3:4–11). The old covenant "engraved in letters on stone" (v. 7) came with a glorious demonstration of God's presence, but it was "transitory" (v. 11) and brought "death" (v. 7) and condemnation (v. 9). Citing what he says he has received "from the Lord," Paul passes on Jesus's words "this cup is the new covenant in my blood" at the Last Supper (1 Cor. 11:23–25).[70] The "new covenant" is far more glorious and (unlike the temporary first covenant) lasts forever (2 Cor. 3:6, 11).

The story of the transfiguration (Luke 9:28–36) also indirectly suggests Jesus's superiority to the Law and the Prophets of the old covenant. In the story Jesus appears on the mountain with Moses (who represents the Law) and Elijah (who represents the Prophets). But then the representatives of the Law and the Prophets disappear, and Jesus is left alone with his three disciples. The voice from heaven declares, "This is my Son, whom I have chosen; listen to him" (v. 35).

Jesus's superiority to the Law and the Prophets in the old covenant also emerges in Jesus's discussion of John the Baptist (Matt. 11:7–15). Jesus says that "all the Prophets and the Law prophesied until John" (v. 13). Jesus considers John the Baptist at least as great as the greatest Old Testament prophets ("Among those born of women there has not risen anyone greater than John the Baptist," v. 11). But then Jesus adds that "whoever is least in the kingdom of heaven is greater than he" (v. 11)—a clear implication that Jesus and his dawning kingdom transcend the Law and the Prophets.

We see a similar claim in the Gospel of John. "The law was given through Moses; grace and truth came through Jesus Christ" (1:17). Clearly what Jesus brings greatly surpasses the law given by Moses. And the next verse underlines John's point: "No one has ever seen God, but the one and only Son, who is himself God and is in closest relationship with the Father, has made him known" (1:18). This statement echoes Jesus's statement in Matthew 11:27:

69. Ephesians 2:19–21 says that Jesus's new multiethnic people is a "holy temple in the Lord" (v. 21) and Jesus is the chief cornerstone. Second Corinthians 6:16–17 also depicts the church as God's temple.
70. So too Luke 22:20; Matthew and Mark do not have the word "new" in most manuscripts.

"No one knows the Father except the Son and those to whom the Son chooses to reveal him." In fact, no one can come to the Father except through Christ (John 14:6). The revelation in Christ clearly transcends the Mosaic law.

N. T. Wright is clearly correct in insisting that Paul (and the rest of the New Testament authors) does not see Jesus initiating something totally new. Rather, he fulfills God's plan all along to bless all nations through Abraham and his descendants (Gen. 12:1–3). In Christ, God brought to fulfillment the long-standing plan to make Israel a light to the nations.[71] The law, however, with its food laws, circumcision, and strict Sabbath observance, has erected a "dividing wall of hostility" (Eph. 2:14) between Jew and gentile. But Christ has set aside the law with its commands (2:15), and the result is one new reconciled humanity of Jew and gentile. That is the mystery of the gospel that has been "hidden for ages" (Col. 1:26). But in fulfilling the promise of the Old Testament, Jesus and his new community transcend and set aside central aspects of the Old Testament.

It is in this context that we must understand Jesus's setting aside of the Old Testament's clear teaching on oaths and an eye for an eye—in fact, Jesus's entire teaching and example against violence. Many devout Jews of Jesus's day fervently believed that God would keep God's ancient promises to Israel by sending a military messiah who would wage violent war against the pagans, destroying them and establishing Jerusalem and a rebuilt temple as the center of the world. Jesus did claim to be the expected Messiah, and he believed that God was fulfilling in him the ancient promise to Abraham to make his descendants a blessing to the whole world. But Jesus taught that loving enemies, not killing them, was God's way. Jesus insisted that children of the heavenly Father must love their enemies. And Jesus modeled that teaching all the way to the cross. Furthermore, God raised him on the third day to demonstrate that Jesus's way was God's way.

The evidence is quite clear. In both his life and his teaching, Jesus rejects the way of violence, loves his enemies, and insists that his disciples must do the same. If one confesses, as the church has for two millennia, that the teacher from Nazareth is God in the flesh, then we dare not say that Jesus is wrong. To reject Jesus's teaching on loving enemies is to deny the deity of Christ.

And if we believe with the early Christians that Jesus Christ is God's final[72] revelation to us, that the old covenant is just a mere shadow of the new covenant in Christ, that the new covenant fulfills by *setting aside* central aspects

71. N. T. Wright, *Jesus and the Victory of God*, 594–97 and elsewhere.
72. Final, until the return of Christ and the establishment of the new heaven and earth. But that does not mean that Jesus in the incarnation revealed everything there is to know about God.

(law, circumcision, temple) of the old covenant, then we must start with Jesus's teaching about who God is and what God demands of God's people. To start with Old Testament statements about violence and insist that Jesus's teaching must be interpreted to fit Old Testament texts flatly contradicts the entire New Testament hermeneutic. The New Testament constantly understands the Old Testament through the lens of the final revelation in Christ.[73] The former is but a shadow. The clear revelation is in Jesus Christ the Lord. To return to the shadow is finally to deny Christ.

That still leaves me without a fully satisfactory answer to the question of how to reconcile Old Testament statements about violence with Jesus and the New Testament. Are these Old Testament statements simply misguided ideas by sinful, societally conditioned human beings? Perhaps, but I do not see how that fits with Jesus's teaching about the Old Testament as the word of God. Did God actually command the slaughter of the Canaanites? Perhaps, and if God did, I accept the truth that finite human beings have no authority or standing to judge the Infinite One. But if Jesus was right in revealing that God is love, indeed so profoundly love that God even submits to the terror of Roman crucifixion out of amazing, unfathomable love for sinful enemies, then I cannot see how the Father of Jesus would command genocide.

It is true that some Old Testament prophets seem to speak of a future messianic time when war will end and peace will prevail. We also know that some of these passages were understood in Jesus's day to refer to a coming Messiah.[74] Jesus certainly claims to be that Messiah and teaches that the messianic kingdom breaking into history means loving enemies, even vicious Roman imperialists. Thus, passages in the Prophets that point toward a future day when God will establish a new covenant and bring a new day when swords will be beaten into plowshares fits well with the understanding that whatever the proper understanding of violence in the Old Testament, we now live under the new covenant with its rejection of killing.

Perhaps this side of eternity, we will never have an adequate answer to the question of violence in the Old Testament. But that lack of clarity in no way leaves uncertain what faithful disciples of Jesus should believe and do. If God's final revelation, the eternal Son of God, calls his disciples to love their enemies, we must obey.

---

73. See the ways the New Testament interprets many Old Testament passages to speak of Christ even though that does not seem to be the meaning of the Old Testament author. See Boyd, *Crucifixion of the Warrior God*, 1:93–140, 504–6.

74. See chap. 1, "Messianic Expectations."

11

What If Most (or All) Christians Became Pacifists?

Repeated headlines remind us that there are powerful terrorist groups that seek to destroy the United States, Israel, and "Western values."[1] Radical Islamic terrorists are only a small part of the global Muslim community. But they have frequently terrorized, raped, beheaded, and slaughtered Christians in the past couple decades. Groups like ISIS and Al-Qaeda are a genuine threat to many people, especially Christians. Like vicious people of the past—Hitler, Stalin, Pol Pot—they seem to respond to nothing except force. The only way to stop their vicious behavior seems to be to fight and kill them.

If most or all Christians became pacifists, would evil not rage unchecked? Would not Christians be slaughtered by the millions? Would not Hitler's racist Nazism, Stalin's totalitarian communism, or Osama bin Laden's ruthless terrorism conquer the world?

It is interesting that a very similar question faced the early church. Sometime about AD 180, a fairly well-informed Roman pagan named Celsus wrote a sharp attack on Christians. One of his central arguments was that since Christians refuse to kill, if all Romans became Christians, barbarians would

1. See the discussion and many citations in Clough and Stiltner, *Faith and Force*, 146–74.

invade and destroy the Roman Empire. "For if all were to do the same as you [Christians] . . . the affairs of the earth would fall into the hands of the wildest and most lawless barbarians."[2]

More than fifty years after Celsus's attack, Origen (perhaps the most widely read Christian author in the first half of the third century) wrote a reply. Origen agrees with Celsus that Christians refuse to kill. But he insists that if all Romans became Christians, God would protect them. "If all the Romans, according to the supposition of Celsus, embrace the Christian faith, they will, when they pray, overcome their enemies; or rather, they will not war at all, being guarded by that divine power." Origen goes on to acknowledge that sometimes God does allow people to persecute Christians. But Christ has overcome the world, and persecution lasts only as long as God allows it. Even when persecution happens, Origen says, Christians will say to their persecutors, "I can do all things, through Christ Jesus our Lord, which strengtheneth me."[3] Origen clearly believes that God would not allow vicious enemies to destroy Christianity. And even though Christianity was an illegal religion and Roman officials martyred many Christians in the second and third centuries, Christianity flourished and expanded rapidly.

I think that the first and most important response to the concern of this chapter (if all Christians refuse to defend themselves by fighting, they may be destroyed) is essentially the response of Origen. Christians believe that the risen Lord Jesus is now "ruler of the kings of the earth" (Rev. 1:5). We know that "all authority in heaven *and on earth* has been given" to him (Matt. 28:18). As Jesus tells Pilate, "You would have no power over me if it were not given to you from above" (John 19:11). Sometimes God allows Christians to suffer martyrdom. Sometimes God marvelously, even miraculously, prevents that. But we know that the gates of hell cannot prevail against the church (Matt. 16:18). We know where history is going. We know the final outcome. We know that in God's time, Christ will return and complete the victory over all evil. Until then, Christ's faithful followers will sometimes experience terrible persecution. But they cannot be defeated. And the Risen One, who is *now* Lord of heaven and earth, has promised, "I am with you always, to the very end of the age" (28:20). Since Jesus has taught his disciples to love rather than kill their enemies, we can trust our Lord to prevent evil persons from destroying his church. And as the evidence of the early church demonstrates, the witness of faithful martyrs trusting the Lord even in death draws more and more people to become disciples.

2. Celsus quoted in Origen's reply, *Contra Celsum* 8.68; quoted in Sider, *Early Church on Killing*, 80.
3. Origen, *Contra Celsum* 8.70; Sider, *Early Church on Killing*, 81.

But that is not the only important thing to say. First, Christians who believe Christ calls them never to kill do not, must not, become passive in the face of evil and injustice. There is a vast range of powerful ways to work nonviolently against injustice. Especially in the last hundred years, courageous leaders like Gandhi and Martin Luther King Jr. have demonstrated that nonviolent action can be an effective way to challenge and overcome evil. As we have seen, daring Christian leaders in Poland and East Germany led the way in nonviolent campaigns that succeeded in overthrowing communist dictators. Similar, successful nonviolent campaigns also overthrew vicious dictators in the Philippines and Liberia.[4] And scholars who have examined the most important armed and unarmed insurrections from 1900 to 2006 discovered that "nonviolent resistance campaigns were nearly twice as likely to achieve full or partial success as their violent counterparts."[5] If most Christians became pacifists, they would invest large resources in preparing for and engaging in nonviolent campaigns against injustice and violence.[6]

Second, pacifist Christians would have a great deal to contribute to resolving the current conflicted relationship between the world's two largest religions, Christianity and Islam. Only a very small number of Muslims are terrorists like ISIS and Al-Qaeda, seeking to kill Christians. But the larger Muslim world has genuine grievances against Christians. Many Muslims still remember the medieval Crusades when European Christians invaded the Holy Land, controlled for centuries by Muslim rulers, and slaughtered tens of thousands of Muslims. For centuries, Arabic Muslim civilization was more advanced than Christian European civilization—whether in philosophy, medicine, mathematics, or science. But in the nineteenth century, white "Christian" European colonial powers used their military superiority to dominate Muslim societies from North Africa to Indonesia. And in the last one hundred years, European and American "Christian" nations have used their economic and military power in ways that vast numbers of Muslims have felt to be unfair. With partial justification, many Muslims blame their poverty and other problems on "Christian" nations.

I do not mean to argue that the "Christian" West is to blame for all or most of the problems—poverty, lack of modern education, dictatorial regimes—in many majority Muslim nations. But we have contributed to part of the problem. And that fact gives some credibility to the Islamic terrorists' claim that the only solution is to seek to destroy the "Christian" West.

4. See Sider, *Nonviolent Action*, chaps. 2, 3, 5, 6, 7, 8.
5. Chenoweth and Stephan, *Why Civil Resistance Works*, 7.
6. See the suggestions in Sider, *Nonviolent Action*, 167–73. They would, of course, also use all the nonviolent peacemaking techniques discussed in Stassen, *Just Peacemaking*.

In the short run, just war Christians need not fear that most Christians will become pacifists in the next decade or two. There will be plenty of just war Christians to fight the military battles they believe are necessary to resist terrorists. But almost every informed Western leader knows (and many say) that radical Islam cannot be defeated only with arms. Susan Thistlethwaite is right: "Only justice will actually, finally, stop terrorism. Violence only creates more violence."[7] The primary struggle with radical Islam is in the realm of ideas. We must help Muslim youth tempted by radical Islamists to see that education, freedom, economic development, scientific advance, and peaceful cooperation are the way forward.

Third, as we saw earlier, in the early 1990s a group of pacifist and just war Christian ethicists began a dialogue that has led to what they call Just Peacemaking. Without resolving their disagreement about whether Christians should ever kill, they agree that there are many effective nonviolent practices that promote peace: fostering sustainable economic development, advancing democracy and human rights, acknowledging responsibility for injustice and seeking forgiveness, promoting cooperative conflict resolution, supporting nonviolent intervention, and encouraging grassroots peacemaking groups and voluntary associations.[8] These scholars insist that "we need *initiatives* to correct the injustices that cause terrorism; *structures of justice* that dry up the sources of recruitment of terrorists."[9] Whereas violence, as Dr. King said, creates more violence, nonviolent alternatives nurture peace and justice.

Obviously, both just war and pacifist Christians can and should work together on nonviolent, just peacemaking initiatives. But pacifists should be especially active. And they are. Mennonite Central Committee (MCC), the relief and development arm of Mennonite churches, invests tens of millions of dollars every year in economic development—including work in poor Muslim nations. MCC has been especially active assisting Syrian refugees from the prolonged war in Syria. Christian Peacemaker Teams (which grew out of Mennonite circles) have been active in Israel-Palestine, using the tactics of nonviolent intervention, seeking to promote peace with justice for both Israelis and Palestinians.[10] (The failure to achieve a just resolution of that long conflict continues to be an effective recruiting tool for Islamic terrorists.) And Christian Peacemaker Teams have inspired and helped train new Muslim Peacemaker Teams and encouraged a growing nonviolent intervention in situations of violent conflict. Mennonite John Paul Lederach has led in developing

7. Thistlethwaite, "New Wars, Old Wineskins," 264.
8. Stassen, *Just Peacemaking*. They discuss ten different practices.
9. Stassen, *Just Peacemaking*, 2 (italics original).
10. Sider, *Nonviolent Action*, 148–50.

peace-building processes in intrastate conflict by bringing together top-level, mid-level, and grassroots leaders.[11]

Precisely because they are not closely identified with the military activities of Western nations in Muslim countries, Christian pacifists have a unique opportunity to initiate dialogue and cooperative programs of social and economic development with Muslims deeply suspicious of Western initiatives. They can begin conversations and programs that would be considered highly suspect and probably rejected if proposed by official representatives of Western nations. Developing effective programs of quality education and economic opportunity will help impoverished Muslim youth see a more promising alternative to terrorist propaganda. Initiating intensive Christian-Muslim dialogue will help promote growing mutual respect between the two major world religions today—and point to a way to affirm each other's right to exist and flourish without denying genuine theological differences.[12] Pacifists have a unique opportunity to lead the way toward greatly reducing one of today's most serious conflicts—one that, if unresolved, could lead to an incredibly destructive "conflict of civilizations."

Muslim-Christian conflict, of course, is not the only area of violence in our world. Selfish violent persons threaten the property and lives of people in every society. Police are intended to help prevent societies from slipping into anarchy. And aggressive nations frequently threaten their neighbors.

To provide any substantial discussion of how Christians who believe that our Lord calls us never to kill should deal with the issues of police and national defense would require at least two other books. Here, in a very few paragraphs, I can only hint at what could be developed at much greater length.

Whether or not it would be possible someday to move to completely nonviolent police work, it is clearly the case that the criminal justice system, including the work of police, could be improved through new approaches of restorative justice and nonviolent policing.

Pacifists have pioneered now widely influential Victim Offender Reconciliation Programs (VORP).[13] These programs seek to provide restitution to victims and create reconciliation between victims and offenders.[14] Programs

---

11. Lederach, *Building Peace*.

12. See, e.g., the invitation to David W. Shenk (the founder of Eastern Mennonite Missions' Christian/Muslim Relations Team) to bring 2,500 copies of a book he coauthored with Muslim scholar Badru D. Kateregga called *A Muslim and a Christian in Dialogue* to distribute in 2017 at the largest annual gathering of American Muslims. See *The Mennonite*, Daily News Posts, July 25, 2017.

13. Zehr, *Changing Lenses*. Howard Zehr is widely recognized as having played a key role in launching VORP.

14. See the vast bibliographical references in the Wikipedia article on "Restorative Justice," https://en.wikipedia.org/wiki/Restorative_justice.

of restorative justice help offenders accept responsibility for their evil actions, face the people they have harmed, and seek to right the damage they have caused. There has been a great deal of research on the vast number of VORPs that have been launched in recent decades. An extensive review of the research has shown that VORPs reduce recidivism, improve the lives of both victims and offenders, and reduce the cost of criminal justice.[15] People who have studied the evidence recommend major expansion of this approach.

An increasing number of police departments use Tasers, which emit a strong electrical charge that temporarily disables (but normally does not permanently harm) an assailant, who then can safely be arrested.[16] The use of Taser guns and pepper spray could be greatly expanded.

In recent decades, "community policing" has been embraced in a number of communities. Using more foot patrols so that officers become known personally in the community and therefore more trusted has tended to reduce crime. In one instance of community policing in Boston, where unarmed patrols of church groups played a key role, the number of homicides dropped from 152 in 1990 to 31 in 1999.[17] If combined with efforts to reduce structural factors nurturing crime (e.g., racism and lack of economic opportunity), much greater adoption of the best community policing efforts would reduce crime in a largely nonviolent way.

Citizen patrols where unarmed local residents volunteer to walk at night to discourage crime have occurred for decades in some neighborhoods. The Christian Peacemaker Teams have modeled a version of this in Cleveland.[18] Pacifists should greatly expand this effort, training large numbers of church members to patrol their neighborhoods and embrace other nonviolent responses to crime.

Is it naive to think that policing could move significantly away from its current use of lethal weapons? "Thirty years ago, much of the police would have considered it ridiculous to try to bring together victims and offenders to talk about the harm that was done in crime. Today we have a restorative justice movement that is effectively growing in leaps and bounds. Perhaps such a paradigm-shift in policing is more within our reach than we might imagine."[19] No one, of course, can accurately predict the future. But there are many ways that pacifists can act now to develop and encourage more widespread use of

15. Sherman and Strong, *Restorative Justice*. See also Sullivan and Tifft, *Restorative Justice*; and Moran, "Restorative Justice."

16. Friesen, "In Search of Security," 69–70.

17. Friesen, "In Search of Security," 69. See also Gingerich, "Breaking the Uneasy Silence," 397.

18. Gingerich, "Breaking the Uneasy Silence," 400.

19. Gingerich, "Breaking the Uneasy Silence," 401–2.

nonviolent methods in policing. Only if we engage in an extensive sustained effort in that direction will we discover what is possible.

Gene Sharp, the most distinguished advocate of Civilian-Based Defense (CBD), defines CBD as a national policy in which "the whole population and the society's institutions become the fighting forces." By training the entire population of a country to oppose invaders with nonviolent noncooperation, preparing for CBD would hopefully deter attack and, if a country was invaded, make consolidation of political control by the invader impossible.[20] Michael Walzer, in his famous book *Just and Unjust Wars*, devotes several pages to Sharp's proposal of CBD. Walzer notes that no nation has abandoned military defense and decided to rely only on CBD to defend itself. So there is no evidence that it works. But he adds, "No nonviolent struggle has ever been undertaken by a people trained in advance in its methods and prepared (as soldiers are in the case of war) to accept its costs, so it might be true."[21] But Walzer believes that, at best, it would work only against an invader who embraced fundamental moral values. It would be useless, he believes, against a Hitler or Stalin who would simply slaughter people until the civilian defenders were cowed into submission.[22]

Actually, there is some evidence that something like CBD partially worked against Hitler. Although they did not organize a national strategy of CBD before Hitler's invasion, both Norway and Denmark engaged in widespread national nonviolent resistance and civil disobedience. In Norway, after Hitler's army quickly conquered the country, the teachers and church leaders successfully resisted the Nazi attempt to take over the schools and churches to indoctrinate the population with fascist ideology. And they successfully saved more than half of Norway's Jewish population. After occupation by Hitler's army, Denmark used widespread noncooperation, from the Danish king to the average citizen, to save 93 percent of Denmark's Jews by secretly helping them escape to neutral Sweden.[23]

Military specialists have urged more intensive study of CBD. General Jacques Pâris de Bollardière, one of France's most highly decorated generals, has urged France to replace its military defense with CBD. Commander Sir Stephen King-Hall, a retired British officer, wrote two books advocating

20. Sharp, *Making Europe Unconquerable*, 2–3. See also Sharp, *Civilian-Based Defense*; and Sharp, *Politics of Nonviolent Action*.
21. Walzer, *Just and Unjust Wars*, 330.
22. Walzer, *Just and Unjust Wars*, 331–33.
23. For the bibliographical evidence, see Sider and Taylor, *Nuclear Holocaust*, 238–43. Pages 231–92 offer an extended discussion of CBD. K. B. Payne and K. I. Payne, *Just Defense*, 223–49, contains a long critique of *Nuclear Holocaust*.

nonmilitary strategies as the best means for defending England against foreign aggression.[24] When Sharp's book *The Politics of Nonviolent Action* appeared with its many examples of nonmilitary defense, US military journals of the army, navy, and air force reviewed it positively and recommended "serious consideration."[25] At one point, the Swedish government authorized its defense minister to set up a special government body to prepare a plan for nonmilitary national defense.[26]

In their famous peace pastoral letter in 1983, *The Challenge of Peace*, the US Catholic bishops cite the work of Sharp and urge further study of CBD. "Nonviolent means of resistance to evil deserve much more study and consideration than they have thus far received. There have been significant instances in which people have successfully resisted oppression without recourse to arms." After citing the cases of Norway and Denmark in the struggle against Hitler, they note the way that governments can organize and train their people in "the techniques of peaceable non-compliance and noncooperation as a means of hindering an invading force." They acknowledge that such an approach would be costly and have no guarantees. But the Catholic bishops conclude, "Before the possibility is dismissed as impractical or unrealistic, we urge that it be measured against the almost certain effects of a major war."[27]

For the past seventy plus years, the great powers have relied on massive nuclear deterrence to protect against foreign invasion. We have hoped that the strategy of mutual assured destruction (MAD)—if the enemy attacks us with nuclear weapons, we can, within less than an hour, obliterate them—would prevent war.[28] Thank God, we have avoided a nuclear war—although we came dangerously close in the Cuban missile crisis, and there have been several instances when for minutes American forces thought the Russians had launched nuclear missiles against the US.[29] Nuclear war has seemed less likely since the collapse of the Soviet Union. But nuclear weapons continue to spread and recent developments in North Korea and Russia underline the continuing danger. A major nuclear exchange would obliterate civilization as we know it. As the Catholic bishops recognized, both morality and realism compel us to explore the possibility of the alternative of nonviolent national self-defense.

24. See Sider and Taylor, *Nuclear Holocaust*, 235, for bibliographic details.
25. Sider and Taylor, *Nuclear Holocaust*, 234–35.
26. Sider and Taylor, *Nuclear Holocaust*, 234.
27. *Challenge of Peace*, §§222–24, pp. 94–95.
28. See Sider and Taylor, *Nuclear Holocaust*, 64–65, for the statements of many American leaders that MAD has been their official policy.
29. See Sider and Taylor, *Nuclear Holocaust*, 55–56, for examples.

What would happen if all the Christians in the US (or the whole world) would decide that Jesus calls us to refuse to kill? We would suffer greatly. Evil people would kill many millions. We would suffer a huge loss of possessions. The suffering would be immense. But using the methods of war has also been deadly. Eighty-six million people died in wars between just 1900 and 1989.[30] The path of killing also has enormous costs.

If all Christians decided to love their enemies rather than try to kill them, I think it is reasonable to expect that fewer people would die from violence in the next one hundred years than in the past century. And sometimes non-violent resistance would be stunningly successful.

There is clear evidence from successful nonviolent campaigns that coura-geous nonviolent resistance sometimes moves the hearts of hardened soldiers. When a million Filipino citizens dared to stand in front of the tanks sent by the ruthless dictator President Marcos to crush them, the soldiers hesitated. One eyewitness reported, "The soldiers atop the armored carriers pointed their guns of every make at the crowd, but their faces portrayed agony. . . . The soldiers did not have the heart to pull the triggers on civilians armed only with their convictions."[31] Praying nuns and unarmed civilians conquered a vicious dictator.

In 1989, stunningly courageous nonviolent campaigns in Poland and East Germany overthrew ruthless communist dictators. In the Soviet Union, Presi-dent Gorbachev initiated significant reforms and allowed elections in the individual republics of the Soviet Union. Boris Yeltsin was elected as leader of the Russian Republic. But on August 18, 1991, hardliners launched a coup d'état against Gorbachev and sent tanks to arrest Yeltsin at the Russian White House in Moscow. Fortunately, thousands of unarmed civilians filled the streets. Yeltsin climbed up on one of the tanks and persuaded the troops to disobey orders to shoot Yeltsin's unarmed supporters. The coup failed.[32] Sometimes the daring actions of nonviolent protesters prove stronger than the commands of military superiors!

Not always, of course. We dare not forget the Tiananmen Square massacre in China in 1989. If all Christians refused to kill, there would be terrible suf-fering and many deaths—probably millions. But would there be as many as in the wars of the twentieth century?

And what would Christ our Lord do if his disciples all chose to face death rather than kill their enemies? Again, we cannot know in advance. The book

30. Glover, *Humanity*, 47.
31. Cited in Sider, *Nonviolent Action*, 74.
32. Sider, *Nonviolent Action*, 79–81, 83–100.

of Acts and early church history show that sometimes God intervened miraculously and sometimes God allowed Christians to be martyred. But if we truly believe our basic confession that the resurrected Jesus is *now* Lord "in heaven and on earth," *now* ruler of the "kings of the earth," then it is not naive to expect that some surprising things would happen if Christians refused to kill those who attacked them. We have Jesus's promise that the gates of hell cannot prevail against the church. We know from church history that the death of martyrs often attracted even more people to confess Christ.

I expect that if most Christians today would decide to love their enemies rather than try to fight them with violence, we would experience perhaps the most amazing epoch of church history. Millions of Christians would suffer and die. But more millions of astonished observers would decide to embrace Christ. I even dare to expect that fewer people would die than if we continue on the path of violent defense, developing ever more lethal weapons. That expectation, of course, is only a hope. Since the third century, most Christians have chosen war rather than nonviolence. We will have empirical evidence of my hopeful expectation only if most Christians dare to decide that their Lord summons them to love their enemies rather than kill them.

12

Nonviolence
and the Atonement

The foundation of Christian nonviolence lies not in some calculation of effectiveness. It rests in the cross. The ultimate ground of the biblical teaching to love one's enemies is the nature of God revealed first in Jesus's teaching and life and then most powerfully in his death.

Jesus does not say that one should practice loving nonviolence because it will always transform vicious enemies into bosom friends. The cross stands as a harsh reminder that love for enemies does not always work—at least not in the short run. Jesus grounds his call to love enemies not in the hope of reciprocity but rather in the very nature of God: "Love your enemies and pray for those who persecute you, *that* you may be children of your Father in heaven. He causes his sun to rise on the evil and the good, and sends rain on the righteous and the unrighteous" (Matt. 5:44–45). Jesus says the same thing in the Beatitudes: "Blessed are the peacemakers, for they will be called children of God" (5:9). God loves God's enemies. Instead of promptly destroying sinners, God continues to shower the good gifts of creation on them. Since that is the way God acts, those who want to be God's sons and daughters must do likewise. One fundamental aspect of the holiness and perfection of God is that God loves God's enemies. Those who seek to reflect God's holiness will likewise love their enemies—even when it involves a cross.

In chapter 1 we discussed both Jesus's unconventional teaching on God's prodigal forgiveness and also his unorthodox view of a suffering Messiah.[1] The link between these central affirmations of Jesus and his teaching on nonviolence now becomes more clear. The divine Father, so eager to forgive repentant sinners, is the one whose love for enemies we are summoned to imitate.

Jesus's conception of the suffering Messiah who goes to the cross as a ransom for sinners underlines most powerfully his teaching on God's way of dealing with enemies. At the Last Supper, Jesus states unequivocally that he is going to die for the sake of others. All four versions of the Eucharistic words,[2] carefully handed down in the early church's oral tradition, contain this central notion. "This is my body, which is for you" (1 Cor. 11:24). "This is my blood of the covenant, which is poured out for many for the forgiveness of sins" (Matt. 26:28). Jesus's death is the sacrificial inauguration of a new covenant. The one who has claimed divine authority (blasphemously, his enemies charge) to forgive sinners now dies for others at the demand of those very enemies. The one who has taught his followers to imitate God's love for enemies now dies with a forgiving prayer on his lips for the enemies who send him to the cross (Luke 23:34).

That the cross is the ultimate demonstration that God deals with God's enemies through suffering love receives its clearest theological expression in Paul. "God demonstrates his own love for us in this: While we were still sinners, Christ died for us. . . . While we were God's *enemies*, we were reconciled to him through the death of his Son" (Rom. 5:8, 10). Jesus's vicarious cross for sinners is the foundation and deepest expression of Jesus's command to love one's enemies. As the substitutionary view of the atonement indicates, we are enemies in the double sense that sinful persons are hostile to God and that the just, holy Creator hates sin (1:18). For those who know the law, failure to obey it results in a divine curse. But Christ has redeemed us from that curse by becoming a curse for us (Gal. 3:10–14). On the cross the one who knew no sin was made sin for us sinful enemies (2 Cor. 5:21). Miroslav Volf puts it well: "As God does not abandon the godless to their evil but gives the divine self for them in order to receive them into divine communion through atonement, so also should we—whoever our enemies."[3]

But to say that plunges one into the midst of intense modern debate about the nature of the atonement. Is the "violence" of the cross inconsistent with Jesus's teaching on nonviolence? Is the cross divine child abuse? Have we

1. See chap. 1, under "Jesus's Gospel of the Kingdom."
2. Except perhaps Luke, where the text is uncertain. See Matt. 26:26–29; Mark 14:22–25; Luke 22:19–20; 1 Cor. 11:23–26.
3. Volf, *Exclusion and Embrace*, 23. So too Boyd, *Crucifixion of the Warrior God*, 1:225.

misunderstood Paul's conception of sin so that the idea that Jesus's death paid the penalty for our sins is a mistake? Is the widespread evangelical idea of substitutionary atonement really what the New Testament says? And if it is, and if Jesus's substitutionary death on the cross is the primary purpose of Jesus's coming to earth (as some evangelicals claim), is there any connection between the atonement and Christian ethics?[4]

In my understanding of the atonement, I seek to embrace all that the New Testament tells us about the cross. I think that includes the three major views of the atonement articulated in Christian history. The moral view of the atonement emphasizes the way the cross reveals the love of God. The *Christus Victor* view stresses the way Christ conquers evil in his life, death, and resurrection. And the substitutionary view focuses on Christ dying in our place so that our sins are forgiven. I believe and will argue that all these metaphors are important, complementary parts of how the New Testament helps us understand the cross. Furthermore, it is essential that we understand all of them in the context of Jesus's announcement that the long-expected messianic kingdom has broken into history in Jesus's life, death, and resurrection. Jesus teaches love for enemies as a central aspect of what it means now to live according to his dawning kingdom. And the most profound foundation for that way of living is that at the cross God (in the second person of the Trinity) has died for sinful enemies. But we must examine some of the central ways that this position, especially the substitutionary view of the atonement, is challenged today.

Challenges to Traditional Understandings of the Atonement

J. Denny Weaver

Weaver is a Mennonite theologian who argues that Jesus's death "accomplishes nothing for the salvation of sinners."[5] Weaver insists that Jesus did not come to die and God did not will Jesus's death on the cross. "Satisfaction atonement *in any form* depends on divinely sanctioned violence."[6] Such a view, Weaver claims, makes God the author of Jesus's death, which is divine child abuse. Furthermore, it nurtures unhealthy attitudes among Christians, encouraging women to accept abuse and racial minorities to accept domination. Finally, it involves a heretical doctrine of the Trinity: to say that Jesus

4. See Boersma, *Violence, Hospitality, and the Cross*, 40n54, for a list of some of the works that link the atonement to violence.

5. J. Weaver, *Nonviolent Atonement*, 89.

6. J. Weaver, *Nonviolent Atonement*, 245 (italics original).

teaches nonviolence but God the Father demands violent punishment so our sins can be forgiven violates a central trinitarian understanding that each person of the Trinity participates in all actions of the Trinity.[7]

I find Weaver's views fundamentally unbiblical at many points. Weaver simply ignores large parts of the New Testament. Jesus says he has come "to give his life as a ransom for many" (Mark 10:45). The Gospels, Acts, and the Epistles all say that Jesus's death on the cross is according to the eternal will of God. That is not to ignore the clear New Testament assertion that sinful people have willed and accomplished Jesus's death. But Acts 2:23 demonstrates that the early Christians see no contradiction in saying both that the powers of evil have caused Jesus's death and that God has willed it: "This man was handed over to you by God's deliberate plan and foreknowledge; and you, with the help of wicked men, put him to death by nailing him to the cross."[8]

Weaver's claim that Jesus's death has no significance for our salvation contradicts numerous New Testament statements. Paul regularly argues that we are reconciled to God by the death of Christ.[9]

What about divine child abuse?[10] If we see an angry God bludgeoning the innocent man Jesus, then of course Weaver and others are right. But that is to ignore the fact that the Trinity is present at the cross. The Father and the Spirit suffer the agony of the cross every bit as much as the Son. The Trinity wills the cross. Karl Barth says that "God's own heart suffered on the cross." It was "no one else but God's own Son, and hence the eternal God himself" who chose and experienced the agony of the cross.[11] Acts 20:28 goes so far as to speak of "the church of God, which he [God!] bought with his own blood." I think John Stott puts it very well:

> Who, then, is the substitute? Certainly not Christ, if he is seen as a third party. Any notion of penal substitution in which three independent actors play a role— the guilty party, the punitive judge and the innocent victim—is to be repudiated with the utmost vehemence. It would not only be unjust in itself but would also reflect a defective Christology. For Christ is not an independent third person, but the eternal Son of the Father, who is one with the Father in his essential being.

7. J. Weaver, *Nonviolent Atonement*, 245–46.

8. Christopher Marshall notes that to claim that Jesus's death was not willed by God "flies in the face of the accumulated weight of the New Testament evidence." C. Marshall, "Atonement, Violence, and the Will of God," 81.

9. Rom. 3:21–25; 5:9–10; Gal. 3:13–14. See the full critique of Weaver by C. Marshall ("Atonement, Violence, and the Will of God") and my critique (Sider, "Critique of J. Denny Weaver's *Nonviolent Atonement*").

10. See also Baker, *Executing God*, 5, 67–72, 78, who also makes this argument.

11. Barth, *Church Dogmatics* II.1, 397–403; quoted in Stott, *Cross of Christ*, 153.

. . . As Dale put it, "the mysterious unity of the Father and the Son rendered it possible for God at once to endure and to inflict penal suffering."[12]

What about Weaver's argument that we are involved in logical contradiction and a heretical doctrine of the Trinity if we say both that Jesus taught nonviolence and God willed Jesus's death? This would be a logical contradiction only if Jesus condemns violence in precisely the same way that God uses violence at the cross. But that is not the case. The action of an infinite God substituting Godself for sinful persons at the cross is not identical with the action of finite persons using violence against other persons. Perhaps an analogy with the Trinity can help. Some people claim that the Christian doctrine that God is both one and three is a logical contradiction. But that would be true only if Christians were claiming that God is one in exactly the same way God is three. But Christians do not say that. God is three in a different way than God is one. In a similar way, God uses violence at the cross in a different way than God in Christ condemns violence. And if that is the case, then it is simply confusion to charge that one person of the Trinity is rejecting what another person of the Trinity does.

It is very important to note that Jesus does not see the contradiction Weaver claims to discover. Jesus clearly lives and teaches nonviolence. He says his followers should love their enemies, thus being children of the heavenly Father, who sends good gifts of sun and rain on the righteous and unrighteous (Matt. 5:43–48). But the same Jesus talks about God's wrath against sinners, divine punishment of evildoers, and eternal separation from God. In fact, in the parable of the last judgment, it is precisely the Son (who taught nonviolent love of enemies) who is the judge who condemns sinners to *eternal* separation from God (25:41–46). *Jesus* does not seem to see the contradiction that Weaver claims.

Nor does the rest of the New Testament. As we will see below, the teaching that God is angry at and punishes sin is all through the New Testament— right alongside the most amazing statements about God's overflowing love. Weaver simply ignores all that in his claim that if God used the Son's death on the cross for our salvation, that contradicts Jesus's teaching of nonviolence.

Finite human beings do not know enough about the infinite God to say that what Jesus and other parts of the New Testament say about God and the cross contradicts Jesus's teaching on nonviolence. We ought to submit to what Jesus and the New Testament tell us about God punishing sinners and the Son taking our place at the cross rather than reject (on the basis of some

12. Stott, *Cross of Christ*, 158.

alleged logical contradiction) one part of what Jesus and the New Testament teach. Weaver seems to see a contradiction where Jesus and the rest of the New Testament do not.

It is also important to remember that the Bible calls on believers to imitate God at some points and not at others. Finite human beings are radically different from God. We do not create out of nothing. Our understanding of how holiness and love, justice and mercy fit together in perfect harmony is dreadfully incomplete.

It is surely important to remember that one of the places where the New Testament specifically forbids persons from imitating God is just at this point. God, the New Testament teaches more than once, does rightly execute vengeance on evildoers (Rom. 12:19; Heb. 10:30; 1 Pet. 2:23). Paul says, "Do not take revenge, my dear friends, but leave room for God's wrath, for it is written: 'It is mine to avenge; I will repay'" (Rom. 12:19). Followers of Jesus must love their enemies as Jesus has taught and not seek vengeance against evil persons. Finite human beings simply do not know enough to rightly combine holiness and love in a way that punishes evil the way God justly does. But that does not mean that God should not. Nor does it mean there is a contradiction in the Trinity or in Jesus's own teaching when the Incarnate One tells us that the trinitarian God both loves God's enemies and punishes sinners. Finite human beings will never, this side of the final kingdom, ever fully understand that double truth. Only an infinite, all-knowing, all-loving, holy God knows how holiness and love fit together perfectly in the very being of God.

One final point: Weaver seems to think that the critique of both the moral and satisfaction views of the atonement by black, feminist, and womanist theologians—that satisfaction atonement thinking encourages women to submit passively to abuse and the oppressed to passively accept oppression—strengthens his arguments against those views of the atonement.[13] But that is to claim too much. One can and should agree that an understanding of the atonement that focuses *exclusively* on Christ as our substitute on the cross so that we can be forgiven by a holy God does cut the link with ethics, does make it easy for white racists and male chauvinists to continue in their sin, does run the danger of nurturing passivity in the face of abuse and oppression. But none of those problems follow if one has a fully biblical understanding of the cross and salvation. Christ not only came to die as a substitute for us.

13. J. Weaver, *Nonviolent Atonement*, 129–218. See Baker, *Executing God*, 29–30, for terrible examples of the misuse of Jesus's submission to the Father. See also Boersma's response in *Violence, Hospitality, and the Cross*, 118.

He also came to bring the in-breaking reign of God; to combat and break the power of evil, including sexism and racism; to transform and empower us so that believers now can live according to the norms of Christ's dawning kingdom and join Christ in the battle against all that enslaves, abuses, and destroys people. The solution to the inadequacies of an *exclusively* substitutionary view of the atonement is not to throw away what that view rightly teaches but to see that metaphor in the much larger context of all the New Testament teaches about the atonement. And also to place all of that within Jesus's proclamation that the messianic kingdom has begun and his disciples can now live the life of that new kingdom.

As N. T. Wright insists again and again, the goal of the atonement is not only forgiveness of sins but also freedom from the power of sin so we can now live the kingdom life Jesus taught.[14] Evangelical theologian Scot McKnight is right: "The atoning work of God of wiping away sins had everything to do with God creating a covenant-based community of faith. . . . [The] atonement is all about creating a society in which God's will is actualized—on planet earth, in the here and now."[15]

C. H. Dodd, "Sins," and Sin

Many scholars, including C. H. Dodd, have argued that for Paul, God's wrath is not divine anger at sins committed but rather an "inevitable process of cause and effect in a moral universe."[16] What the cross needs to accomplish, therefore, is not forgiveness of *sins* but liberation, deliverance, from the enslaving power of *Sin*.[17] Consequently, the atonement involves Christ conquering evil (*Christus Victor*), not Christ offering himself as a substitute for our sins.

That the New Testament does sometimes talk of Christ's atoning work in this way is clear (e.g., Heb. 2:14–15; 1 John 3:8).[18] But an *exclusive* emphasis on this understanding of the atonement ignores other clear texts that speak of "sins" in the plural and say that Christ became our substitute to offer sinners forgiveness for our sins. And Christ's substitutionary death happened because God, who is both holiness and love and hates and punishes sins, freely chose out of unfathomable love to accomplish our forgiveness that way.

14. E.g., N. T. Wright, *Day the Revolution Began*, 223 and elsewhere.
15. McKnight, *Community Called Atonement*, 11.
16. Dodd, *Romans*, 23.
17. Gathercole, *Defending Substitution*, 43–45.
18. And of course Christ's battle with the demons during his public ministry. See Sider, *Good News and Good Works*, 97–98.

Frequently Paul talks about sins in the plural. "Blessed are those whose transgressions are forgiven, whose sins are covered" (Rom. 4:7).[19] "Paul frequently refers to the human plight in terms of sins, transgressions and trespasses, and so it is no surprise to see reference to Christ's death as dealing with these—even summarizing his gospel this way."[20]

Furthermore, Paul quite clearly says that Jesus became our substitute, taking our guilt for our sins on himself.[21] In Romans 5:6–11, Paul reflects on Christ as our substitute at the cross by alluding to the considerable body of Greco-Roman literature that discusses the idea of one person dying as the substitute for another. But there is one shocking difference in the case of Christ: Jesus dies as the substitute not for good people but for sinners— indeed enemies![22]

Paul clearly states that Jesus became sin and took on a curse for us. "God made him [Christ] who had no sin to be sin for us, so that in him we might become the righteousness of God" (2 Cor. 5:21). No one can be justified before God by works of the law since all who fail to do everything written in the law are under a curse (and no one keeps the law perfectly). But "Christ redeemed us from the curse of the law by becoming a curse for us" (Gal. 3:10–13). God no longer reckons or imputes our sins to us (2 Cor. 5:19). When we trust not in our good deeds but in God, "who justifies the ungodly," our faith is credited as justification (Rom. 4:4–6). And Paul goes on to explain what that justification means by quoting Psalm 32:1–2, which says that that person is blessed whose sins are forgiven rather than being counted against him or her (Rom. 4:7–8). And, as Paul explains a bit earlier, that justification comes through faith in Jesus's death on the cross (3:21–26).

N. T. Wright repeatedly emphasizes that when Paul uses the word *dikaiosynē* and its cognates, he is thinking of the setting of a law court. The one who is "justified freely" by grace (Rom. 3:24) stands forgiven. "Since in Romans 3, Paul's point is that the whole human race is in the dock, guilty before God, 'justification' will always then mean 'acquittal.'"[23] Justification ("righteousness" is another translation) in Romans 3 "remains the status that you possess as a result of the judge's verdict. For the defendant in the law court (Rom. 3:19–20) it simply means 'acquitted,' 'forgiven,' 'cleared,' 'in good standing in the com-

---

19. Also Rom. 11:27; 1 Cor. 15:3. See the lengthy list of Gathercole, *Defending Substitution*, 48–50.

20. Gathercole, *Defending Substitution*, 50 (italics original).

21. See Gathercole's extensive commentary on 1 Cor. 15:3 in this regard. Gathercole, *Defending Substitution*, 61–77.

22. See the extensive discussion in Gathercole, *Defending Substitution*, 85–107.

23. N.T. Wright, *Justification*, 90.

munity as a result of the judge's pronouncement.'"[24] And that happens, as Romans 3:25 says and Wright explains, through the cross of Jesus, whom "God 'put forward' (the language is sacrificial) to be the place and means of propitiation (*hilastērion*)."[25]

God's Wrath

Does Jesus's cross deal with God's wrath? Does God's wrath require Jesus's death so that God may forgive sinful enemies? And if so, does that contradict Jesus's teaching that God loves God's enemies?

Many modern people want to dismiss the idea of God's wrath and speak only of God's love. But the New Testament speaks of God's wrath at least thirty times.[26] Does that mean God is angry at sinners?

C. H. Dodd and others, as we have seen, have argued that God's wrath is an impersonal process of cause and effect built into the structure of the universe. As Paul says in Romans 1, God gives sinners over to the natural destructive consequences of their evil acts (1:24, 26, 29). The fact that sinful actions produce destructive results does not mean that God is angry at sinners.[27] God is angry only at sin. In a moment, we will see that this approach fits some but not all of the biblical statements on God's wrath. But even in this understanding of God's wrath, it is still the case that God the Creator designed the universe in such a way that sin is punished. So God is still responsible, even in Dodd's view, for the punishment of sin.

But the article on *orgē* (wrath, anger) in the *Theological Dictionary of the New Testament* says that in some New Testament verses, "the idea of

24. N.T. Wright, *Justification*, 213. But that is not to deny that Paul also uses the word *dikaiosynē* to refer to personal and social transformation. The lengthy article on *dikaiosynē* in *TDNT* says: "In Paul, therefore, *dikaiosynē* can denote both the righteousness which acquits and the living power which breaks the bondage of sin" ("δικαιοσύνη," *TDNT* 2:209–10). Yoder was quite right to insist, in his chapter on this topic, that Paul's understanding of *dikaiosynē* includes both personal forgiveness and the social transformation that reconciles Jew and gentile (*Politics of Jesus*, 212–27). N. T. Wright, of course, vigorously agrees (e.g., all through *Justification*, see esp. 248).

25. N.T. Wright, *Justification*, 204. Both Wright and Scot McKnight emphasize that Paul sees this justification of sinners in the larger context of God, at the cross, keeping God's longstanding promise to Abraham to bless all nations through him by reconciling Jew and gentile. See McKnight, *Community Called Atonement*, 90–91; N. T. Wright, *Day the Revolution Began*, 314–15, 336–51; and N. T. Wright, *Justification*, 10, 24–28, 94, 132–36.

26. McKnight, *Community Called Atonement*, 67.

27. Greg Boyd's discussion of God's wrath as God's withdrawal that allows the consequences of sin to work themselves out in history is an example of this basic argument. Boyd, *Crucifixion of the Warrior God*, 2:768–821.

an actual attitude of God cannot be disputed."[28] God is angry because of sin. Sometimes the object of God's wrath is sin itself (e.g., Rom. 1:18). But in other passages, the object of God's wrath is evildoers (Luke 21:23; John 3:36; Rom. 2:5; 1 Thess. 2:16). Sin, as David recognized so clearly in confessing his sexual sin, is first of all an offense against God: "Against you, you only, have I sinned" (Ps. 51:4; cf. 41:4).[29] After listing a number of sins, Ephesians 5:6 says, "Because of such things God's wrath comes on those who are disobedient."[30]

Repeatedly the Bible says that death is a central aspect of the punishment of sin. "The wages of sin is death" (Rom. 6:23). But Christ has taken the curse of sin on himself, dying as our substitute so that those who have faith in Christ are now justified, forgiven. As McKnight says, "Jesus dies 'for us'—his death forgives our sin, 'declares us right,' absorbs the wrath of God against us."[31]

But does that mean that God could not have forgiven us unless Christ had died as our substitute? Some evangelicals say that. Thus J. I. Packer and Mark Dever write that given God's holiness, "there was no alternative" to Jesus's death for our sins.[32] Jesus's penal substitution "had its effect first on God, who was hereby *propitiated*"; Christ's death was a "*satisfaction* for sins, satisfaction which *God's own character dictated as the only means whereby* his no to us could become a yes."[33] Even Stott (one of my favorite Christian leaders) says that "the doctrine of substitution affirms not only a fact (God in Christ substituted himself for us) but its *necessity* (*there was no other way* by which God's holy love could be satisfied and rebellious human beings be saved)."[34]

I believe the New Testament clearly says that God *did* accomplish our justification through Christ's substitutionary death on the cross. But I know of no biblical passage that states that Christ's death was the only way our holy God could forgive us.[35] That the trinitarian God chose to substitute Godself underlines in a most astounding way that God is both love and holiness. It demonstrates more clearly than anything I can imagine that sin is a terrible reality that our holy God refuses to ignore. But the crucifixion of God

28. "ὀργή E II 2," *TDNT* 5:424–25. See the helpful chapter by Lane, "Wrath of God."

29. Obviously David also sinned against Bathsheba and her husband.

30. Darrin Belousek (who denies that the Bible teaches "*penal* wrath") clearly says: "The Old Testament, then, gives ample witness to God's personal wrath on humans on account of evildoing." Belousek, *Atonement, Justice, and Peace*, 211.

31. McKnight, *Community Called Atonement*, 69.

32. Packer and Dever, *In My Place*, 24.

33. Packer and Dever, *In My Place*, 72 (italics original in first two instances; other italics added). See also p. 40.

34. Stott, *Cross of Christ*, 160 (italics added).

35. J. I. Packer and John Stott cite no evidence for their astounding claim!

Incarnate does not mean that that was the only way God could forgive us. It simply reveals in a most amazing way that God is both holiness and love.[36]

God could have chosen to forgive us without suffering Roman crucifixion. An infinite, all-knowing, all-loving God could have chosen any number of ways to forgive us. That God chose to undergo crucifixion certainly under-lines in a most awesome way how serious sin is. But God's love for sinners is clearly greater than God's wrath against sin. We must tremble at the way the cross underlines the gravity of sin. But we should never say what the Bible never says, namely, that Christ dying as our substitute was the only way God could forgive us. There is no biblical basis for such a statement. And it may even obscure the persistent biblical teaching that God's love is greater than God's wrath.

But does not Hebrews 9:22 say that "without the shedding of blood there is no forgiveness"? Some think that means that God could not forgive our sins unless Jesus died for us. To interpret that statement in that way, however, ignores the first part of the verse: "The *law* requires that *nearly everything* be cleansed with blood, and without the shedding of blood there is no forgive-ness." The text is talking about the situation in the Old Testament. And even there, the text says, there were exceptions.[37]

It is striking that on Israel's annual day of atonement, when the high priest made atonement "for all the sins of the Israelites" (Lev. 16:34), the goat that bore those sins was not even killed! Chapter 16 has detailed instructions for this annual day of atonement. The high priest selects a bull and two goats. He kills the bull for a sin offering for himself and his household (16:11). He also kills one goat as a "sin offering for the people" (16:15). But then the text describes in detail how the high priest is to place all the sins of Israel on the live goat—which is *not* killed. "He is to lay both hands on the head of the live goat and confess over it all the wickedness and rebellion of the Israelites—all their sins—and put them on the goat's head. He shall send the goat away into the wilderness. . . . The goat will carry on itself all their sins to a remote place" (16:21–22). Apparently God has chosen to forgive the sins of the Israelites without requiring—in fact explicitly forbidding—the slaughter of the goat that bears their sins.

A number of texts in the Old Testament say that God forgives sins without any mention of a blood sacrifice. Isaiah 6 describes the prophet's dramatic encounter with the holy God. Isaiah feels overwhelmed by his sin. But an angel

36. See, for example, Gwyn and coauthors: "God's righteousness . . . remains inexorably hostile toward evil while blessing those who commit it." Gwyn et al., *Declaration on Peace*, 20.
37. See Belousek, *Atonement, Justice, and Peace*, 193.

touches his lips with a coal from the altar: "See, this has touched your lips; your guilt is taken away and your sin atoned for" (v. 7). There is no mention of any blood sacrifice. Frequently, the Psalms speak of God forgiving sins without any mention of sacrifice (Pss. 25; 32; 103; 130). Psalm 40:6 even says God does not want burnt offerings and sacrifices.

John the Baptist preaches "a baptism of repentance for the forgiveness of sins" (Luke 3:3; Mark 1:4). There is no mention of John telling people who repent to offer sacrifices at the temple. Baptism, not a temple sacrifice, seems to be the way to forgiveness.

Jesus repeatedly declares, on his own authority, without any requirement that sacrifice must be offered at the temple, that people's sins are forgiven (Mark 2:1–12).[38] In the story of the sinful woman who washes Jesus's feet with her tears, Jesus tells her, "Your sins are forgiven" (Luke 7:48).[39] Clearly, both Testaments teach us that God normally uses sacrifices (animals in the Old Testament, Jesus's death in the New Testament) as God forgives sins and also that God sometimes forgives sins without any blood sacrifice.

The fact that God chose to accomplish our forgiveness through the incarnate Son's death on the cross reveals most vividly that God is both love and holiness. But that does not mean that God's wrath against sin and sinners is equal to God's love for everyone. God is love in a way that God is not wrath.

Exodus 34:6–7 declares that whereas God's punishment for sin lasts only briefly, God's steadfast love (*hesed*) endures for a thousand generations. When the prophet Hosea announces God's impending judgment for Israel's sin, he depicts God as deeply grieved by the punishment God plans: "How can I hand you over, Israel? . . . My heart is changed within me; all my compassion is aroused. I will not carry out my fierce anger" (Hosea 11:8–9). The prophet depicts God's attitude to Israel with the image of an ever-faithful husband repeatedly seeking the return of his repeatedly unfaithful wife (Hosea 9–14).[40] In a similar way, the prophet Joel announces God's coming punishment but also insists that God is "slow to anger and abounding in love" (Joel 2:13). Again and again, the Psalms declare that God's "love endures forever."[41] God's "anger lasts only a moment, but his favor lasts a lifetime" (Ps. 30:5). Repeatedly the Old Testament insists that even when God punishes Israel for their sins, God's purpose is restoration of right relations: "I take no pleasure in

38. See the parallel passages in Matt. 9:1–8 and Luke 5:17–26.
39. See Belousek, *Atonement, Justice, and Peace*, 206–7.
40. See Belousek, *Atonement, Justice, and Peace*, 399.
41. E.g., Pss. 106:1; 107:1; 118:1, 2, 3, 4, 29. See further Belousek, *Atonement, Justice, and Peace*, 403–4.

the death of the wicked, but rather that they turn from their ways and live" (Ezek. 33:11).[42]

The Trinity is love from all eternity. Before the rebellion of angels and humanity, God had no wrath. God's holy wrath follows human sin. As Volf says, "A nonindignant God would be an accomplice in injustice, deception and violence."[43] But it is God's love that prompts God's anger at sinners. Precisely because God loves all people with unfathomable love, God is angry when people harm and destroy themselves and others. "The wrath of God is the truth-telling force of God's love."[44] And God's love continues even as God punishes. Jeremiah seems to suggest that God weeps as God punishes the chosen people with exile because of their sin (Jer. 9:10). Nowhere is God's love more powerfully revealed than at the cross, where the Trinity somehow experiences crucifixion as the eternal Son becomes a curse for us and dies for our sins.

If crucifixion were the end of the story, then we would have to conclude that God's wrath is at least equal to God's love. But the story continues on Easter morning. The resurrection declares loudly that God's love for sinful enemies far outweighs God's wrath against sinners. The resurrection of the one who died for our sins proves that Jesus was right in teaching that God is like the father of the prodigal son. God stands with arms stretched wide open, eager to forgive our sins and welcome us back as forgiven sons and daughters. As Emil Brunner has rightly said, God's wrath is "not the ultimate reality; it is the divine reality which corresponds to sin. But it is not the essential reality of God. In Himself God is love."[45]

Multiple, Complementary Metaphors of the Atonement[46]

I agree with the many theologians and biblical scholars who find all these metaphors complementary and important.[47] Rejecting any one metaphor involves ignoring or denying significant parts of what the New Testament says about

42. Deut. 29:22–30:10. See Belousek, *Atonement, Justice, and Peace*, 409–14. C. Marshall writes, "God's justice is a restorative or reconstructive justice before it is punitive or destructive justice." C. Marshall, *Beyond Retribution*, 52.

43. Volf, *Exclusion and Embrace*, 297. See similarly Boersma, *Violence, Hospitality, and the Cross*, 49.

44. Schertz, "Partners in God's Passion," 173.

45. Brunner, *Mediator*, 519–21; quoted in Lane, "Wrath of God," 160–61.

46. This section includes material from Sider, *Good News and Good Works*, 95–100.

47. See, e.g., Boersma, *Violence, Hospitality, and the Cross*, esp. 112–204; Gathercole, *Defending Substitution*, 112 and elsewhere; McKnight, *Community Called Atonement*, 107–14; Treat, *Crucified King*, 174–226 (who emphasizes both penal substitution and *Christus Victor*).

the atonement. It is also, as I have said earlier, absolutely essential to understand the atonement within the context of Jesus's gospel of the kingdom.[48]

The moral metaphor. In this metaphor, Jesus's basic role is that of teacher and example, because one fundamental human problem is ignorance. The locus of Jesus's activity is Galilee, where he teaches, and Golgotha, where he reveals God's love on the cross. The focus is on expanding our knowledge and understanding by activities that teach and model God's love and will.

This metaphor is obviously rooted in key New Testament teaching. The Gospels feature in a prominent way Jesus's teaching about how his disciples live in the kingdom he announced. At the cross, too, Jesus continues to offer revelation: "This is how we know what love is: Jesus Christ laid down his life for us" (1 John 3:16). This metaphor focuses well the ethical demands of Christian faith, including love for enemies.

By itself, however, this metaphor of the atonement is inadequate. Unfortunately, evil in the world lies much deeper than mere ignorance. It rests in radically self-centered persons who need not only knowledge but also divine forgiveness and power to change. Evil also resides in demonic forces and the social structures they have helped distort. We need a powerful Savior who can conquer the forces that enslave us.

The substitutionary metaphor. In this metaphor Jesus's role is that of substitute, because one fundamental aspect of our problem is that sinners stand condemned as guilty before a holy God. The locus of saving activity is Calvary, where Christ takes our guilt on himself. The outcome is forgiveness, renewed relationship with God, and life eternal rather than eternal separation from the Holy One.

As we have seen, a great deal of biblical material contains this metaphor. "God made him who had no sin to be sin for us, so that in him we might become the righteousness of God" (2 Cor. 5:21). The fact that the one hanging limp on the middle cross was the Second Person of the Trinity shows that it was actually God who took our place at the cross, thus holding together God's love and holiness.

Taken *by itself*, however, the substitutionary metaphor of the atonement is also inadequate. By itself, the substitutionary view largely ignores Christ's teaching and proclamation of the kingdom and his victory over the forces of evil during his life and at Easter. If one reduces the atonement merely to Jesus's death for our sins, one abandons the New Testament understanding of the gospel of the kingdom and severs the connection between the cross

---

48. McKnight, *Community Called Atonement*, 141, 143, and elsewhere; and Treat, *Crucified King*, especially emphasize this point.

and ethics. Understood that way, the cross seems totally disconnected from Jesus's summons to love our enemies.

The Christus Victor *metaphor.* In this view of the atonement, Jesus's primary role is conqueror of evil, because one fundamental part of our problem is the power of evil, whether seen in demonic beings, corrupt social structures, or death itself. The central locus is twofold: Galilee, where Christ casts out demons, and Easter morning, when Christ conquers death. Here the focus is not on canceling guilt but on defeating the forces of evil. Christ does that by battling Satan, casting out demons, healing the sick, challenging an unjust status quo, and finally defeating death.

Again, this metaphor is rooted solidly in the New Testament. First John 3:8 is very clear: "The reason the Son of God appeared was to destroy the devil's work." Hebrews says the Son became flesh "so that by his death he might break the power of him who holds the power of death—that is, the devil—and free those who all their lives were held in slavery by their fear of death" (2:14–15). The *Christus Victor* metaphor moves beyond an exclusively individualistic understanding of sin and salvation and points to the social and cosmic aspects of salvation. And it focuses Jesus's work in both Galilee and Jerusalem. Above all, it highlights the victory of Easter morning.

Taken *by itself*, however, this view too is inadequate. Because this metaphor points to the evil forces *outside* the individual, it is easy for proponents of this view to underemphasize the personal side of sin, guilt, and responsibility. This is especially obvious in some theologies of liberation where sin resides largely in unjust social structures.

Are these three different metaphors of the atonement complementary or contradictory? Some people seem to think they are incompatible, but I see no need whatsoever to reject one biblical perspective in order to affirm another. It is only when we take one view and emphasize it in a one-sided or exclusive way that we have problems.[49] Rather, we need to see how the three views complement one another. Placing them in the context of the gospel of the kingdom helps us understand Jesus's interrelated roles as teacher, victor, and substitute.

49. See Martin Luther's statement that justification by faith is "the principal article of all Christian doctrine" (Luther, *Epistle to the Galatians*, 143). Also, the evangelical statement: "Justification by faith appears to us, as it does to all evangelicals, to be the heart and hub, the paradigm and essence, of the whole economy of God's saving grace. Like Atlas, it bears a world on its shoulders, the entire evangelical knowledge of God's love in Christ toward sinners" (Beckwith, Duffield, and Packer, *Across the Divide*, 58). To say that justification by faith in Christ's substitutionary death for our sins is the really important thing in contrast to other biblical metaphors of the atonement and other aspects of salvation is flatly *unbiblical* and a major source of the cheap grace and neglect of sanctification and ethics in evangelical circles.

As messianic proclaimer of the kingdom of God, Jesus taught a radical ethic of love. From his Sermon on the Mount through his death on the cross, he taught and modeled the way of love, even for enemies. Living his costly ethics, however, is possible only as forgiven sinners who are empowered by the Spirit.

As nonviolent messianic conqueror, Jesus inaugurated the kingdom, battling with Satan and all the forces of evil. He conquered diseases and demons in his public ministry. On the cross he broke the power of Satan, and on Easter morning he arose triumphant over death itself, enabling his disciples in the power of the Spirit to live Jesus's kingdom ethics now.

As Isaiah's suffering servant, Jesus died on the cross as our substitute. As we trust in Jesus, who took our place and became a curse for us, we are forgiven. And since Jesus is the incarnate Son of God, it is the Trinity who substitutes Godself for us.

Understanding the atonement in the context of Jesus's gospel of the kingdom underlines the community-building aspect of Jesus's saving work. Jesus not only preached the gospel of the kingdom, he formed a new kingdom community of women and men, prostitutes and royal servants, tax collectors and respectable folk. From the calling together of Israel as a redeemed community, through Jesus's circle of disciples to the community of the early church, establishing a reconciled community was central to God's plan of salvation. That is why Titus 2:14 says that Christ "gave himself for us to redeem us from all wickedness and to purify for himself a *people*." McKnight is right: the "atonement is all about creating a society in which God's will is actualized—on planet earth, in the here and now."[50] And that includes loving our enemies.

That God Incarnate died for sinful enemies is the deepest foundation for Jesus's call to love our enemies. Rather than being a problem for a nonviolent Christian ethic, the atonement provides the most solid foundation. The cross is not an angry God bludgeoning an innocent man. It is the three persons of the Trinity together embracing the agony of Roman crucifixion to accomplish our salvation. That the Trinity chose that awful reality to accomplish our forgiveness demonstrates with unspeakable clarity that God is both holy and loving. But the fact that God substitutes Godself for us at the cross demonstrates that God's wrath is but for a moment and God's love is everlasting.[51]

---

50. McKnight, *Community Called Atonement*, 11.

51. That is not to forget that Jesus and the New Testament authors clearly say that some people experience eternal separation from God. But I think Miroslav Volf is right that for those who experience that terrible reality, "it will not be because they have done evil, but because they have resisted to the end, the powerful lure of the open arms of the crucified Messiah." Volf, *Exclusion and Embrace*, 298.

It is true that if one claims that the substitutionary view of the atonement is the only important view, then one cuts the link between the atonement and ethics. But that is a one-sided, unbiblical position. It ignores the clear New Testament teaching on the moral and *Christus Victor* metaphors of the atonement. And it fails to place the cross in the context of Jesus's gospel of the kingdom. At the heart of Jesus's gospel is the teaching that the members of Jesus's dawning kingdom should love their enemies. And the fact that the Trinity somehow embraces Roman crucifixion for sinful enemies is the deepest foundation for that teaching.

At the cross God suffered for God's enemies. Certainly we can never fathom all the mystery there. But it is precisely because the one hanging limp on the cross was the Word who became flesh that we are absolutely sure of two interrelated things: first, that a just God mercifully loves sinful enemies, and second, that God wants us to go and treat all our enemies in the same self-sacrificial, loving way.

Since Jesus commands his followers to love their enemies and then dies as the incarnate Son to demonstrate that God reconciles his enemies by suffering love, any rejection of the nonviolent way in human relations seems to me to involve an inadequate doctrine of the atonement.[52] If God in Christ has reconciled God's enemies by God's suffering servanthood, should not those who want to follow Christ also treat their enemies in the same way?

It is a tragedy of our time that many of those who appropriate the biblical understanding of Christ's vicarious cross fail to see its direct implications for the problem of war and violence. And it is equally tragic that some of those who emphasize pacifism and nonviolence fail to ground it in Christ's atonement. The sentimental view of Jesus as merely a noble martyr to truth and peace is an inadequate ground for nonviolence. The cross is much more than "Christ's witness to the weakness and folly of the sword,"[53] although it certainly is that. In fact, the cross is such a witness precisely because the incarnate Word's death for our sins demonstrates that the Sovereign of the universe is a merciful Lover who reconciles God's enemies through self-sacrificial love.

52. Dale Brown calls it a heretical doctrine of the atonement. See Brown, *Brethren and Pacifism*, 121.

53. R. Jones, *Church, the Gospel, and War*, 5.

13

Christians and Killing in Church History

For two thousand years now, Christians have sought—more or less seriously, more or less successfully—to follow Jesus. What can we learn about our topic from the history of the church? From the early church, before Emperor Constantine in AD 313 decreed the end of persecution of Christians? From the time, post-Constantine, when the Roman emperors favored Christians? From medieval Christianity, when only small minorities of Christians were pacifists? From the small but growing number of Christian pacifists from the sixteenth through nineteenth centuries? From the large number of new denominations in the last century that were originally pacifist? And from the recent official support for pacifism in the Catholic Church?

Pre-Constantinian Christianity

Scholars have offered contradictory views about Christians' thinking and practice about killing in the centuries between the end of the New Testament and the decree of Constantine in AD 313. Some modern scholars have claimed that the early church was essentially pacifist.[1] Others have argued that the thinking of the early church on killing (especially in warfare) was "small, divided and ambiguous."[2]

1. E.g., Bainton, *Christian Attitudes*; Yoder, *Christian Attitudes to War*.
2. Leithart, *Defending Constantine*, 278.

Among those who claim that we have few relevant texts on the topic and
that the texts we do have are divided in their views are people like Peter J.
Leithart, James Turner Johnson, and Jean Bethke Elshtain. Leithart claims to
find a diversity of viewpoints in the relevant texts (including some that suggest the just war concept) and even argues that vigorous critics of Christian
participation in the Roman army like Tertullian and Origen may have been
a small articulate minority that did not represent the majority of Christians.[3]
Elshtain says that in the "first generations of Christian life after the crucifixion
of Jesus, there is little evidence that the faithful were enjoined from serving
in either the Roman army or police forces."[4] One scholar has argued that
"there is practically no evidence from the Fathers which would support the
argument that the early church denied enlistment on the ground that killing
and war were opposed to the Christian ethic."[5]

In spite, however, of myriad books and articles on the early church's views
on killing, no one had ever collected in one volume all extant relevant sources
(literary and archaeological). I did that in *The Early Church on Killing: A
Comprehensive Sourcebook on War, Abortion, and Capital Punishment*. It
is now possible to say with some precision what the Christians before Constantine said and did.[6]

There is not a single extant Christian author before Constantine who says
killing or joining the military by Christians is ever legitimate. Whenever our
extant texts mention killing—whether in abortion, capital punishment, or
war—they always say Christians must not do that. And the authors of these
writings include many of the important writers of the early church: Justin
Martyr, Irenaeus, Tertullian, Origen, Cyprian, and Lactantius.

There are a substantial number of passages written over a period of many
years that explicitly say that Christians must not and/or do not kill or join the
military. Nine different Christian writers in sixteen different treatises explicitly say that killing is wrong. Four writers in five treatises clearly argue that
Christians do not and should not join the military. In addition, four writers
in eight works strongly imply that Christians should not join the military.
At least eight times, five authors apply the messianic prophecy about swords
being beaten into plowshares (Isa. 2:4) to Christ and his teaching. Ten different authors in at least twenty-eight different places cite or allude to Jesus's
teaching to love enemies and, in at least nine of these places, they connect

3. Leithart, *Defending Constantine*, 259, 268, 270, 272. See also Johnson, *Quest for Peace*,
14–15.
4. Elshtain, *Just War*, 52.
5. Helgeland, "Christians and the Roman Army," 764–65.
6. See my summary in Sider, *Early Church on Killing*, 163–95.

that teaching to some statement about Christians being peaceful, ignorant of war, opposed to attacking others, and so forth. All of this represents a considerable body of evidence.[7]

There is virtually no basis in the texts for describing the early Christian view as "divided and ambiguous." There are no authors who argue that killing or joining the military is permissible for Christians. On these questions, every writer who mentions the subject takes the same position. Some pre-Constantinian Christian writers say more about these topics than others. Some do not discuss them at all. But to conclude from this relative silence or paucity of some surviving texts that other writers disagreed with the extant texts would be sheer speculation. Every extant Christian statement on killing and war up until the time of Constantine says Christians must not kill, even in war.

No early Christian writer stated the absolute prohibition of all killing more firmly than Lactantius (AD 250–325). Writing at the court of the emperor Diocletian during a widespread persecution of Christians, Lactantius wrote *The Divine Institutes*, a brilliant defense of Christian faith in superb Ciceronian Latin. He condemned every kind of killing: abortion, infanticide, capital punishment, gladiatorial contests, and war.

> For when God forbids us to kill, he not only prohibits us from open violence, which is not even allowed by the public laws, but he warns us against the commission of those things which are esteemed lawful among people. Thus it will be neither lawful for a just man [a Christian] to engage in military service . . . nor to accuse anyone of a capital charge because it makes no difference whether you put a person to death by word or rather by sword, since it's the act of putting to death itself which is prohibited. Therefore with regard to this precept of God, there ought to be no exception at all but that it is always unlawful to put to death a person, whom God willed to be a sacred creature."[8]

It is also true that in the late second century and then increasingly in the later third century and the first decade of the fourth century, there is evidence (both in Christian writings and in archaeological data) that some Christians were serving in the Roman army—at least a few by AD 173 and a substantial number by the late third and early fourth centuries.[9] Unfortunately, our sources do not enable us to say how many.

7. Sider, *Early Church on Killing*, 168–79. Helmut Koester says that Jesus's command to love enemies is the most frequently cited saying of Jesus in the second century (*Synoptische Überlieferung*, 44, 76; cited in Swartley, *Love of Enemy*, 8). But I have not been able to confirm that.

8. Lactantius, *Divine Institutes* 6.20; quoted in Sider, *Early Church on Killing*, 110.

9. Sider, *Early Church on Killing*, 185–90.

Apparently in the later third and early fourth centuries, an increasing number of Christian laity did not live what their Christians leaders taught. That
disconnect between teaching and preaching has continued throughout church
history. Today vast numbers of Christians ignore what Christian leaders say
about divorce and materialism. But the teaching of all extant Christian writings
up to the time of Constantine is clear. Killing is always wrong for Christians.
Every extant Christian author who discusses killing forbids it. Paul Ramsey,
perhaps the leading just war Christian advocate of the last generation, summarizes the data this way:

> For almost two centuries of the history of the early church, Christians were
> universally pacifists. . . . There can be no doubt that early Christian pacifism
> was on the main a consistent deduction from the new foundation laid by
> Christ in the lives of men for a new kind of exercise, in intention and in
> practice, of love for every man for whom Christ died. How could anyone,
> who knew himself to be classed with transgressors and the enemies of God
> whom Christ came to die to save, love his own life and seek to save it more
> than that of his own enemy or murderer?[10]

What do the historical facts about the early church mean for our question about whether Christians should ever kill? It certainly does not settle
the question for us today. Jesus and the Scriptures, not the early fathers, are
our final authority. But the Christians of the second and third centuries were
much closer to Jesus and the writers of the New Testament than we are. They
read the New Testament in the same language in which it was written. Their
world was substantially closer to the world of Jesus than is ours.[11] It is not
unreasonable to conclude that they had at least as good an understanding,
and perhaps better, of what Jesus meant than Christians living two thousand
years later. The fact that every Christian writer up until Constantine who
mentions killing insists that Jesus's disciples should not kill strengthens the
argument that this is what Jesus intended.

Constantinian Christianity and Killing

When Constantine, one of the contenders for emperor, placed Christian symbols on his soldiers' military emblems before a decisive military victory in AD
312, and then one year later issued the decree that made it legal to be a Christian,

10. Ramsey, *War and the Christian Conscience*, xv–xvi.
11. So Yoder, *Christian Attitudes to War*, 43.

Christians entered a dramatically new period of history. It took many more years for Constantine to completely vanquish his rivals and establish himself as sole emperor. Since some of his rivals favored continued persecution of Christians, it is hardly surprising that Christians wanted Constantine to win, cheering his military victories. Vastly more Christians joined the Roman army, and within one hundred years *only* Christians could serve in the Roman army.

In the one hundred years after Constantine, leading Christian theologians—especially Ambrose (ca. 340–397), bishop of Milan, and Augustine (354–430), bishop of Hippo in North Africa—developed the basic framework of the just war tradition.[12] As Augustine wrestled with his views on Christian participation in war, barbarian attacks were threatening the very existence of the newly "Christian" Roman Empire. Borrowing from Cicero, Augustine wrote that war may be just only if it cannot be avoided to defend the state and the intention is peace and justice, not revenge. And war itself must be conducted justly. In the subsequent centuries, Christian thinkers refined and developed the just war criteria. But from the fifth century to the present, the just war tradition has been the "official" position of most Christians.[13]

During the Middle Ages, Christian theologians and leaders (including Thomas Aquinas) continued to reflect on and seek to apply the tradition. There were efforts to reduce war. Those promoting the peace of God sought to greatly expand the categories of people exempt from attack. Those advancing the Truce of God sought to limit the time when military campaigns could be undertaken (not on Sundays, Fridays, or holy days). Unfortunately, the church itself launched the Crusades as a holy war willed by Christ to capture and free the Holy Land from centuries of Muslim control. Christ summoned Christians, prominent church leaders proclaimed, to slaughter the infidels controlling the Holy Land.

The pacifist tradition continued in the Middle Ages only among fringe Christian groups. The Cathari were gnostic heretics who opposed war. When they grew numerous in southern France, the church launched a crusade to wipe them out.

A small but significant pacifist movement emerged in the middle of the fifteenth century. After Jan Hus, a prominent preacher in Prague, was burned at the stake in 1415 for his rejection of some Catholic teaching, several streams

12. In the Eastern church, however, the teaching against Christians killing in war remained stronger. See Belousek, *Atonement, Justice, and Peace*, 77.

13. For the development of the tradition, see Biggar, *In Defence of War*; Johnson, *Quest for Peace*; Ramsey, *Just War*; Ramsey, *War and the Christian Conscience*; Bainton, *Christian Attitudes*; Yoder, *Christian Attitudes to War*; Cahill, *Love Your Enemies*; and the many books cited by those authors.

of Hussite thought emerged. One stream, led by Petr Chelcicky (who rejected all killing on the basis of Jesus's teaching) coalesced at midcentury as the Unity of Brethren (*Unitas Fratrum*). One part of this movement was totally pacifist and survived into the sixteenth century and beyond.[14]

The Reformation

The mainstream Protestant Reformers—Lutheran, Calvinist, and Anglican—not only affirmed and taught the just war tradition as the proper Christian understanding of war; by incorporating it into their official creeds, they also declared it to be Christian orthodoxy.[15]

Anabaptists. The Anabaptists disagreed with the mainstream Reformers. After working closely for a few years with the Protestant Reformer Ulrich Zwingli in Zurich, a group of young Reformers rejected infant baptism and in 1525 (re)baptized adults who made a mature confession of faith. They insisted that the church should manage its own life free of interference by the state. They also taught that Christians should never kill.[16] The Anabaptists thus rejected two central pieces of Christian life—the state church and the just war tradition—that had prevailed for over a thousand years. Other Christians were furious. And they all—Catholics, Lutherans, Anglicans, Zwinglians, and Calvinists—executed the new "heretics." Anabaptists died by the hundreds.

Anabaptists survived by fleeing to remote places and occasionally finding a prince who tolerated their "heretical" ideas because they were excellent farmers and artisans. After a disastrous violent episode in the city of Münster (1534–35), a former Dutch priest named Menno Simons gathered together discouraged Anabaptists into successful communities, which eventually took the name Mennonite. Again and again, they emigrated to places around the world where rulers tolerated their refusal to participate in war. They have especially flourished in North America, where the Mennonites are known as one of the major denominations belonging to the "Historic Peace Churches."

The Quakers. The Quakers emerged out of the Puritan party in the civil wars in England in the middle of the seventeenth century. Disillusioned by the violence and failure of Puritan Thomas Cromwell's revolution against the king, leaders like George Fox (1624–91) emerged who taught that Christians

14. Yoder, *Christian Attitudes to War*, 146–49.
15. See the Augsburg Confession (art. 16), the Westminster Confession (art. 23/2), and the Thirty-Nine Articles of the Church of England (art. 37). See also citations in Yoder, *Christian Attitudes to War*, 123.
16. See Yoder, *Christian Attitudes to War*, 161–95. Not all Anabaptists rejected all killing in the early years (183, 188).

should reject all killing. Moved by powerful personal religious experiences and a sense of an inner light, as well as their reading of the New Testament, the Quakers (also called Friends) became a vigorous, albeit minority, pacifist voice in late seventeenth-century England. Like the Anabaptists, they rejected the Constantinian union of church and state. But they were somewhat more hopeful about moving the larger society toward peace.[17]

The opportunity for an amazing experiment in that way emerged when the king of England repaid a debt to the father of the young Quaker nobleman William Penn (1644–1718) and gave Penn a large tract of land in America, now called Pennsylvania. As the first governor, Penn set out to establish peaceful, just relations with the Indigenous peoples living in his colony. Roland Bainton says that "no finer example of the treatment of aborigines is to be found in history."[18] Peace with the Indigenous peoples lasted for about seventy-five years (1682–1756). Quakers, who controlled the colony's legislature, refused to vote for military expenditures until 1756. But the king of England, not the Quakers, appointed the governor of Pennsylvania and set the foreign policy of all of Britain's North American colonies. In addition, although some of the many European colonists moving into Pennsylvania were pacifists (e.g., Mennonites), others were not (Anglicans and Scots-Irish Presbyterians). When the French and Indian War broke out in 1756, the Quaker majority in the Pennsylvania legislature faced a huge decision. With great reluctance, they voted for a bill that exempted Quakers but funded the military campaign. But after intense internal discussion in Quaker circles, the Quakers simply refused to run as candidates in the next election and nonpacifists took over the legislature.[19]

Quaker pacifism, however, continued as a substantial influence in Pennsylvania and a number of other colonies. With Mennonites, Quakers issued the first public condemnation of slavery in British North America. Through their American Friends Service Committee and other Quaker (Friends) organizations, they continue to the present as an important pacifist voice in the United States and around the world.

Early Holiness and Pentecostal Denominations

In their earlier years, several evangelical denominations and a majority of Pentecostal denominations embraced pacifism. In fact, after a careful study of

---

17. See Bainton, *Christian Attitudes*, 157–65; and Yoder, *Christian Attitudes to War*, 219–52.

18. Bainton, *Christian Attitudes*, 171.

19. Bainton, *Christian Attitudes*, 170–72. See Yoder's argument that this seventy-five year pacifist experiment in running a government was not a failure, in *Christian Attitudes to War*, 240–52.

early Pentecostal denominations, Jay Beaman reports that "thirteen of twenty-one, or 62 percent, of [Pentecostal] groups formed by 1917 give evidence of being pacifist at some point. Twenty-four of forty-eight, or 50 percent, of those groups formed by 1934 give evidence of pacifism."[20] Murray Dempster, who seeks to modify Beaman's argument somewhat, nevertheless says, "The claim that pacifism pervaded all branches of the Pentecostal movement can be demonstrably documented."[21]

Wesleyan Methodists. The official *Discipline of the Wesleyan Methodist Connection* from 1844 declares, "We believe the Gospel of Christ to be every way opposed to the practice of war."[22] Along with other Holiness groups that were also working to abolish slavery, the Wesleyan Methodists (now the Wesleyan church) were pacifists for some time. But when the Civil War broke out, their opposition to slavery led them to support the North in the war.[23]

Church of God (Anderson, Indiana). Quakers and Mennonites were active in some of the movements that led to the emergence of Holiness denominations in the latter part of the nineteenth century.[24] That was certainly true of the Church of God, which emerged in Indiana about 1880. A number of articles in the denominational paper, *The Gospel Trumpet*, in the first decade of the twentieth century clearly advocated pacifism.[25] A declaration signed by top leaders of the church states, "It is contrary to my religious convictions as a follower of Christ for me to take human life. My religion and my conscience forbid my taking up arms for the slaughter of my fellowmen."[26] By the time of World War I, this group had officially registered with the US government claiming exemption from the draft and involvement in war as "inconsistent with our religious stand" on the basis of principles "for years . . . definitely expressed in the standard literature of the church."[27] But by the end of the war, *The Gospel Trumpet* softened its stand, and many church members joined the army. Then in the 1930s, a pacifist commitment returned. In 1932, the general ministerial assembly of the church declared, "We will never again sanction or participate in any

20. Beaman, "Extent of Early Pentecostal Pacifism," 12.
21. Dempster, "Crossing Borders," 127. Murray Dempster points out (what Jay Beaman also acknowledges) that there is evidence of nonpacifist voices in early Pentecostalism.
22. D. Dayton and L. Dayton, "Historical Survey of Attitudes," 137.
23. D. Dayton and L. Dayton, "Historical Survey of Attitudes," 137–42.
24. Beaman, *Pentecostal Pacifism*, 10.
25. Beaman and Pipkin, *Pentecostal and Holiness Statements*, 75.
26. Beaman and Pipkin, *Pentecostal and Holiness Statements*, 76.
27. Quoted in D. Dayton and L. Dayton, "Historical Survey of Attitudes," 144. See also pp. 144–47 for an indication of pacifists in the Pilgrim Holiness Church and Free Methodists and other Holiness groups.

war."[28] But again in World War II, a majority of church members who were drafted joined the US army.

The Churches of Christ. In the first half of the nineteenth century, Alexander Campbell was the most prominent leader in the formation of a restorationist movement called the Disciples of Christ. Campbell himself was an absolute pacifist.[29] Later in the nineteenth century, a church split led to the formation of the Churches of Christ, which continued to be pacifist. Even though the strong pacifism of the editor of their paper, *Gospel Advocate*, during the American Civil War led to threats on his life, David Lipscomb persisted in rejecting Christian participation in war.[30] The Churches of Christ remained largely pacifist until 1917. But when the government threatened the editors of the group's magazines with arrest, they stopped printing articles opposed to the war.[31]

The Assemblies of God. Started in 1914, the Assemblies of God today is the largest Pentecostal denomination, with approximately seventy million adherents around the world.[32] In 1917, the General Council of the Assemblies of God issued a strong pacifist statement. Citing a number of biblical statements, including Jesus's "love your enemies," they stated, "Whereas these and other scriptures have always been accepted and interpreted by our churches as prohibiting Christians from shedding blood or taking human life: therefore . . . we are constrained to declare we cannot conscientiously participate in war and armed resistance which involves the actual destruction of human life, since this is contrary to our view of the clear teachings of the inspired Word of God which is the sole basis of our faith."[33] This statement became the official position of the Assemblies of God until 1967.

It is true that there were some early leaders who supported participation in World War I.[34] But the statement from 1917 was an official statement sent to President Woodrow Wilson by the top leaders of the church.[35] Many articles in the church's magazine, *The Pentecostal Evangel* (including ones written

28. Quoted in Strege, "Uncertain Voice for Peace," 116.
29. Beaman, *Pentecostal Pacifism*, 14.
30. Casey, "Religious Outsiders to Insiders," 457–58.
31. Alexander, *Peace to War*, 72; Casey, "Religious Outsiders to Insiders," 463–70.
32. Alexander, *Peace to War*, 29–30. For more recent statistics see https://ag.org.
33. Beaman and Pipkin, *Pentecostal and Holiness Statements*, 144.
34. Dempster argues, on the basis of these people, that in spite of the official statement endorsing pacifism, only a "prophetic minority" in the early Assemblies of God were actually pacifists. See Dempster, "Crossing Borders." But both Alexander (*Peace to War*, 38–45) and Beaman ("Response: Pacifism among the Early Pentecostals," esp. 85–90) successfully challenge Dempster.
35. Dempster, "Pacifism in Pentecostalism," 31.

by three different General Superintendents), endorsed pacifism. In 1938, the General Superintendent reprinted the church's pacifist position. In October 1940, *The Pentecostal Evangel* ran an article saying, "The universal feeling in the ranks of the Assemblies of God [is] that military service is incompatible with the gospel of Jesus Christ."[36]

The fact that many Assemblies of God men joined the US military in World War II (although about half chose noncombatant service) prompted the church's General Council to appoint a committee in 1947 to review the church's article on military service. After careful study, however, the committee opposed any change, saying they were "unable to formulate an article on Military Service that will better represent the attitude of the Assemblies of God than that which is now part of our General Council by-laws."[37] The pacifist statement remained as the official position of the church. In fact, pacifism remained the official stance of the Assemblies of God until 1967.[38]

Church of God (Cleveland, Tennessee). Now another one of the larger Pentecostal denominations, the Church of God (Cleveland, Tennessee) emerged in the early twentieth century. The founder, Ambrose Jessup Tomlinson, was a strong pacifist. In 1917, he cited Jesus's command to love our enemies and insisted that "it is not the spirit of the Master to fight." He continues, "Our attitude toward war can be no other than that taught by our Lord."[39] In another article, Tomlinson wrote, "If any of our members should in any way advocate war, or try to persuade any of these registrants [for the draft] to go on to war or urge or enthuse them into a desire to fight, such members will be considered disloyal to the Church . . . and continuance of the same may lead to the necessary action (expulsion) under our laws and principles."[40] And the "Teachings" document of the church in 1917 says simply, "Against members going to war."[41] The church remained pacifist until 1945.[42]

Church of God in Christ (COGIC). With over six million members in the United States, COGIC is the largest African American Pentecostal denomination. It was founded in 1895 by Bishop C. H. Mason, COGIC's first general overseer. Mason repeatedly stated in official documents that "the creed of our church is now and has been ever since its organization . . . adverse to war and bloodshed. . . . The members of said church are not allowed to carry arms or

36. Quoted in Alexander, *Peace to War*, 44.
37. Alexander, *Peace to War*, 45.
38. Alexander, *Peace to War*, 228.
39. Tomlinson, "Awful World War," 152.
40. Tomlinson, "War Notice."
41. Beaman and Pipkin, *Pentecostal and Holiness Statements*, 152–53.
42. Beaman, *Pentecostal Pacifism*, 26.

to shed the blood of any man and still be members of said church."[43] Mason and his church members experienced extensive attack from government and popular opinion during World War I.[44] Still today, however, the church's official position remains opposed to Christians participating in war.[45]

As we saw above, almost two-thirds of the Pentecostal bodies established by 1917 were originally pacifist. Pacifism was so widespread in the early years of Pentecostalism that an article in *The Weekly Evangel* (the publication of the Assemblies of God) could state in 1917 with regard to Pentecostalism in North America and Europe: "From the very beginning, the movement has been characterized by Quaker principles. The laws of the Kingdom, laid down by our elder brother, Jesus Christ, in His Sermon on the Mount, have been unqualifiedly adopted, consequently the movement has found itself opposed to the spilling of blood of any man, or of offering resistance to any aggression. Every branch of the movement, whether in the United States, Canada, Great Britain or Germany, has held to this principle."[46]

Prominent Individual Pacifists from the Past Two Hundred Years

Some prominent individuals such as Martin Luther King Jr. and Dorothy Day are widely known as pacifists. Others, such as Dwight L. Moody and Charles Spurgeon, are not so known for this.

Moody was one of the most famous evangelists in the late nineteenth century. Among many other things, he founded the Moody Bible Institute, which today is a conservative school both theologically and sociopolitically. But Moody was a lifelong pacifist. The first edition of *The Life of Dwight L. Moody* (written by his son William) reported that during the Civil War, Moody was quite clear that "he could not conscientiously enlist." Moody himself said, "There has never been a time in my life when I felt I could take a gun and shoot down a fellow human being. In that respect I am a Quaker."[47] But a reprint of the biography in 1930 rewrote this section, greatly watering down Moody's pacifism.[48]

43. Beaman and Pipkin, *Pentecostal and Holiness Statements*, 155.
44. Alexander, *Peace to War*, 74–75.
45. Hall, "What the Church Teaches about War." David Hall was CEO of the COGIC publishing house.
46. Quoted in Beaman, *Pentecostal Pacifism*, 33. See also Beaman, "Extent of Early Pentecostal Pacifism," 14–17, and the entire article for discussion of how many Pentecostals actually joined the military.
47. Moody, *Life of Dwight L. Moody*, 81, 82.
48. D. Dayton and L. Dayton, "Historical Survey of Attitudes," 133.

Catherine Booth (1829–90), cofounder of the Salvation Army, and her son Herbert Booth were both pacifists.[49]

Spurgeon (1834–92), a theological conservative, was one of the most popular preachers of his day. His vast number of sermons and commentaries are still widely read today. He was also a pacifist: "I always mourn to find a Christian a soldier, for it seems to me that when I take up Christ Jesus, I hear one of His laws: 'I say unto you, resist not evil. Put up your sword into its sheath.'"[50]

William Lloyd Garrison (1805–79), one of the most prominent American abolitionists, was a pacifist all of his life. Garrison grew up in a Baptist home and knew the Bible thoroughly, but later in life he rejected orthodox Christianity.[51] Garrison was a key leader of the pacifist New England Non-Resistance Society (1838–c. 1850), and many of its members were evangelicals.[52]

William Jennings Bryan (1860–1925), theological conservative, prominent presidential candidate, and then Secretary of State under President Wilson, was a pacifist and admirer of Leo Tolstoy for a number of years.[53]

Martin Niemoller (1892–1984) was the commander of a German submarine in World War I. But he later opposed Hitler and became a pacifist.[54]

John Stott (1921–2011; perhaps the second most influential evangelical after Billy Graham in the second half of the twentieth century) became a pacifist as a young Christian. As he read Jesus's words on loving enemies, "he couldn't begin to understand how you could be a Christian and fight."[55] To the horror of his father, who was fighting in the British army in World War II, John refused to enlist and joined the Anglican Pacifist Society.[56] Later, however, Stott resigned and embraced a just war stance.

Stanley Hauerwas is one of the most influential Christian ethicists in the past forty years. In numerous books, he has argued a strong pacifist position.[57]

There were, of course, many other famous Christian pacifists in the twentieth century: Martin Luther King Jr., Archbishop Desmond Tutu of South Africa, Archbishop Dom Hélder Câmara of Brazil, and Nobel Prize winner Adolfo Pérez Esquivel of Argentina.[58] In his speech before the US Congress

---

49. Beaman and Pipkin, *Pentecostal and Holiness Statements*, 118–19.
50. Spurgeon, "Christ Our Peace." See also Swartz, "Christian Pacifism of Charles Spurgeon."
51. Brock, *Pacifism in the United States*, 527, 534, 589, 681–85, 697–701, 922.
52. Brock, *Pacifism in the United States*, 542–82.
53. Brock, *Pacifism in the United States*, 934–36.
54. Brown, *Biblical Pacifism*, 143.
55. Steer, *Basic Christian*, 37.
56. Steer, *Basic Christian*, 37–48.
57. E.g., Hauerwas, *Peaceable Kingdom*; Hauerwas, *Against the Nations*; Hauerwas, *War and the American Difference*.
58. See Esquivel's *Christ in a Poncho*.

on September 24, 2015, Pope Francis mentioned four "great Americans." Two were Catholic pacifists: Dorothy Day and Thomas Merton.[59]

Evangelical scholar Ben Witherington, professor of New Testament at Asbury Theological Seminary, is a pacifist. Jesus, Witherington writes, "was a hard core pacifist." Witherington insists that embracing Jesus's teaching against killing demands that we be "truly pro-life across the board" and that "one needs to be opposed to abortion, capital punishment and war."[60]

Liberal Pacifism in the 1920s and 1930s

Revulsion against the horrors of World War I prompted a major embrace of pacifism in liberal theological circles.[61] Optimistic about the power of education and believing in the basic goodness of human nature, large numbers of Protestants adopted a pacifist stand in the 1920s and 1930s.[62] But as Reinhold Niebuhr soon pointed out, this pacifism was based on a naively optimistic view of the basic goodness of human nature. It fundamentally ignored the historic Christian teaching on the depth and pervasiveness of human sinfulness. Niebuhr's blistering critique and the outbreak of World War II largely squelched this short-lived, widespread liberal pacifism.[63]

Nuclear Pacifism

As both the Soviet Union and the United States developed large numbers of nuclear weapons in the decades after World War II, a number of prominent just war Christians became nuclear pacifists as they applied the just war criteria of intention (the intent must be the restoration of justice, not revenge), reasonable hope of success, and noncombatant immunity. Nuking the Soviet Union after it had hit the United States with nuclear weapons would be an act of revenge, not an act to restore justice. A major nuclear exchange would probably destroy civilization as we know it—thus violating the criterion of a

---

59. See Lisa Cahill's discussion of both in her *Love Your Enemies*, 213–23. See also George Weigel's discussion of both plus Catholic pacifist Gordon Zahn and his acknowledgment of the growing influence of Catholic pacifists. Weigel, *Tranquillitas Ordinis*, 148–64.

60. Witherington, "Long Journey." Scot McKnight is another widely read evangelical scholar who is a pacifist. See his *Sermon on the Mount*, 123–38.

61. But pacifism also existed in some evangelical circles. In 1934, the Swedish Baptist General Conference approved a resolution that said that "all Christians should absolutely refuse to take up arms against fellow men." Gehrz, "Unexpected Sites of Christian Pacifism."

62. Yoder, *Christian Attitudes to War*, 278–84.

63. See Niebuhr, "Why the Christian Church Is Not Pacifist."

reasonable chance of success. And almost any nuclear exchange would likely kill millions of noncombatants.

Writing in *Christianity Today*, John Stott says, "Because they [nuclear weapons] are indiscriminate in their effects, destroying combatants and non-combatants alike, it seems clear to me that they are ethically indefensible, and that every Christian, whatever he may think of the possibility of 'just' use of conventional weapons, must be a nuclear pacifist."[64]

In their pastoral letter *The Challenge of Peace*, the US Catholic bishops argue that the just war criteria would not allow any use of nuclear weapons. But they do accept the continued, *temporary* possession of nuclear weapons. They insist that these weapons must never be used.[65]

Many prominent Christian leaders have rejected even the possession of nuclear weapons. In 1978, a number of Christians signed "A Call to Faithfulness" and pledged to not cooperate with the US government's preparations for nuclear war. "On all levels—research, development, testing, production, deployment and actual use of nuclear weapons—we commit ourselves to resist in the name of Jesus."[66] Those signing this document included not only prominent mainline Protestants and Catholics but also well-known evangelicals: Jay Kesler, President of Youth for Christ; Frank Gaebelein, former coeditor of *Christianity Today*; and Vernon Grounds, longtime president of Conservative Baptist Theological Seminary. Even President Ronald Reagan's pastor said, "I must be a nuclear pacifist."[67]

Growing Catholic Affirmation of Pacifism

Catholic scholars recognize that the Catholic Church's attitude toward pacifism has changed substantially since World War II.[68] In World War II, Catholic Church officials refused to support pacifists. In 1956, Pope Pius XII said pacifism was unacceptable as a moral posture.[69] As late as 1962, the papal Holy Office was issuing directions saying Catholics could not be conscientious objectors.[70] But in the next few decades, the pope and bishops endorsed pacifism as an equally valid Catholic stance alongside the just war position.

64. Stott, "Calling for Peacemakers," 45.
65. *Challenge of Peace*, §§178–99, pp. 76–84.
66. Printed in *Sojourners*, May 1978 with the names of signers.
67. Sider and Taylor, *Nuclear Holocaust*, 81. Others, of course, strongly disagreed. See, e.g., Payne and Coleman, "Christian Nuclear Pacifism."
68. See Christiansen, "Contemporary Just War Tradition," 25–30, 35–36; Weigel, *Tranquillitas Ordinis*, 237–56; Shannon, *War or Peace?*, x, 19–23; Allman, *Who Would Jesus Kill?*, 95–97.
69. Shannon, *War or Peace?*, 17.
70. Christiansen, "Contemporary Just War Tradition," 35.

This dramatic change began with Pope John XXIII and Vatican II (1963–65). In 1965, the encyclical Pastoral Constitution on the Church in the Modern World (*Gaudium et Spes*) stated its intention "to undertake an evaluation of war with an entirely new attitude." The result was praise for pacifism and a call for legal protection for conscientious objectors who refuse to bear arms.[71] This encyclical stated, "We cannot fail to praise those who renounce the use of violence in the vindication of their rights."[72]

There had been prominent Catholic pacifists like Dorothy Day (1897–1980), and pacifist Catholic publications like *The Catholic Worker*, but *Gaudium et Spes* was very different. This was an official recognition of the legitimacy of pacifism at the highest level of the Catholic Church. As a result, in 1983 in their pastoral letter *The Challenge of Peace* the US Catholic bishops recognized the validity of two Catholic positions on war: "While the just war teaching has clearly been in possession for the past 1,500 years of Catholic thought, the 'new moment' in which we find ourselves sees the just-war teaching and nonviolence as distinct but interdependent methods of evaluating warfare. . . . They share a common presumption against the use of force as means of settling disputes."[73] The importance of this statement is underlined by the fact that it is part of an extensive positive discussion of pacifist nonviolence—with mention of pacifism in the early church and modern pacifists like Day and King.[74]

In his 1991 encyclical *Centesimus Annus*, Pope John Paul II underlined the fact that the defeat of the communist dictatorships in Eastern Europe in 1989 "was accomplished almost everywhere by means of peaceful protest." He noted that it had seemed that the division of Europe into communist and democratic nations could be ended only by war. "Instead," he marveled, "it has been overcome by the nonviolent commitment of people who, while always refusing to yield to the force of power, succeeded time after time in finding effective ways of bearing witness to the truth." And Pope John Paul II concluded, "I pray that this example will prevail in other places and other circumstances. May people learn to fight for justice without violence."[75]

The official *Catechism of the Catholic Church* also affirms pacifism: "Those who renounce violence and bloodshed, and in order to safeguard human rights,

71. Shannon, *War or Peace?*, 21.
72. *Gaudium et Spes*, 78; quoted in Gremillion, *Gospel of Peace and Justice*, 315.
73. *Challenge of Peace*, §120, p. 51. See the similar stance of the United Methodist bishops in *In Defense of Creation* (1986); see Cahill, *Love Your Enemies*, 2–8.
74. *Challenge of Peace*, §§111–21, pp. 48–52.
75. *Centesimus Annus*, 23. For a discussion of the nonviolent campaigns that overthrew communist dictators in 1989, see Sider, *Nonviolent Action*, 79–100.

make use of those means of defense available to the weakest, bear witness to evangelical charity."[76]

In 2007, Pope Benedict XVI commented on Jesus's command to "love your enemies": "This Gospel passage is rightly considered the *magna carta* of Christian nonviolence. . . . For Christians, nonviolence is not merely tactical behavior, but a person's way of being, the attitude of one *who is so convinced of God's love and power* that [one] is not afraid to tackle evil with the weapons of love and truth alone. Love of one's enemy constitutes the nucleus of the 'Christian revolution.'"[77] Clearly official contemporary Catholic teaching not only encourages much greater use of nonviolent methods. It also affirms, in ways that it has not for fifteen hundred years, that pacifism is a valid, significant Christian stance.

Many Christians today are pacifists. Perhaps today more than at any time since the three centuries before Constantine, significant numbers of Christians believe that Jesus calls them to refuse to kill their enemies.

76. *Catechism of the Catholic Church* §2306, p. 614.
77. Quoted in Allman, *Who Would Jesus Kill?*, 112 (italics original).

14

If Jesus Is Lord

At the center of historic Christian faith is the belief that the teacher of love from Nazareth is true God as well as true man. If one accepts that teaching of the church for two millennia, one must embrace and seek to live Jesus's ethical teaching. For every person who affirms historic Christian orthodoxy, the most important question for our topic is clearly: What did Jesus tell us about killing our enemies?

The historical record is clear. Jesus of Nazareth lived at a time when violent Jewish rebels frequently urged their people to take up arms against the oppressing Roman imperialists. In Jesus's day, there was widespread expectation among the Jewish people that a military messiah would appear to drive out the Romans in a violent military victory. The Jewish historian Josephus reports a number of violent Jewish rebellions against Rome in the decades before and after the lifetime of Jesus. Josephus also reports that this Jewish messianic expectation eventually led to the Jewish War against Rome (AD 66–70) and the total destruction of Jerusalem.

Indirectly at first, but then clearly, Jesus claimed to be that long-expected Messiah. He said the messianic kingdom of justice and peace was actually arriving in his own person and work. But Jesus dramatically redefined the role of the Messiah. He said that in the new dawning messianic kingdom, his followers must love their enemies, not kill them, as the violent Jewish revolutionaries demanded. He repeatedly told his followers that (contrary to every contemporary messianic expectation) he would accomplish his messianic mission by submitting to Roman crucifixion. In his clearest public messianic claim, he rode into Jerusalem not on a military conqueror's warhorse but on a humble donkey. On the cross, he lived his call to love one's enemies, asking God to forgive those who crucified him.

Matthew clearly presents the Sermon on the Mount as Jesus's teaching about how he expects his followers to live in the dawning messianic kingdom. His followers must reject the central proposal of Old Testament jurisprudences (an eye for an eye) and instead respond with love (although not passivity) to oppressors. That even includes responding to Roman soldiers (who are enforcing imperialist oppression) by offering to carry their packs not just the legally mandated one mile but even a second mile. In fact, Jesus gives the unprecedented command to his followers to love their enemies—a teaching contrary to the practice of virtually every human society that has ever existed.

Rejecting the narrow nationalism of much Jewish messianic expectation, Jesus says his dawning kingdom is for everyone: despised Samaritans, sinners of all sorts, even oppressive Romans. "I say to you that many will come from the east and the west, and will take their places at the feast with Abraham, Isaac and Jacob in the kingdom of heaven" (Matt. 8:11).

Both Jewish and Roman leaders decided that Jesus's radical messianic claims and teaching were a threat to their power. So they arranged his crucifixion. The implications for Jesus's followers were painfully obvious. Every Jew in Jesus's day knew that anyone who claimed to be the expected Messiah and then was crucified was a fraud. There is absolutely no evidence of followers of a messianic claimant continuing to believe in that leader after his opponents killed him. For Jews of Jesus's day, there was only one conclusion on the day after the crucifixion: Jesus was a fake, a fraud, and his movement was finished. Nothing short of meeting the resurrected Jesus could have convinced his discouraged disciples that Jesus's messianic proclamation was true and that they could now tell the world that his peaceful messianic kingdom had truly broken into history.

There is evidence all through the rest of the New Testament after the Gospels that the early church understood and embraced Jesus's message of peace. The word "peace" (*eirēnē*) appears ninety-nine times in the New Testament. Peter and Paul sometimes use the word "peace" to sum up the whole Christian message. Peter learns, in his encounter with Cornelius, that Jesus's peaceful kingdom includes even Roman imperialists—the national enemies of the Jews. Ephesians explains that the overcoming of the worst ethnic prejudice and hostility at that time in history is central to Jesus's gospel of peace. We see in the Epistles, especially clearly in Romans (12:14–21), echoes of Jesus's rejection of an eye for an eye. Frequently, New Testament writers command Christians to imitate Christ at the cross, where he loved even his enemies. And we know from the writings of Christians up until the time of Constantine that the early church's teachers taught that Jesus intended that his followers should never kill anyone. Every extant writing by Christians (up until Constantine) that discusses the topic of killing says clearly that Christians should never kill.

The most profound theological foundation for the conviction that Christians should love, not kill, their enemies is the cross. Jesus taught in the Sermon on the Mount that his followers should love their enemies because that is what God does. And Paul wrote that at the cross, Christ died for *sinful enemies*! We will never fathom the full mystery, but Christians believe that the trinitarian God—Father, Son, and Holy Spirit—suffered the agony of Roman crucifixion, somehow taking our sins on Godself to accomplish the forgiveness and reconciliation of God's enemies. Since that is the way God treats God's enemies, Christ's followers must treat their enemies in the same way.

It is interesting that no one states this more clearly than the prominent just war advocate Paul Ramsey. After saying that for almost two centuries, the early Christians "were universally pacifists," Ramsey explains their pacifism with the comment "How could anyone, who knew himself to be classed with transgressors and the enemies of God whom Christ came to die to save, love his own life and seek to save it more than that of his own enemy or murderer?"[1] That ethical/theological conclusion, it seems to me, remains as true today as in the second and third centuries.

The evidence of the New Testament is quite clear. Jesus called his followers to love their enemies, not kill them. One can conclude, with people like Reinhold Niebuhr, that although that is what Jesus said, it does not work in the real world. Therefore we should ignore what Jesus taught. But that option is simply not available to anyone with an orthodox Christology. If Jesus is true God as well as true man, then it is profoundly heretical to say Jesus's followers should reject one of his central teachings. Evangelicals and other historically orthodox Christians simply dare not do that.

If Jesus is God incarnate; if Jesus was truly the expected Jewish Messiah; if Jesus taught his followers to love, not kill, their enemies; if Jesus's messianic kingdom has begun in his life, death, and resurrection; if the church, in the power of the Holy Spirit, is called to live now the lifestyle of the already dawning kingdom modeled by Jesus; and if the crucified and risen Jesus is *now* Lord of all earthly kingdoms, then Christians today must refuse to kill their enemies. Miroslav Volf is right: "If one decides to put on soldier's gear instead of carrying one's cross, one should not seek legitimation in the religion that worships the crucified Messiah."[2]

1. Ramsey, *War and the Christian Conscience*, xv, xvi.
2. Volf, *Exclusion and Embrace*, 306.

BIBLIOGRAPHY

Alexander, Paul Nathan. *Peace to War: Shifting Allegiances in the Assemblies of God.* Scottdale, PA: Herald, 2009.

———, ed. *Pentecostals and Nonviolence: Reclaiming a Heritage.* Eugene, OR: Pickwick, 2012.

Allman, Mark J. *Who Would Jesus Kill? War, Peace, and the Christian Tradition.* Winona, MN: St. Mary's Press, 2008.

Arendt, Hannah. *The Human Condition.* 2nd ed. Chicago: University of Chicago Press, 1998.

———. *On Violence.* New York: Harcourt, Brace and World, 1969.

Arndt, William F., and F. Wilbur Gingrich. *Greek-English Lexicon of the New Testament.* 4th ed. Cambridge: Cambridge University Press, 1952.

Augsburger, Myron. "Beating Swords into Plowshares." *Christianity Today*, November 21, 1975: 7–9.

Bainton, Roland H. *Christian Attitudes toward War and Peace.* New York: Abingdon, 1960.

Baker, Sharon L. *Executing God: Rethinking Everything You've Been Taught about Salvation and the Cross.* Louisville: Westminster John Knox, 2013.

Barrett, C. K. *The Gospel according to St. John.* London: SPCK, 1962.

Barth, Karl. *Church Dogmatics.* 4 vols. Edited by Thomas F. Torrance and Geoffrey William Bromiley. Edinburgh: T&T Clark, 1936–77.

Bartsch, Hans-Werner. "The Foundation and Meaning of Christian Pacifism." In *New Theology No. 6*, edited by Martin E. Marty and Dean G. Peerman, 185–98. London: Macmillan, 1969.

Bauckham, Richard. *The Theology of the Book of Revelation.* Cambridge: Cambridge University Press, 1993.

Beaman, Jay. "The Extent of Early Pentecostal Pacifism." In Alexander, *Pentecostals and Nonviolence*, 3–38.

———. *Pentecostal Pacifism*. 1989. Repr., Eugene, OR: Wipf & Stock, 2009.

———. "Response: Pacifism among the Early Pentecostals; Conflicts Within and Without." In Schlabach and Hughes, *Proclaim Peace*, 82–93.

Beaman, Jay, and Brian K. Pipkin, eds. *Pentecostal and Holiness Statements on War and Peace*. Eugene, OR: Pickwick, 2013.

Beckwith, R. T., G. E. Duffield, and J. I. Packer. *Across the Divide*. Basingstoke, UK: Lyttelton, 1977.

Bell, Daniel M., Jr. *Just War as Christian Discipleship: Recentering the Tradition in the Church Rather Than the State*. Grand Rapids: Brazos, 2009.

Belousek, Darrin W. Snyder. *Atonement, Justice, and Peace: The Message of the Cross and the Mission of the Church*. Grand Rapids: Eerdmans, 2012.

Bergmann, Michael, Michael J. Murray, and Michael C. Rea, eds. *Divine Evil? The Moral Character of the God of Abraham*. Oxford: Oxford University Press, 2011.

Biggar, Nigel. *In Defence of War*. Oxford: Oxford University Press, 2013.

Black, Matthew. "'Not Peace but a Sword': Matt. 10:34ff; Luke 12:51ff." In *Jesus and the Politics of His Day*, edited by Ernst Bammel and C. F. D. Moule, 287–94. Cambridge: Cambridge University Press, 1984.

Blomberg, Craig L. *Matthew*. New American Commentary 22. Nashville: Broadman, 1992.

Bock, Darrell L. *Luke 9:51–24:53*. Exegetical Commentary on the New Testament. Grand Rapids: Baker, 1996.

Boersma, Hans. *Violence, Hospitality, and the Cross: Reappropriating the Atonement Tradition*. Grand Rapids: Baker Academic, 2004.

Boettner, Loraine. *The Atonement*. Grand Rapids: Eerdmans, 1941.

———. *The Christian Attitude toward War*. 3rd ed. Phillipsburg, NJ: P&R, 1985.

Boyd, Gregory A. *Crucifixion of the Warrior God*. 2 vols. Minneapolis: Fortress, 2017.

Brock, Peter. *Pacifism in the United States: From the Colonial Era to the First World War*. Princeton: Princeton University Press, 1968.

Brown, Dale W. *Biblical Pacifism*. 2nd ed. Nappanee, IN: Evangel, 2003.

———. *Brethren and Pacifism*. Elgin, IL: Brethren, 1970.

Bruce, F. F. *Romans*. Tyndale New Testament Commentaries. Grand Rapids: Eerdmans, 1963.

Bruner, Frederick Dale. *Matthew: A Commentary*. 2 vols. Rev. ed. Grand Rapids: Eerdmans, 2004.

Brunner, Emil. *The Mediator*. Philadelphia: Westminster, 1947.

Cahill, Lisa Sowle. *Love Your Enemies: Discipleship, Pacifism, and Just War Theory*. Minneapolis: Fortress, 1994.

Caird, G. B. *The Gospel of St. Luke.* The Pelican New Testament Commentaries. Baltimore: Penguin, 1963.

Calvin, Jean. *Commentaries Sur le Nouveau Testament.* Meyrueis, 1854.

Carter, Craig A. *The Politics of the Cross: The Theology and Social Ethics of John Howard Yoder.* Grand Rapids: Brazos, 2001.

Casey, Michael W. "From Religious Outsiders to Insiders: The Rise and Fall of Pacifism in the Churches of Christ." *Journal of Church and State* 44, no. 3 (Summer 2002): 455–75.

Catechism of the Catholic Church. New York: Image, 1995.

The Challenge of Peace: God's Promise and Our Response; A Pastoral Letter on War and Peace by the National Conference of Catholic Bishops. Washington, D.C.: United States Catholic Conference, 1983.

Channing, William Ellery. *Discourses on War.* Boston: Ginn & Co., 1903.

Charles, J. Daryl. *Between Pacifism and Jihad: Just War and Christian Tradition.* Downers Grove, IL: InterVarsity, 2005.

Charles, J. Daryl, and Timothy J. Demy. *War, Peace, and Christianity: Questions and Answers from a Just-War Perspective.* Wheaton: Crossway, 2010.

Chenoweth, Erica, and Maria J. Stephan. *Why Civil Resistance Works: The Strategic Logic of Nonviolent Conflict.* New York: Columbia University Press, 2011.

Childress, James F. "Reinhold Niebuhr's Critique of Pacifism." *The Review of Politics* 36, no. 4 (October 1974): 467–91.

Christiansen, Drew. "The Contemporary Just War Tradition." In *Just War, Lasting Peace: What Christian Traditions Can Teach Us,* edited by John Kleiderer, Paula Minaert, and Mark Mossa, 24–29. Maryknoll, NY: Orbis, 2006.

Clark, Robert E. D. *Does the Bible Teach Pacifism?* Surrey: Fellowship of Reconciliation, 1976.

Clifford, George. "Legalizing Selective Conscientious Objection." *Public Reason* 3, no. 1 (2011): 22–38.

Clough, David L., and Brian Stiltner. *Faith and Force: A Christian Debate about War.* Washington, DC: Georgetown University Press, 2007.

Cole, Darrell. *When God Says War Is Right: The Christian's Perspective on When and How to Fight.* Colorado Springs: Waterbrook, 2002.

Collins, Adela Yarbro, and John J. Collins. *King and Messiah as Son of God: Divine, Human, and Angelic Messianic Figures in Biblical and Related Literature.* Grand Rapids: Eerdmans, 2008.

Collins, John J. *Does the Bible Justify Violence?* Minneapolis: Fortress, 2004.

———. *The Scepter and the Star: The Messiahs of the Dead Sea Scrolls and Other Ancient Literature.* New York: Doubleday, 1995.

Copan, Paul, and Matthew Flannagan. *Did God Really Command Genocide? Coming to Terms with the Justice of God.* Grand Rapids: Baker Books, 2014.

Cowles, C. S. "The Case for Radical Discontinuity." In *Show Them No Mercy: Four Views on God and Canaanite Genocide*, edited by Stanley N. Gundry, 11–46. Grand Rapids: Zondervan, 2003.

Craigie, Peter C. *The Problem of War in the Old Testament*. Grand Rapids: Eerdmans, 1978.

Cranfield, C. E. B. *The Epistle to the Romans*. 2 vols. Edinburgh: T&T Clark, 1975–79.

———. *The Gospel according to St. Mark*. The Cambridge Greek Testament Commentary. Cambridge: Cambridge University Press, 1963.

———. "Some Observations on Romans XIII:1–7." *New Testament Studies* 6, no. 3 (1959–60): 241–49.

Cromartie, Michael, ed. *Peace Betrayed? Essays on Pacifism and Politics*. Washington, DC: Ethics and Public Policy Center, 1990.

Crossan, John Dominic. *God and Empire: Jesus against Rome, Then and Now*. San Francisco: HarperSanFrancisco, 2007.

Cullmann, Oscar. *The Christology of the New Testament*. Philadelphia: Westminster, 1959.

Davis, Harry R., and Robert C. Good, eds. *Reinhold Niebuhr on Politics*. New York: Scribner's Sons, 1960.

Dayton, Donald, and Lucille Dayton. "A Historical Survey of Attitudes toward War and Peace within the American Holiness Movement." In *Perfect Love and War*, edited by Paul Hostetler, 132–52. Nappanee, IN: Evangel, 1974.

Dechow, Jon F. "The 'Gospel' and the Emperor Cult: From Bultmann to Crossan." *Forum* Third Series 3, no. 2 (Fall 2014): 63–88.

Dempster, Murray W. "Crossing Borders: Arguments Used by Early American Pentecostals in Support of the Global Character of Pacifism." In Alexander, *Pentecostals and Nonviolence*, 121–42.

———. "Pacifism in Pentecostalism: The Case of the Assemblies of God." In Schlabach and Hughes, *Proclaim Peace*, 31–57.

Dodd, C. H. *The Epistle of Paul to the Romans*. London: Fontana, 1959.

Douglass, James W. *The Non-Violent Cross: A Theology of Revolution and Peace*. New York: Macmillan, 1969.

Driver, John. *How Christians Made Peace with War: Early Christian Understandings of War*. Scottdale, PA: Herald, 1988.

———. *Understanding the Atonement for the Mission of the Church*. Scottdale, PA: Herald, 1986.

Duchrow, Ulrich, ed. *Lutheran Churches—Salt or Mirror of Society: Case Studies on the Theory and Practice of the Two Kingdoms Doctrine*. Geneva: Lutheran World Federation, 1977.

Duffey, Michael K. *Peacemaking Christians: The Future of Just War, Pacifism, and Nonviolent Resistance*. Kansas City, MO: Sheed and Ward, 1995.

Dunn, J. D. G. *Romans*. 2 vols. Word Biblical Commentaries 38A–B. Dallas: Word, 1988.

Eller, Vernard. *War and Peace: From Genesis to Revelation*. Scottdale, PA: Herald, 1981.

Ellner, Andrea, Paul Robinson, and David Whetham, eds. *When Soldiers Say No: Selective Conscientious Objection in the Modern Military*. Burlington, VT: Ashgate, 2014.

Ellul, Jacques. *Violence: Reflections from a Christian Perspective*. Translated by Cecelia Gaul Kings. New York: Seabury, 1969.

Elshtain, Jean Bethke. *Just War against Terror: The Burden of American Power in a Violent World*. New York: Basic Books, 2003.

Enns, Peter. *The Bible Tells Me So . . . : Why Defending Scripture Has Made Us Unable to Read It*. New York: HarperOne, 2014.

———. *Inspiration and Incarnation: Evangelicals and the Problem of the Old Testament*. 2nd ed. Grand Rapids: Baker Academic, 2015.

Esquivel, Adolfo Pérez. *Christ in a Poncho: Testimonials of the Nonviolent Struggles of Latin America*. Edited by Charles Antoine. Maryknoll, NY: Orbis, 1983.

Evans, Craig A. *Matthew*. New Cambridge Bible Commentary. Cambridge: Cambridge University Press, 2012.

Fahey, Joseph J. *War and the Christian Conscience: Where Do You Stand?* Maryknoll, NY: Orbis, 2005.

Fiensy, David A., and Ralph K. Hawkins, eds. *The Galilean Economy in the Time of Jesus*. Atlanta: Society of Biblical Literature, 2013.

Finn, Daniel. "Morality, Government and the Common Good: Understanding How Coercive Power Operates Morally in Our Daily Lives." In *Catholics and Evangelicals for the Common Good*, edited by Ronald J. Sider and John Borelli, 153–59. Eugene, OR: Wipf & Stock, 2018.

France, R. T. *The Gospel of Matthew*. New International Commentary on the New Testament. Grand Rapids: Eerdmans, 2007.

Friesen, Duane K. *Artists, Citizens, Philosophers: Seeking the Peace of the City; An Anabaptist Theology of Culture*. Scottdale, PA: Herald, 2000.

———. *Christian Peacemaking and International Conflict: A Realist Pacifist Perspective*. Scottdale, PA: Herald, 1986.

——— "In Search of Security." In Friesen and Schlabach, *At Peace and Unafraid*, 37–82.

———. "Power: An Ethical Analysis from a Christian Perspective." In Swartley, *Essays on Peace Theology*, 73–101.

Friesen, Duane K., and Gerald W. Schlabach, eds. *At Peace and Unafraid: Public Order, Security, and the Wisdom of the Cross*. Scottdale, PA: Herald, 2005.

Gathercole, Simon. *Defending Substitution: An Essay on Atonement in Paul*. Grand Rapids: Baker Academic, 2015.

Gehrz, Chris. "Unexpected Sites of Christian Pacifism: Baptists During WWII and Vietnam." *Patheos*, February 7, 2017. http://www.patheos.com/blogs/anxiousbench/2017/02/pacifism-baptists-wwii-vietnam.

Gingerich, Jeff. "Breaking the Uneasy Silence: Policing and the Peace Movement in Dialogue." In Friesen and Schlabach, *At Peace and Unafraid*, 389–403.

Glover, Jonathan. *Humanity: A Moral History of the Twentieth Century*. New Haven: Yale University Press, 1999.

Goossen, Rachel Waltner. "Defanging the Beast: Mennonite Responses to John Howard Yoder's Sexual Abuse." *Mennonite Quarterly Review* 89, no. 1 (January 2015): 7–80.

Grayson, A. K. *Assyrian Rulers of the Early First Millennium BC I (1114–859 BC)*. Toronto: University of Toronto Press, 1991.

Green, Joel B. *The Gospel of Luke*. Grand Rapids: Eerdmans, 1997.

Gremillion, Joseph, ed. *The Gospel of Peace and Justice: Catholic Social Teaching Since Pope John*. Maryknoll, NY: Orbis, 1976.

Grimsrud, Tim. "Anabaptist Faith and 'National Security.'" In Friesen and Schlabach, *At Peace and Unafraid*, 311–27.

Guelich, Robert. *The Sermon on the Mount*. Waco: Word, 1982.

Gundry, Robert H. *Matthew: A Commentary on His Handbook for a Mixed Church Under Persecution*. 2nd ed. Grand Rapids: Eerdmans, 1994.

Gwyn, Douglas, George Hunsinger, Eugene F. Roop, and John Howard Yoder. *A Declaration on Peace: In God's People the World's Renewal Has Begun*. Scottdale, PA: Herald, 1991.

Hall, David A., Sr. "What the Church Teaches about War: A COGIC Conscientious Objection Principle." In Alexander, *Pentecostals and Nonviolence*, 205–14.

Häring, Bernard. *The Healing Power of Peace and Nonviolence*. New York: Paulist, 1986.

Hauerwas, Stanley. *Against the Nations: War and Survival in a Liberal Society*. Minneapolis: Winston, 1985.

———. "Pacifism: Some Philosophical Considerations." *Faith and Philosophy* 2, no. 2 (April 1985): 99–104.

———. *The Peaceable Kingdom: A Primer in Christian Ethics*. Notre Dame, IN: University of Notre Dame Press, 1983.

———. *Should War Be Eliminated? Philosophical and Theological Investigations*. Milwaukee: Marquette University Press, 1984.

———. *War and the American Difference: Theological Reflections on Violence and National Identity*. Grand Rapids: Baker Academic, 2011.

Hauerwas, Stanley, Chris K. Huebner, Harry J. Huebner, and Mark Thiessen Nation, eds. *The Wisdom of the Cross: Essays in Honor of John Howard Yoder*. Grand Rapids: Eerdmans, 1999.

Hays, Richard B. *The Moral Vision of the New Testament: A Contemporary Intro-duction to New Testament Ethics*. New York: HarperOne, 1996.

Helgeland, John. "Christians and the Roman Army from Marcus Aurelius to Constan-tine." *Aufstieg und Niedergang der römischen Welt* 23.1:724–834. Part 2, *Principat*, 23.1. Edited by H. Temporini and W. Haase. New York: de Gruyter, 1979.

———. "Roman Army Religion." *Aufstieg und Niedergang der römischen Welt* 16.1:1470–505. Part 2, *Principat*, 16.1. Edited by H. Temporini and W. Haase. New York: de Gruyter, 1978.

Hendricks, Obery M., Jr. *The Politics of Jesus: Rediscovering the True Revolutionary Nature of What Jesus Believed and How It Was Corrupted*. New York: Doubleday, 2006.

Hendriksen, William. *New Testament Commentary: Luke*. Grand Rapids: Baker, 1978.

Hengel, Martin. *Christ and Power*. Translated by Everett R. Kalin. Philadelphia: Fortress, 1977.

———. *Victory over Violence*. Translated by David E. Green. London: SPCK, 1975.

———. *Was Jesus a Revolutionist?* Translated by William Klassen. Philadelphia: Fortress, 1971.

———. *The Zealots: Investigations into the Jewish Freedom Movement in the Period from Herod I until 70 AD*. Translated by David Smith. Edinburgh: T&T Clark, 1989.

Hershberger, Guy Franklin. *War, Peace, and Nonresistance*. Scottdale, PA: Herald, 1953.

Hertz, Karl H., ed. *Two Kingdoms and One World: A Sourcebook in Christian Ethics*. Minneapolis: Augsburg, 1976.

Hoekema, David A. "A Practical Christian Pacifism." *Christian Century* (October 22, 1986): 917–19.

Holmes, Arthur F. "The Just War." In *War: Four Christian Views*, edited by Robert G. Clouse, 115–35. 2nd ed. Downers Grove, IL: InterVarsity, 1991.

———, ed. *War and Christian Ethics: Classic and Contemporary Readings on the Morality of War*. 2nd ed. Grand Rapids: Baker Academic, 2005.

Horsley, Richard A. *Archaeology, History and Society in Galilee: The Social Context of Jesus and the Rabbis*. Valley Forge, PA: Trinity Press International, 1996.

———. "Ethics and Exegesis: 'Love Your Enemies' and the Doctrine of Non-Violence." *Journal of the American Academy of Religion* 54, no. 1 (Spring 1986): 3–31.

———. *Jesus and the Spiral of Violence: Popular Jewish Resistance in Roman Pal-estine*. Minneapolis: Fortress, 1993.

Horsley, Richard A., and John S. Hanson. *Bandits, Prophets, and Messiahs: Popular Movements in the Time of Jesus*. Minneapolis: Winston, 1985.

Hunt, Gaillard T. "Selective Conscientious Objection." *Catholic Lawyer* 15, no. 3 (Summer 1969): 221–37.

Jeremias, Joachim. *Jerusalem in the Time of Jesus*. Philadelphia: Fortress, 1975.

―――. *Jesus' Promise to the Nations*. Naperville, IL: Allenson, 1958.

Johnson, James Turner. *Just War Tradition and the Restraint of War: A Moral and Historical Inquiry*. Princeton: Princeton University Press, 1981.

―――. *The Quest for Peace: Three Moral Traditions in Western Cultural History*. Princeton: Princeton University Press, 1987.

Jones, L. Gregory, and Célestin Musekura. *Forgiving as We've Been Forgiven: Community Practices for Making Peace*. Downers Grove, IL: InterVarsity, 2010.

Jones, Rufus M. *The Church, the Gospel, and War*. New York: Harper, 1948.

Josephus. *Antiquities*. Translated by William Whiston. In *The Works of Josephus*, 27–542. Peabody, MA: Hendrickson, 1987.

―――. *The Jewish War*. Translated by H. St. J. Thackeray. Cambridge: Harvard University Press, 1961.

Kearney, Milo, and James Zeitz. *World Saviors and Messiahs of the Roman Empire, 28 BCE –135 CE: The Soterial Age*. Lewiston, NY: Mellen, 2009.

Keegan, John. *A History of Warfare*. New York: Vintage Books, 1993.

Keener, Craig S. *Acts: An Exegetical Commentary*. 4 vols. Grand Rapids: Baker Academic, 2012–14.

―――. *A Commentary on the Gospel of Matthew*. Grand Rapids: Eerdmans, 1999.

―――. *The Gospel of John*. 2 vols. Peabody, MA: Hendrickson, 2003.

―――. *The Historical Jesus of the Gospels*. Grand Rapids: Eerdmans, 2009.

―――. *The IVP Bible Background Commentary: New Testament*. 2nd ed. Downers Grove, IL: IVP Academic, 2014.

Kirk, J. Andrew. *Theology Encounters Revolution*. Downers Grove, IL: InterVarsity, 1980.

Klassen, William. "Coals of Fire: Sign of Repentance or Revenge?" *New Testament Studies* 9, no. 4 (July 1963): 337–50.

―――. "Jesus and the Zealot Option." In Hauerwas et al., *Wisdom of the Cross*, 131–49.

―――. *Love of Enemies: The Way to Peace*. Philadelphia: Fortress, 1984.

―――. "'Love Your Enemies': Some Reflections on the Current Status of Research." In Swartley, *Love of Enemy*, 1–31.

―――. "Vengeance in the Apocalypse of John." *Catholic Biblical Quarterly* 28 (1966): 300–311.

Koester, Helmut. *Synoptische Überlieferung bei den apostolischen Vätern*. Berlin: Akademie-verlag, 1957.

Koontz, Ted. "Response: Pacifism, Just War, and Realism." In Schlabach and Hughes, *Proclaim Peace*, 217–29.

Kraybill, Donald B. *The Upside-Down Kingdom*. Scottdale, PA: Herald, 1978.

Kreider, Alan, Eleanor Kreider, and Paulus Widjaja. *A Culture of Peace: God's Vision for the Church*. Intercourse, PA: Good Books, 2005.

Küng, Hans. *On Being a Christian*. Translated by Edward Quinn. New York: Pocket, 1978.

Lamb, David T. *God Behaving Badly: Is the God of the Old Testament Angry, Sexist and Racist?* Downers Grove, IL: InterVarsity, 2011.

Lane, Tony. "The Wrath of God as an Aspect of the Love of God." In *Nothing Greater, Nothing Better: Theological Essays on the Love of God*, edited by Kevin J. Vanhoozer, 138–67. Grand Rapids: Eerdmans, 2001.

Larsen, Timothy. "When Did Sunday Schools Start?" *Christianity Today*, August 2008. https://www.christianitytoday.com/history/2008/august/when-did-sunday-schools-start.html.

Lasserre, Jean. *War and the Gospel*. Translated by Oliver Coburn. Scottdale, PA: Herald, 1962.

Lecky, W. E. H. *History of European Morals*. New York: Appleton, 1927.

Lederach, John Paul. *Building Peace: Sustainable Reconciliation in Divided Societies*. Washington, DC: United States Institute of Peace Press, 1997.

Leithart, Peter J. *Defending Constantine*. Downers Grove, IL: IVP Academic, 2010.

Lewis, C. S. "Why I Am Not a Pacifist." In *The Weight of Glory and Other Addresses*, 64–90. San Francisco: HarperSanFrancisco, 2001.

Lewy, Guenter. *Peace and Revolution: The Moral Crisis of American Pacifism*. Grand Rapids: Eerdmans, 1988.

Licona, Michael R. *The Resurrection of Jesus*. Downers Grove, IL: IVP Academic, 2010.

Liddell, Henry George, and Robert Scott, eds. *A Greek-English Lexicon*. Oxford: Clarendon, 1996.

Lind, Millard C. *Yahweh Is a Warrior: The Theology of Warfare in Ancient Israel*. Scottdale, PA: Herald, 1980.

Loewen, Howard John. *One Lord, One Church, One Hope, and One God: Mennonite Confessions of Faith in North America*. Elkhart, IN: Institute of Mennonite Studies, 1985.

Longman, Tremper, III. "The Messiah: Explorations in the Law and Writings." In *The Messiah in the Old and New Testaments*, edited by Stanley E. Porter, 13–34. Grand Rapids: Eerdmans, 2007.

Luther, Martin. *Commentary on St. Paul's Epistle to the Galatians*. London: James Clarke & Co., 1953.

———. *Commentary on the Sermon on the Mount*. Philadelphia: Lutheran Publication Society, 1892.

Macfarland, Charles S., ed. *The Churches of Christ in Time of War*. New York: Federal Council of the Churches of Christ in America, 1917.

Macgregor, G. H. C. *The New Testament Basis of Pacifism and the Relevance of an Impossible Ideal*. Rev. ed. Nyack, NY: Fellowship Publications, 1960.

Marshall, Christopher D. "Atonement, Violence, and the Will of God: A Sympathetic Response to J. Denny Weaver's *The Nonviolent Atonement*." *Mennonite Quarterly Review* 77 (January 2003): 69–92.

———. *Beyond Retribution: A New Testament Vision for Justice, Crime, and Punishment*. Grand Rapids: Eerdmans, 2001.

Marshall, I. Howard. *Commentary on Luke*. Grand Rapids: Eerdmans, 1978.

Mauser, Ulrich. *The Gospel of Peace: A Scriptural Message for Today's World*. Louisville: Westminster John Knox, 1992.

McKnight, Scot. *A Community Called Atonement*. Nashville: Abingdon, 2007.

———. *The Jesus Creed: Loving God, Loving Others*. Brewster, MA: Paraclete, 2014.

———. *Sermon on the Mount*. The Story of God Bible Commentary. Grand Rapids: Zondervan, 2013.

McSorley, Richard. *New Testament Basis of Peacemaking*. Washington, DC: Georgetown University Center for Peace Studies, Georgetown University, 1979.

Merton, Thomas. *Faith and Violence: Christian Teaching and Christian Practice*. Notre Dame, IN: University of Notre Dame Press, 1968.

———, ed. *Gandhi on Non-Violence: A Selection from the Writings of Mahatma Gandhi*. New York: New Directions, 1964.

Metzger, B. M. *A Textual Commentary on the Greek New Testament*. 3rd ed. London: United Bible Societies, 1971.

Miller, Marlin, and Barbara Nelson Gingerich, eds. *The Church's Peace Witness*. Grand Rapids: Eerdmans, 1994.

Moo, Douglas J. *The Epistle to the Romans*. Grand Rapids: Eerdmans, 1996.

Moody, William. *The Life of Dwight L. Moody*. New York: Revell, 1900.

Moran, Katie L. "Restorative Justice: A Look at Victim Offender Mediation Programs." *21st Century Social Justice* 4, no. 1 (2017). https://fordham.bepress.com/swjournal/vol4/iss1/4.

Morris, Leon. *The Atonement: Its Meaning and Significance*. Downers Grove, IL: IVP Academic, 1983.

———. *The Book of Revelation*. 2nd ed. Grand Rapids: Eerdmans, 1987.

———. *The Gospel according to St. Luke*. Grand Rapids: Eerdmans, 1974.

Moule, C. F. D. *The Gospel according to Mark*. The Cambridge Bible Commentary. Cambridge: Cambridge University Press, 1965.

———, ed. *The Significance of the Message of the Resurrection for Faith in Jesus Christ*. London: SCM, 1968.

Mounce, Robert H. *The Book of Revelation*. Rev. ed. New International Commentary on the New Testament. Grand Rapids: Eerdmans, 1997.

Mouw, Richard. "Christianity and Pacifism." *Faith and Philosophy* 2, no. 2 (April 1985): 105–11.

Murphy, Nancey. "John Howard Yoder's Systematic Defense of Christian Pacifism." In Hauerwas et al., *Wisdom of the Cross*, 45–68.

Nation, Mark Thiessen. *John Howard Yoder: Mennonite Patience, Evangelical Witness, Catholic Convictions*. Grand Rapids: Eerdmans, 2006.

Neufeld, Thomas R. Yoder. *Killing Enmity: Violence and the New Testament*. Grand Rapids: Baker Academic, 2011.

Ng, Larry, ed. *Alternatives to Violence: A Stimulus to Dialogue*. New York: Time-Life Books, 1968.

Niditch, Susan. *War in the Hebrew Bible: A Study in the Ethics of Violence*. New York: Oxford University Press, 1993.

Niebuhr, Reinhold. *Interpretation of Christian Ethics*. New York: Harper, 1935.

———. "Why the Christian Church Is Not Pacifist." In *The Essential Reinhold Niebuhr: Selected Essays and Addresses*, edited by Robert McAfee Brown, 102–19. New Haven: Yale University Press, 1986.

Nietzsche, Friedrich. *The Birth of Tragedy and the Genealogy of Morals*. Translated by Francis Golffing. Garden City, NY: Doubleday, 1956.

Nugent, John C. *The Politics of Yahweh: John Howard Yoder, the Old Testament, and the People of God*. Eugene, OR: Cascade, 2011.

O'Donovan, Oliver. *The Just War Revisited*. Cambridge: Cambridge University Press, 2003.

Packer, J. I., and Mark Dever. *In My Place Condemned He Stood: Celebrating the Glory of the Atonement*. Wheaton: Crossway, 2007.

Patterson, Eric. *Just War Thinking: Morality and Pragmatism in the Struggle against Contemporary Threats*. Lanham, MD: Lexington, 2007.

Payne, Keith B., and Jill E. Coleman. "Christian Nuclear Pacifism and Just War Theory: Are They Compatible?" *Comparative Strategy* 7, no. 1 (1988): 75–89.

Payne, Keith B., and Karl I. Payne. *A Just Defense: The Use of Force, Nuclear Weapons, and Our Conscience*. Portland, OR: Multnomah, 1987.

Perrin, Andrew B. "From Qumran to Nazareth: Reflections on Jesus' Identity as Messiah in Light of Pre-Christian Messianic Texts among the Dead Sea Scrolls." *Religious Studies and Theology* 27, no. 2 (2008): 213–30.

Pickus, Robert, and Robert Woito. *To End War: An Introduction: Ideas, Books, Organizations, Work That Can Help*. Rev. ed. New York: Harper and Row, 1970.

Piper, John. *"Love Your Enemies": Jesus' Love Command in the Synoptic Gospels and the Early Christian Paraenesis*. Cambridge: Cambridge University Press, 1979.

Powers, Gerard F., Drew Christiansen, and Robert T. Hennemeyer, eds. *Peacemaking: Moral and Policy Challenges for a New World*. Washington, DC: United States Catholic Conference, 1994.

Ramsey, Paul. *Basic Christian Ethics*. New York: Charles Scribner's Sons, 1950.

———. *The Just War: Force and Political Responsibility*. New York: University Press of America, 1983.

———. *War and the Christian Conscience: How Should Modern War Be Conducted?* Durham, NC: Duke University Press, 1961.

Ramsey, Paul, and Stanley Hauerwas. *Speak Up for Just War or Pacifism: A Critique of the United Methodist Bishops' Pastoral Letter, "In Defense of Creation."* University Park: Pennsylvania State University Press, 1988.

Ringe, Sharon H. *Luke*. Louisville: Westminster John Knox, 1995.

Roth, John D. *Choosing against War: A Christian View*. Intercourse, PA: Good Books, 2002.

Rutenber, Culbert G. *The Dagger and the Cross: An Examination of Christian Pacifism*. New York: Fellowship Publications, 1950.

Sampson, Cynthia, and John Paul Lederach, eds. *From the Ground Up: Mennonite Contributions to International Peacebuilding*. New York: Oxford University Press, 2000.

Sanders, E. P. *Jesus and Judaism*. Philadelphia: Fortress, 1985.

Sanders, John, ed. *Atonement and Violence: A Theological Conversation*. Nashville: Abingdon, 2006.

Schertz, Mary H. "Partners in God's Passion." In Friesen and Schlabach, *At Peace and Unafraid*, 167–78.

Schlabach, Gerald W. "Just Policing and the Christian Call to Nonviolence." In Friesen and Schlabach, *At Peace and Unafraid*, 405–21.

Schlabach, Theron S., and Richard T. Hughes, eds. *Proclaim Peace: Christian Pacifism in Unexpected Quarters*. Urbana: University of Illinois Press, 1997.

Schrage, Wolfgang. *The Ethics of the New Testament*. Philadelphia: Fortress, 1988.

Schweizer, Eduard. *The Good News according to Matthew*. Translated by David E. Green. Louisville: John Knox, 1975.

Seibert, Eric A. *The Violence of Scripture: Overcoming the Old Testament's Troubling Legacy*. Minneapolis: Fortress, 2012.

Sen, Amartya. *Identity and Violence: The Illusion of Destiny*. New York: Norton, 2006.

Senior, Donald. *Matthew*. Abingdon New Testament Commentaries. Nashville: Abingdon, 1998.

Shannon, Thomas A., ed. *War or Peace? The Search for New Answers*. Maryknoll, NY: Orbis, 1980.

Sharp, Gene. *Civilian-Based Defense: A Post-Military Weapons System*. Princeton: Princeton University Press, 1990.

———. *Making Europe Unconquerable: The Potential of Civilian-Based Deterrence and Defense*. Cambridge, MA: Ballinger, 1985.

———. *The Politics of Nonviolent Action*. 3 vols. Boston: Porter Sargent, 1973.

Shenk, David W., and Badru D. Kateregga. *A Muslim and a Christian in Dialogue.* Scottdale, PA: Herald, 1980.

Shepherd, Michael B. "Targums, the New Testament, and Biblical Theology of the Messiah." *Journal of the Evangelical Theological Society* 51, no. 1 (March 2008): 45–58.

Sherman, Lawrence W., and Heather Strong. *Restorative Justice: The Evidence*. London: The Smith Institute, 2007.

Showalter, Nathan D. *The End of a Crusade: The Student Volunteer Movement for Foreign Missions and the Great War*. Lanham, MD: Scarecrow, 1998.

Shriver, Donald W., Jr. *An Ethic for Enemies: Forgiveness in Politics*. New York: Oxford University Press, 1995.

Sider, Ronald J. *Christ and Violence*. Scottdale, PA: Herald, 1979.

———. "A Critique of J. Denny Weaver's *Nonviolent Atonement*." *Brethren in Christ History and Life* 35, no. 1 (April 2012): 212–41.

———, ed. *Cry Justice: The Bible on Hunger and Poverty*. Downers Grove, IL: InterVarsity, 1980.

———, ed. *The Early Church on Killing: A Comprehensive Sourcebook on War, Abortion, and Capital Punishment*. Grand Rapids: Baker Academic, 2012.

———. *Good News and Good Works: A Theology for the Whole Gospel*. Grand Rapids: Baker, 1993.

———. *Just Politics: A Guide for Christian Engagement*. Grand Rapids: Brazos, 2012.

———. *Nonviolent Action: What Christian Ethics Demands but Most Christians Have Never Really Tried*. Grand Rapids: Brazos, 2015.

———. *Rich Christians in an Age of Hunger: Moving from Affluence to Generosity*. 6th ed. Nashville: Nelson, 2015.

———. *The Scandal of the Evangelical Conscience*. Grand Rapids: Baker Books, 2005.

Sider, Ronald J., and Diane Knippers, eds. *Toward an Evangelical Public Policy: Political Strategies for the Health of the Nation*. Grand Rapids: Baker Books, 2005.

Sider, Ronald J., and Oliver O'Donovan. *Peace and War: A Debate about Pacifism*. Grove Books on Ethics 56. Nottinghamshire, UK: Grove Books, 1985.

Sider, Ronald J., and Richard K. Taylor. *Nuclear Holocaust and Christian Hope: A Book for Christian Peacemakers*. Downers Grove, IL: InterVarsity, 1982.

Skillen, James W. *With or Against the World? America's Role among the Nations*. New York: Rowman and Littlefield, 2005.

Smith, Morton. *Studies in Historical Method, Ancient Israel, Ancient Judaism*. Vol. 1, *Studies in the Cult of Yahweh*, edited by Shaye Cohen. Leiden: Brill, 1996.

Sparks, Kenton L. *Sacred Word, Broken Word: Biblical Authority and the Dark Side of Scripture*. Grand Rapids: Eerdmans, 2012.

Speak Truth to Power: A Quaker Search for an Alternative to Violence. Philadelphia: American Friends Service Committee, 1955.

Sprinkle, Preston, with Andrew Rillera. *Fight: A Christian Case for Nonviolence.* Colorado Springs: David C. Cook, 2013.

Spurgeon, Charles H. "Christ Our Peace." *Christian Classics Ethereal Library.* https://www.ccel.org/ccel/spurgeon/sermons59.lii.html.

Stassen, Glen H., ed. *Just Peacemaking: The New Paradigm for the Ethics of Peace and War.* 2nd ed. Cleveland: Pilgrim, 2008.

Stassen, Glen H., and David P. Gushee. *Kingdom Ethics: Following Jesus in Contemporary Context.* Downers Grove, IL: InterVarsity, 2003.

Stassen, Glen H., and Michael L. Westmoreland-White. "Defining Violence and Nonviolence." In *Teaching Peace: Nonviolence and the Liberal Arts*, edited by J. Denny Weaver and Gerald Biesecker-Mast, 17–36. Lanham, MD: Rowman & Littlefield, 2003.

Steer, Roger. *Basic Christian: The Inside Story of John Stott.* Downers Grove, IL: InterVarsity, 2009.

Stone, Lawson G. "Early Israel and Its Appearance in Canaan." In *Ancient Israel's History: An Introduction to Issues and Sources*, edited by Bill T. Arnold and Richard S. Hess, 127–64. Grand Rapids: Baker Academic, 2014.

Storkey, Alan. *Jesus and Politics: Confronting the Powers.* Grand Rapids: Baker Academic, 2005.

Stott, John R. W. "Calling for Peacemakers in a Nuclear Age, Part 1." *Christianity Today* (February 8, 1980): 44–45.

———. *The Cross of Christ.* 2nd ed. Downers Grove, IL: InterVarsity, 2006.

———. *The Message of the Sermon on the Mount (Matthew 5–7): Christian Counter-Culture.* Downers Grove, IL: InterVarsity, 1978.

Strege, Merle D. "An Uncertain Voice for Peace: The Church of God (Anderson) and Pacifism." In Schlabach and Hughes, *Proclaim Peace*, 115–26.

Sullivan, Dennis, and Larry Tifft. *Restorative Justice: Healing the Foundations of Our Everyday Lives.* Monsey, NY: Criminal Justice, 2001.

Swalm, E. J., ed. *Nonresistance under Test.* Nappanee, IN: E. V. Publishing House, 1949.

Swartley, Willard M., ed. *Essays on Peace Theology and Witness.* Occasional Papers 12. Elkhart: Institute of Mennonite Studies, 1988.

———, ed. *The Love of Enemy and Nonretaliation in the New Testament.* Louisville: Westminster John Knox, 1992.

———. *Slavery, Sabbath, War and Women: Core Issues in Biblical Interpretation.* Scottdale, PA: Herald, 1983.

Swartz, David. "The Christian Pacifism of Charles Spurgeon." *EthicsDaily.com*, September 1, 2015. https://www.ethicsdaily.com/the-christian-pacifism-of-charles-spurgeon-cms-22908/.

Swidler, Leonard. *Biblical Affirmations of Woman*. Philadelphia: Westminster, 1979.

Taylor, Vincent. *The Gospel according to St. Mark*. London: Macmillan, 1952.

Thistlethwaite, Susan, ed. *A Just Peace Church*. New York: United Church Press, 1986.

———. "New Wars, Old Wineskins." In *Strike Terror No More: Theology, Ethics, and the New War*, edited by Jon L. Berquist, 264–79. St. Louis: Chalice, 2002.

Tolstoy, Leo. *A Confession and Other Religious Writings*. Translated by Jane Kentish. New York: Penguin, 1987.

———. *Writings on Civil Disobedience and Nonviolence*. Philadelphia: New Society Publishers, 1987.

Tomlinson, Ambrose Jessup. "The Awful World War" (1917), in *Pentecostal and Holiness Statements on War and Peace*, ed. Jay Beaman and Brian K. Pipkin, 152–53. Eugene, OR: Pickwick, 2013.

———. "War Notice." *Evangel* (August 4, 1917): 3.

Treat, Jeremy R. *The Crucified King: Atonement and Kingdom in Biblical and Systematic Theology*. Grand Rapids: Zondervan, 2014.

Trocmé, André. *Jesus and the Nonviolent Revolution*. Translated by Michael H. Shank and Marlin Miller. Scottdale, PA: Herald, 1973.

Volf, Miroslav. *Exclusion and Embrace: A Theological Exploration of Identity, Otherness, and Reconciliation*. Nashville: Abingdon, 1996.

Walzer, Michael. *Arguing about War*. New Haven: Yale University Press, 2004.

———. *Just and Unjust Wars: A Moral Argument with Historical Illustrations*. 5th ed. New York: Basic Books, 2015.

Watson, G. R. *The Roman Soldier*. Ithaca, NY: Cornell University Press, 1969.

Weaver, Dorothy Jean. "Transforming Nonresistance from *Lex Talionis* to 'Do Not Resist the Evil One.'" In Swartley, *Love of Enemy*, 32–71.

Weaver, J. Denny. *The Nonviolent Atonement*. 2nd ed. Grand Rapids: Eerdmans, 2011.

Weaver, J. Denny, and Gerald Biesecker-Mast, eds. *Teaching Peace: Nonviolence and the Liberal Arts*. Lanham, MD: Rowman and Littlefield, 2003.

Webster, Alexander F. C. *The Pacifist Option: The Moral Argument against War in Eastern Orthodox Theology*. San Francisco: International Scholars Publications, 1998.

Weigel, George. "Five Theses for a Pacifist Reformation." In Cromartie, *Peace Betrayed?*, 67–85.

———. *Tranquillitas Ordinis: The Present Failure and Future Promise of American Catholic Thought on War and Peace*. New York: Oxford University Press, 1987.

Weinberg, Arthur, and Lila Weinberg, eds. *Instead of Violence: Writings by the Great Advocates of Peace and Nonviolence throughout History*. Boston: Beacon, 1963.

Wells, Ronald A. *The Wars of America: Christian Views*. Grand Rapids: Eerdmans, 1981.

Westermarck, Edward. *The Origin and Development of the Moral Ideas*. 2 vols. London: Macmillan, 1906–8.

Wink, Walter. *Engaging the Powers: Discernment and Resistance in a World of Domination*. Minneapolis: Fortress, 1992.

————. *Jesus and Nonviolence: A Third Way*. Minneapolis: Fortress, 2003.

————. "Neither Passivity nor Violence: Jesus' Third Way (Matt. 5:38–42 par.)." In Swartley, *Love of Enemy*, 102–25.

————. *The Powers That Be: Theology for a New Millennium*. New York: Doubleday, 1998.

————. *Violence and Nonviolence in South Africa: Jesus' Third Way*. Philadelphia: New Society, 1987.

Witherington, Ben, III. "The Long Journey of a Christian Pacifist." *Patheos*, October 3, 2012. http://www.patheos.com/blogs/bibleandculture/2012/10/03/the-long-journey -of-a-Christian-pacifist.

————. *The Paul Quest*. Downers Grove, IL: InterVarsity, 1998.

Wright, Christopher J. H. *The God I Don't Understand: Reflections on Tough Questions of Faith*. Grand Rapids: Zondervan, 2008.

Wright, N. T. *The Day the Revolution Began*. San Francisco: HarperOne, 2016.

————. *Jesus and the Victory of God*. Minneapolis: Fortress, 1996.

————. *Justification: God's Plan and Paul's Vision*. Downers Grove, IL: IVP Academic, 2009.

————. *The Kingdom New Testament: A Contemporary Translation*. New York: HarperOne, 2011.

————. *The New Testament and the People of God*. Minneapolis: Fortress, 1992.

————. *The Resurrection of the Son of God*. Minneapolis: Fortress, 2002.

————. *Surprised by Hope: Rethinking Heaven, the Resurrection, and the Mission of the Church*. New York: HarperOne, 2008.

Yoder, John Howard. *Body Politics: Five Practices of the Christian Community before the Watching World*. Nashville: Discipleship Resources, 1992.

————. *Christian Attitudes to War, Peace, and Revolution*. Edited by Theodore J. Koontz and Andy Alexis-Baker. Grand Rapids: Brazos, 2009.

————. *The Christian Witness to the State*. Institute of Mennonite Studies Series 3. Newton, KS: Faith and Life Press, 1964.

————. *Discipleship as Political Responsibility*. Scottdale, PA: Herald, 2003.

————. *For the Nations: Essays Public and Evangelical*. Grand Rapids: Eerdmans, 1997.

————. *Karl Barth and the Problem of War*. Nashville: Abingdon, 1970.

———. *Nevertheless: The Varieties of Religious Pacifism*. Scottdale, PA: Herald, 1971.

———. *Nonviolence: A Brief History; The Warsaw Lectures*. Edited by Paul Martens, Matthew Porter, and Myles Werntz. Waco: Baylor University Press, 2010.

———. *The Original Revolution: Essays on Christian Pacifism*. Scottdale, PA: Herald, 1971.

———. *The Politics of Jesus: Vicit Agnus Noster*. 2nd ed. Grand Rapids: Eerdmans, 1994.

———. *The Priestly Kingdom: Social Ethics as Gospel*. Notre Dame, IN: University of Notre Dame Press, 1984.

———. *Reinhold Niebuhr and Christian Pacifism*. Church Peace Mission Pamphlets 6. Washington, DC: The Church Peace Mission, 1966.

———. *Royal Priesthood: Essays Ecclesiological and Ecumenical*. Edited by Michael G. Cartwright. Grand Rapids: Eerdmans, 1994.

———. *The War of the Lamb: The Ethics of Nonviolence and Peacemaking*. Edited by Glen Harold Stassen, Mark Thiessen Nation, and Matt Hamsher. Grand Rapids: Brazos, 2009.

———. *What Would You Do? A Serious Answer to a Standing Question*. Scottdale, PA: Herald, 1983.

———. *When War Is Unjust: Being Honest in Just-War Thinking*. Maryknoll, NY: Orbis, 1996.

Zahn, Gordon C. "The Case for Christian Dissent." In *Breakthrough to Peace*, edited by Thomas Merton, 117–38. New York: New Directions, 1962.

———. *German Catholics and Hitler's Wars: A Study in Social Control*. New York: Sheed and Ward, 1962.

Zehr, Howard. *Changing Lenses: A New Focus for Crime and Justice*. Scottdale, PA: Herald, 1990.

Zerbe, Gordon. "Paul's Ethic of Nonretaliation and Peace." In Swartley, *Love of Enemy*, 177–222.

SUBJECT AND NAME INDEX

SCRIPTURE INDEX